D1244156

ANALYTICAL POLITICAL PHILOSOPHY:
FROM DISCOURSE, EDIFICATION

DAVID BRAYBROOKE

Analytical Political Philosophy: From Discourse, Edification

UNIVERSITY OF TORONTO PRESS
Toronto Buffalo London

© University of Toronto Press Incorporated 2006
Toronto Buffalo London
Printed in Canada

ISBN 0-8020-3867-0

Toronto Studies in Philosophy
Editors: Donald Ainslie and Amy Mullin

Printed on acid-free paper

Library and Archives Canada Cataloguing in Publication

Braybrooke, David
    Analytical political philosophy : from discourse, edification / David
Braybrooke.

    Includes bibliographical references and index.
    ISBN 0-8020-3867-0

    1. Political science – Philosophy.   I. Title

JA71.B725 2006   320'.01   C2005-907376-4

University of Toronto Press acknowledges the financial assistance to
its publishing program of the Canada Council for the Arts and the
Ontario Arts Council.

University of Toronto Press acknowledges the financial support for
its publishing activities of the Government of Canada through the
Book Publishing Industry Development Program (BPIDP).

To my wife Michiko,
who has enlivened
my sunset years
and made them happy

Table of Contents

Acknowledgments

Unlike the two of my books just preceding this one in the series of four published by University of Toronto Press, this book does not emerge from my teaching any specific course. The impetus for it came from certain events at the Department of Government, The University of Texas at Austin, which provoked me into assembling a defence of analytical political philosophy and of my work under that head. In the course of the assembly, the unity, and in particular the programmatic unity, of my work became visible – more visible to me than it had ever been before.

I have drawn money from the research funds attached to my chair at The University of Texas at Austin to provide a subsidy for publication. I am grateful for being able to do this. I trust University of Toronto Press is grateful, too. It has spared me and the Press from having to apply to the Canadian Federation for the Humanities and Social Sciences. That is a departure from the regular policy of the Press, but it is a good thing, insofar as it frees up money from Ottawa for other Canadian authors. However, in accordance with the regular policy of the Press, the present book has been refereed by two external readers; and before final acceptance it has been reviewed, along with those readers' reports – in effect refereed for a third time – by a University of Toronto professor of philosophy sitting on the Manuscript Review Committee of the Press. Three rounds should suffice. I thank all three readers for their efforts. Comments by the external readers led to substantial improvements in the book.

I also wish to thank, comprehensively, the students and colleagues who have assisted me year by year in my work. Discussions with students in many different courses have affected what I say. Students and colleagues near and far have supplied helpful objections and criticisms. Most prominent and telling have been the objections and criticisms from Richmond Campbell of the Dalhousie University philosophy department, who, to my great benefit, dealt with the whole manuscript; his criticisms, combining in force with criticisms from the external readers, led among other things to a drastic reordering of the chapters and to major revisions in the presentation of the logic of rules. Peter K. Schotch, the Dalhousie logician, my collaborator on several occasions and my mentor in logic, has considered the presentation as it now stands and found it free of glaring errors. Steven Burns at Dalhousie and Benjamin Gregg at the Department of Government at Texas dealt, like Richmond Campbell, with the whole manuscript, with less dramatic results, but still with much appreciated encouragement. I cite in some chapters below a number of people who had a part in thinking out in their original form the chapters that, in part or as wholes, were published elsewhere. For help with other chapters and passages written from scratch for the present book, I thank Sharon Lloyd, who read some of the things that I say about John Rawls's work; and in respect to the chapter on evil, Mats Furberg, Benjamin Gregg again, and my grandson Frank Braybrooke Portman. Benjamin Gregg welcomed my trying to say something about how to prevent the evils that I survey; and because of his comment, I have made more of prevention in the chapter, though surely not enough. I wish to thank Catherine Wilson for encouragement with the present book and with the book just preceding (*Utilitarianism: Restorations; Repairs; Renovations*); and for the idea from which the subtitle of the present book sprang.

Brenna Troncoso, my never-failing research assistant, now doing research in turbulent circumstances in Bolivia, helped again – and again – with this book, at one stage of its preparation after another. I hope she knows how deeply grateful to her I am. Staff at the Department of Government, The University of Texas at Austin, have continually supported my activities; so have staff at the Dalhousie Department of Philosophy. I want to single out for grateful mention Patrick Couture, during the preparation of the book from the beginning to within sight of the end, the computer consultant in the Department of Government at The University of Texas. My daughter, Linda McAdams, again made proofreading fun for both of us by joining me in doing it. (Perhaps I should write more books so that this fun will not have to come to a stop.) At University of Toronto Press, I want to thank Ron Schoeffel, now retired, who got this series of my books underway; Len Husband, who succeeded him as editor in charge of books in the series; and Frances Mundy, the managing editor for this book as for the preceding one. No one has ever had more congenial help from editors. I have again benefited from Catherine Frost's careful attention to the text in copyediting; I have remedied many of the things that she thought needed remedy and very likely should have remedied more.

Thanks to my appointment at The University of Texas at Austin, I have had a prolonged career; and working on into my eighty-first year has enabled me, among other things, to bring a number of my projects to full completion or close to it to an extent that I could not have brought them otherwise. Both at Texas and at Dalhousie I have had continual professional excitement; and I am especially grateful for having been welcome to participate during part of every year in the astonishingly continuous and vigorous milieu of philosophical discussion at Dalhousie.

I shall now cite the permissions that I have been given by the copyright holders to reprint material already published elsewhere: In chapter 1, on needs, I reprint an article written for a collection, *Necessary Goods: Our Responsibilities to Meet Others' Needs* (Lanham, Md., 1998), edited by Gillian Brock; and I do so with the permission of the publisher Rowman & Littlefield. In chapter 3, on rights, I draw heavily, with permission of Random House, on the first part of my book *Three Tests for Democracy: Personal Rights, Human Welfare, Collective Preference* (New York, 1968). Chapter 4, also on rights, under the title 'Our Natural Bodies, Our Social Rights,' was originally published by *Noûs* 14 (May 1980); I have permission from the present copyright-holder, Blackwell, to reprint it. One of my contributions to the book I edited, *Social Rules: Origin, Character, Logic, Change* (Boulder and Oxford, 1996) reappears here, with important additions, in chapter 5, on the logic and definition of rules; Westview Press has given me permission to reprint. Chapter 8, except for some interpolations and an appended comment, appeared in the *Canadian Journal of Philosophy* 3 (December 1973), as a review essay under the title 'Utilitarianism with a Difference: Rawls's Position in Ethics'; I have permission from the journal to reprint it. Paul Lyon invited what here appears as chapter 9, 'Sidgwick's Critique of Nozick,' as a contribution to the online website on utilitarianism that Lyon has set up and kept running; the copyright question in this case is unclear to me, but Lyon has given me to understand that there is no obstacle to my reprinting the contribution here. Chapter 10, 'Social Contract Theory's Fanciest Flight,' on David Gauthier's work, first appeared, under the same title, in *Ethics* 97 (July 1987), © 1987 by The University of Chicago. All rights reserved. I have permission to reprint. Chapter 12, the final chapter, 'The Relation of Utilitarianism and Natural Law Theory,' first appeared in *The Good Society* 12:3 (2003), and is reprinted with permission. Chapter 2, 'Where Does the Moral Force of Needs Reside, and When?' was intended to appear in the journal *Philosophy,* along with other contributions to the 2003 Durham conference of the Royal Institute of Philosophy, before the publication of the present book. If it appears there before the publication of this book, the copyright permission might flow from *Philosophy* in the direction of this book; if it appears there after the publication of this book, the copyright permission might flow from University of Toronto Press in the direction of *Philosophy.* I believe that a statement from University of Toronto Press to *Philosophy* has the effect of assuring mutual permission in either case.

DB
Halifax, Nova Scotia;
Austin, Texas
September 2005;
January 2006

ANALYTICAL POLITICAL PHILOSOPHY:
FROM DISCOURSE, EDIFICATION

Introduction

The main business of this book is to demonstrate the usefulness of analytical political philosophy, first, in the relatively humble work of clarifying terms in received moral and political discourse; and, second, in the more exalted work of generating a grand program for political action. I shall offer specimens of my own work on the terms 'needs,' 'rights,' and 'rules,' then aggregate these terms, clarified, in a grand program, which will also incorporate an analytical-philosophical account of familiar practice in assessing the consequences of political choices.

My subtitle, *From Discourse, Edification*, suggests, a little playfully, a link with the concerns of post-modernism and deconstruction. The edification that I attempt in this book is for the most part too straightforward to amount to deconstruction, though perhaps I can claim to do a little deconstructing in the course of discrediting, explicitly or implicitly, some uses of the term 'needs' and some uses of the term 'rights.' In the case of 'rules,' my analysis may not touch upon any uses of the term that call for discrediting; but there I try to solve one problem that has been evaded even in a literature dedicated to discussing rules: to find an appropriate non-circular way of defining the term.

People not habituated to analytical philosophy often feel that little or no benefit comes from analysis of this sort. I answer that clarification of the terms 'needs,' 'rights,' and 'rules' can hardly help but be useful to thinking about politics, and indeed to political activity. People do often discuss how needs are to be met and how far they and their government have a responsibility to meet needs. The discussants, and their discussion, may be confronting a practical problem in real-life politics; or merely be rehearsing ideas that could be used in such a confrontation.

In either case, the discussants, and their discussion, do really benefit if it is known, from results that analytical political philosophy can supply, that to establish something as a need is not automatically to establish it as a right; that there are ways of attending systematically to meeting needs other than establishing rights; that since it costs something to shoulder the burden of upholding rights and the rules for rights, it may in some circumstances be better to rely, in meeting the needs, on less burdensome ways. They benefit further from analytical political philosophy when it shows them how to keep the appeal to meeting needs within reasonable bounds; and just what sort of evidence establishes claims to be making headway in meeting them.

The clarifications supplied by analytical political philosophy will be more useful, of course, if the points that they make are by and large well founded. It is rash and unwarranted for any philosopher to claim to have established beyond doubt any points of clarification; but I think that I can reasonably claim that the points that I most want to make in the texts assembled in this book do clarify the terms 'needs,' 'rights,' and 'rules' in a convincing and reliably useful way. They are terms that are continually in use in thinking about politics and in disputes about public policies. Clarification – edification on these points, obtained from received discourse by analysing it – leads to a more precise mastery of the concepts at issue with the terms, a mastery aware of the logical connections of the concepts and of their limits as well as their powers. Without clarification, some headway no doubt can be made – has been made, since political disputants do not wait for advice from philosophers – with questions about (for example) whether new rights should be established to make sure of meeting certain needs. Yet will not the discussion of such questions be more alert and more thorough if the discussants know better just what they are talking about? (On some occasions, ironically, they may be wise not to press their clarifications upon other people; agreement may be easier to come by if the terms are left a bit vague. Better an imperfect peace, which may, in fact, last for years, than heightened acrimony.)

Are the benefits important ones? I think I just answered this question in part. However, the benefits of clarifying individual terms do not stop with those that I have already mentioned. The clarifications can be added up in something like a grand program for political action, a program, especially suitable for democratic politics, that calls for meeting certain needs as the basic purpose of public policy, with rules established to make sure of meeting them, among the rules as a matter of practical efficacy rules for rights when the help that rights can give gives the best sort of help. Aggregated in a grand program, the clarifications answer the call for improved political philosophy that Mark Lilla makes in a review of the life and work of Raymond Aron. Lilla expresses great admiration for Aron's sustained attention, in one political crisis after another, to the details of current issues rather than to the grand themes of political ideology. Lilla complains, however, that Aron never did enough to 'inspire' his readers 'to pursue the ends that he found worthy.' Lilla says, 'Officials and trained experts are expected to do their jobs in modern liberal democracies, and generally they manage to do so with an acceptable level of competence ... Nonetheless, one cannot ignore the sense of disquiet, a nagging impression that the public space is too sedate, that political debate has atrophied, and that no one – neither political leaders nor intellectuals – can offer a compelling, synthetic account of our present situation and how to address the new challenges of our time. Periodically, this disquiet is expressed in nostalgia for the age of Sartre or the spirit of the sixties, a childish and foolish wish. Behind it, however, there lurks a longing to render political life more coherent, more just [nobler].'[1]

Meeting needs with a suitable array of rules, rights, and rules about rights lays the groundwork for a program that, though ready for testing by political controversy, renders political life more coherent, more just, and even nobler; and it does so with continual practical attention to the details of current issues (and of issues that it would make current). A lot that answers to such a program is already being done by officials and experts carrying out established policies. In the eyes of some (those who would like to revive the rapturous anti-capitalism of Sartre, for example? – but not only they) this might seem to make the program a rather humdrum matter of cleaning up details. Yet details (as Aron would insist) are important; some of them, which call for attention and remedy under the program of meeting needs, are poignant. In my mind, as I write, is a little boy in a western American state whose brain has evidently been damaged by the toxic dust surrounding his home, dust that accumulated there during old mining operations.[2] The boy struggles to learn to read and prays every night that his struggles will succeed, but he cannot easily retain the words that he learns one day for use in the next. How can pollution or the details of reducing pollution be thought humdrum with such an example in mind? It is an example that might move even George W. Bush to more than pious words. Tens of millions of Americans share the exposure to pollution in its various manifestations. Tens of millions of Americans, in a very rich country, have to do without the universal access to adequate medical care enjoyed in Canada and other advanced countries. Scores of millions of Americans are working too hard, holding several jobs at once, with no reasonable job security in any of them; their lives are used up in unnecessary ways, often to serve other people's frivolous tastes. Is it not noble to commit oneself to political efforts that will eliminate such troubles, and nobler still when it is more the fate of one's fellow-citizens than one's own that is at stake?

The grand program that rests on the clarifications of 'needs,' 'rights,' and 'rules' invites comparison with other grand programs associated with analytical political philosophy, offered, most famously, by authors including Rawls and Nozick, and somewhat less famously, but at least equally impressively, by David Gauthier. To show this, I include in the book some of my writings about these authors and match against their programs the program that results from adding up my clarifications. Like theirs, my program expresses a vision of the basic structure that a politically organized society should adopt. If this program is not so systematic as Rawls's or Gauthier's nor so formally rigorous as Gauthier's, it is less distant from current real-world politics than either of them – the terms important to the program are terms prominent in daily politics and used there in the same ways (though not only in these ways). My program is certainly less distant from current politics (and always will be) than Nozick's historical fantasy, which, as he acknowledged, is bankrupt so far as current application goes. Moreover, there is some system to the program that I offer, and some rigour. I shall be found deploying, for example, the notion of satiation-limit lexicographical priority as the formal framework for meeting needs in the way that the program calls for. What could be more visionary, or nobler, once understood, than that? It would save other children from toxic dust; make sure of providing adequate medical care to everyone; and even reform the character and burdens of daily work.

The main business of the book is thus a two-part argument. The first part demonstrates the results extracted for edification from disaggregated, free-standing attention to certain specific terms ('needs,' 'rights,' 'rules') that figure incessantly in moral and political discourse. The second part aggregates – adds up the results – and shows that in combination they can be reasonably compared with other grand programs familiar in analytical political philosophy. With the three grand programs offered by Rawls, Nozick, and Gauthier, respectively, I align a program, comparable in scope, that combines refined ideas about needs, rights, and rules.

In addition to the main business of the book, I want to mention and lay to rest two further charges that may be raised against analytical political philosophy (and have been raised in my vicinity): first, that it is useful only in settled times and cannot cope with far-reaching social change; second, that it and its results do not speak in any way to the enormous evils into which politics has at many times, in many places, degenerated in recent generations. As regards the latter charge, I am mindful of what I think is the most searching of Leo Strauss's adverse judgments on American political thought, namely, that American politi-cal scientists have taken too bland a view of politics, oddly unaffected by the way in which politics has been played for keeps, with life-or-death stakes, in Europe and elsewhere. More realistic than most univer-sity political scientists, Mr Dooley maintained, 'Politics ain't bean-bag'; but even he did not think of politics, as Strauss did, and Carl Schmitt and Machiavelli before him, as the scene of literally cut-throat conflict.

I do say something in this book, in the chapter on rules, about changes in rules and the importance of such changes to social change generally. What I say in chapter 6, the keystone chapter (Part Two), about how deliberation about changes deals with consequences also bears upon the topic. However, my main answer to the first of these further charges, of not being able to cope with important social change, is to be found in another book, *Logic on the Track of Social Change*, written with Peter K. Schotch and Bryson Brown (and including contributions by Laura Byrne).[3] I think it may be claimed that this book demonstrates in a substantial way how analytical political philosophy can come to grips with understanding social change, even of the most sweeping and unsettling sort, with abundant implications for policies that guide and embody such change.

To answer the second charge, I offer a substantial treatment of evil, which will be found in Part Three, 'Analytical Political Philosophy Deals with Evil.' I shall answer that it can, by identifying the basic forms of evil that come up in social life and sorting out the relation between natural events, evil intentions, and evil consequences. The analysis will serve, I believe, to show that, horrifying and to a degree mysterious as the crimes of Auschwitz may be, we have concepts to deal with them and in the main understand how they came about. Analytical political philosophy, in this connection and others, will do at least as well as any other approach to political philosophy in generating practical remedies for current evils. It is not enough to denounce the evils, even when the denunciations invest themselves with the language of canonical philosophers and invoke the preoccupations ascribed to them.

Some of the issues taken up in analytical political philosophy during its vigorous last half-century, will not figure in this book. Their presence in my own work is manifest in the three other books of mine published in recent years by University of Toronto Press (the most scholarly current publishers of Erasmus and John Stuart Mill). Together with the present book, those three (*Moral Objectives, Rules, and the Forms of Social Change* [1998]; *Natural Law Modernized* [2001]; *Utilitarianism: Restorations; Repairs; Renovations* [2004]) form an intersecting and mutually reinforcing corpus. As a joke, but not merely a joke, I call the corpus *Summa Philosophica Latirivuli* (putting 'latus' for 'bray,' i.e., 'broad'). The corpus includes, as this book does not, analytical studies of political philosophers of the past – St Thomas, Hobbes, Locke, Hume, Rousseau, and Marx – and an elaborate discussion of utilitarianism, which, like the works of the canonical authors just cited, is both a topic of current philosophical discussion and a historical study. So it is a mistake to think of analytical political philosophy as opposed to historical studies. Because the present, fourth book brings the corpus – the *Summa* – to a close, I include in Part Five, the last part of the book, a chapter on the relation of utilitarianism to natural law theory, which will add two more grand programs to the programs already surveyed in this book: Rawls's; Nozick's; Gauthier's; the needs-focused combination program aggregated in this book from my free-standing studies; and, now, fifth, utilitarianism, and, sixth, natural law theory.

Yet other lines of effort in analytical political philosophy might be mentioned: work on rational choice and on social choice theory; work inspired by the theory of games; work on political deliberation. I have made some contributions to all of these, but, except to some extent in the case of political deliberation, they have been peripheral to my chief persisting interests. What philosophers have done about political deliberation can, in my view, be elaborated in illuminating ways by bringing to bear, on instances of deliberation, the logic of rules and the logic of questions, informal logic, argumentation theory, and discourse analysis, this last in the sense used, not by post-modernists, preoccupied with deconstruction and subtexts, but by philosophers using formalistic techniques in the study of language. Without doing more than brush against formal discourse analysis, on the other lines of effort mentioned I have tried do something in my little book *Traffic Congestion Goes Through the*

Issue-Machine,[4] a study of political deliberation in the United Kingdom, and in an article proposing an alliance between what I call 'issue-processing' and what specialists in argumentation theory at the University of Amsterdam call (accurately, if somewhat opaquely) 'pragma-dialectical analysis.'[5] What I say in this book will make out a robust defence of analytical political philosophy, even if it falls far short, as any one book inevitably would fall, of covering the whole range of its efforts and its uses.

PART ONE

FREE-STANDING STUDIES OF POLITICAL TERMS

SECTION A: NEEDS

1

The Concept of Needs, with a Heart-Warming Offer of Aid to Utilitarianism

My assigned task in the paper from which this chapter derives was to set forth a brief reprise of my account of the concept of needs in *Meeting Needs*.[1] I shall carry out that task, but in the course of doing so I shall introduce some nuances to increase the flexibility of the account. I shall also give a prominent place to the ways in which the concept of needs, on such an account, can assist in making good the project of utilitarianism.

Bentham's original impulse, to hold social policies accountable to effective evidence of their impacts on human welfare, has enabled utilitarianism to survive the long-standing embarrassment of not being able to make anything effective of the felicific calculus. It has even survived the more recent embarrassments that come from redefining utility as simply a matter of realizing preferences and, in consequence, of having projects of aggregating personal preferences founder in the self-stultifying renunciations of welfare economics and in the paradoxes of social choice theory. For utilitarianism keeps in view an indispensable project, even if it does so in a form not realized and for practical purposes of doubtful realization forever. What alternative is there, in ethics or in ethics applied to politics, to the central project of utilitarianism (in some sense, broad if not narrow), namely, having impacts of policies on human welfare considered? And how (though philosophers and economists have made it a puzzle exactly how) can such impacts not be considered (whatever else is) in evaluating social policies? Utilitarianism with its project thus stands in the right place to look to for a principle to guide policy evaluation.

If utilitarianism is to be more than an unfinished project in the right place, however, it has to be recast; and the most promising way of recasting it is to make use of the concept of needs. There are at least three substantial uses that utilitarianism can make of the concept of needs:

first, to explain how, by operating through surrogate concepts like the concept of needs, utilitarianism, or tendencies of thought congenial to utilitarianism, have had practical effects on policy evaluation and policy choice while the calculus has remained unfinished and un-applied;

second, to provide a means of recasting the principle of utility so that it gives something like lexicographical priority to meeting needs (and thereby at once escapes by and large both the embarrassment of not having an applicable calculus in hand and the embarrassments of social choice theory);

third, to show how even if it is not so recast, the principle of utility can be safeguarded from common objections about unjustified personal sacrifices in the same way as comparisons respecting meeting needs.

To be really useful in any of these connections, however, the concept of needs has to be, if not recast itself, at least extricated from the incessant confusion with which it is commonly used. Not everything that people intensely want – invisibility, the power of unaided flight, fame, another life, death – is something that in every case, or sometimes in any case, they need even adventitiously, for some goal both optional and feasible. What within human powers (even powers carried as far as we could expect research to go) can give them invisibility without being annihilated, another life, or the power of unaided flight? What further goal is to be achieved in all the cases in which they intensely want fame or death? Not everything that people do need in order to reach adventi-tious goals is something that they need without qualification. They may need jewellery or a limousine to impress neighbours or customers, or a set of golf clubs to play golf; on the other hand, they would cease to need these things if they ceased to pursue the goals at stake. They cannot cease, during the whole course of their lives, to need food, shelter, clothing, safety, companionship.

The everyday claims made under the concept of needs, however, often do not, in practice, heed the cautions just mentioned. The way to make sure that they are heeded, and that the concept can be used effectively to evaluate policies, is to seize upon certain features of familiar usage that can be exhibited in a systematic construction.

The construction begins by assuming that there is a Reference Population, whose needs are under consideration; and a Policy-Making Population,[2] which may not be identical with the Reference Population, whose understanding of the concept of needs will be decisive for the policies adopted for the Reference Population. The simplest case is one in which the Reference Population is identical with the Policy-Making Population, and that is the case that will be treated here; but the case in which the two populations are wholly separate is important for policies affecting the economic and political development of the Third World.

The construction leads to a schema with a number of dimensions in which agreement will, in practice, almost always come about (if it comes about at all) only after protracted discussion, which should be open to general participation by the Population (in both its Reference and its Policy-Making capacities). For expository convenience, I shall postpone dealing with the complications that the multiple dimensions create for discussion. The Policy-Making Population, let us suppose, has to agree on two things: the needs to be met in that population, taken here as the Reference Population, too; then, once that issue has been fully defined and settled, the arrangements, that is to say, the policies, to meet them.

What is the issue now about defining needs? It, too, can be taken to have two parts, first, fixing upon a List of Matters of Need; then, fixing upon the Minimum Standards of Provision for each Matter of Need on the List. The List on which discussion settles may vary; perhaps everyone will agree to put food, shelter, and clothing on the List, but (considering that the List is to guide social policies) not everyone would perhaps agree to put sexual activity there, or recreation. The Minimum Standards of Provision will vary with discussion even more: in respect to persons provided for – one person will need more food daily than others; in respect to generosity of provisions; in respect to differences in culture. Even were the List of Matters of Need – food, clothing, shelter, and other things – to remain the same, variation in the kinds of resources, religion, and other factors will make some provisions eligible under the conventions of one culture that are not eligible at all in another. It will be no help to offer pork as provisions in an Islamic culture. In the present paper, to be sure, we are dealing in the simplest case with one population and one culture. However, it removes a lot of the uneasiness about the fluidity of the concept of needs to recognize that Matters of Need can remain the same, while provisions, and hence Minimum Standards of Provision, vary with conventions.

Conventional variation does not prevent us from making the definition both of Matters of Need and of Minimum Standards of Provision answer to a Criterion. Any of a family of Criteria having to do with life and death and, short of these things, with social functioning might do. Many people, however, would find persuasive a Criterion according to which something was a Matter of Need and provisions for it were enough to meet the Minimum Standards of Provision if without such provisions the persons in question would no longer be able to carry out fully four basic social roles: as citizens, as workers, as parents, and as householders. Even here some disagreement is to be expected; and what provisions are required is something often settled by settling in accordance with prevailing views upon minimal packets of provisions, with ingredients not strictly defensible as necessary by the Criterion. However, if the List and the Minimum Standards of Provision become uncomfortably inflated, the Schema of the List and the Minimum Standards can always be contracted, and the ingredients of the packets reduced in variety or quantity, until effective agreement is reached. Or the Schema can be expanded, on evidence that the ingredients of current packets do not suffice to prevent observable impairment of the functioning of the people provided for.

How is it told whether the needs of the population as a whole are being met, or met better under one set of policies than under another? The basic form for telling and for making comparisons is given by the census-notion, and this is to be understood, insofar as it is looked to for guidance in adopting policies, as something used in conjunction with a Principle of Precedence, a Revisionary Process, and a Gains-Preservation Principle.[3] (I shall explain what these amount to when they are introduced, one by one, below.)

The census-notion requires observations that (unlike measurements of utility) are philosophically unproblematical and well within the compass of familiar, everyday practice. Suppose that inquiry is to be made into the extent to which shelter as a Matter of Need has been provided for in the Reference Population. The Minimum Standard of Provision is set after discussion as having a place to sleep that is dry, well ventilated, and in the winter heated to 68 degrees Fahrenheit. Then, after observations have been made, everyone in the Population (or everyone in a statistically valid sample) will have been assigned to one category or another in a table like the following, which assumes a Population of 100 or a sample of that size from a larger Population:

With Shelter   70

Without Shelter   30.

Someone proposes a new policy for shelter, which promises to increase provisions to cover half the number of people now without shelter. A comparative census table taking both the present policy into account and the new policy would take the form

Status Quo	New Policy
With Shelter 70	With Shelter 85
Without Shelter 30	Without Shelter 15.

Other things being equal, the new policy would bring in a clear improvement in meeting the need for shelter.

At this point, the Principle of Precedence may come into play. Moving to the new policy may be possible only if some of the people who have shelter in the status quo give up some goods. The Principle of Precedence requires them to give up goods that they themselves do not require to meet their needs under the Minimum Standards of Provision applicable, if only in this way can the Minimum Standards of Provision be met for some members of the Reference Population. We can think of the Principle of Precedence as something that members of the Policy-Making Population accept along with accepting responsibility for meeting, with respect to a certain Reference Population, the Minimum Standards of Provision for a List of Matters of Need.

Other things being equal, the Principle of Precedence, invoked with a rigour that for descriptive purposes will have to be relaxed later, here calls for the new policy to be adopted, even if for some people (say, 10 of the 70 under the Status Quo policy) it reduces provisions over and above what they require to meet their needs. They might prefer to keep these provisions, but the Principle of Precedence overrides such preferences (and thus defies the Pareto Welfare Principle, which licenses only moves that heed more people's preferences without running counter to the preferences of anybody). On the other hand, the Principle of Precedence does not require people to give up meeting their own needs to meet the needs of others, or to give other people's mere preferences more weight than their own.

The Principle of Precedence will call for advances in provision up and down the List of Matters of Need and will continue to call for them, falling silent only when for all the people in the Reference Population all the Matters of Need on the List have been met at the Minimum Standards of Provision. This goal is thus treated as a lexicographical priority, strictly speaking, a priority that is lexicographical only up to a satiation limit that is the conjunction of the satiation limits for all the Matters of Need. The goal is the conjunction; the conjuncts are the Minimum Standards of Provision (a range of minima, varying from person to person, for each Matter of Need).

'Satiation' is the correct technical term, borrowed from economics; but the technical use clashes incongruously on the present topic with the connotation of its ordinary use. To make the clash unobtrusive, I shall refer to 'SL-lexicographical' rather than to 'satiation-limit-lexico-graphical priority.' With SL-lexicographical priority, until every Minimum Standard of Provision for every person in the Reference Population and every Matter of Need has been reached, matters of preference only, a residual category not associated with Matters of Need on the List, have to wait in everybody's case.

Is this practical? Waiving for the moment the point that people may not be ready to conform with such rigour to the Principle of Precedence, it is practical so long as the resources available to the Policy-Making Population, here identical with the Reference Population, allow it under suitable arrangements to meet all Matters of Need at the Minimum Standards of Provision and still leave a surplus, if only a vanishingly little surplus, for other purposes. It may take some time to find the most suitable arrangements. The market may prove effective in some connections but not in others, and arrangements to supplement the market without impairing its effectiveness, so far as it is effective, are notoriously controversial. Nonetheless, SL-lexicographical priority for Matters of Need will turn out to be practical if it can be honoured within the limits of the resources that can be made available to honour it. Moreover, any worry about having room to work with within such limits seems to be based on a very far-fetched hypothesis: citing estimates by the World Bank, Partha Dasgupta says, 'The financial requirement for a broadly based human resource development strategy designed to meet basic needs would total approximately 5.5% of GNP' even in countries in sub-Saharan Africa (where military expenditures have been running at 4.2% of GNP).[4] That would leave a considerable surplus after needs have been met, which, unfortunately, does not guarantee meeting them.

The Revisionary Process operates in conjunction with the Gains-Preservation Principle. The latter prescribes that none of the 70 people now provided for in respect to shelter should cease being provided for. How often will there be clear improvements in view, straightforwardly satisfying both the Principle of Precedence and the Gains-Preservation Principle? In comparisons confined to one Matter of Need, perhaps quite often. The List of Matters of Need, however, presents more than one Matter of Need to be provided for; and combinations of policies that would bring in clear improvements in respect to one Matter of Need may actually worsen provisions for another, or at least bring the provisions for some people whose needs are now being met below the Minimum Standards of Provision for them. A favourable comparison offered by the census-notion on one issue might thus be offset by an unfavourable comparison on another.

The operation of the Revisionary Process, however, transcends this limitation. In the Process I mean to include any forms of taking into account suggestions from any source of revisions in existing options or suggestions of new policy proposals that, like the revisions, offer ways of avoiding difficulties with the existing options. Suppose the new policy for providing shelter would make an advance in meeting the need for shelter, but reduce below the Minimum Standards of Provision the provisions for a number of people in respect to education (say, by diverting funds that would have been used to repair schools), or simply leave many people without such provisions (because new schools will not be built). People concerned to apply the Principle of Precedence will turn to the Revisionary Process to find a combination of policies that will increase provisions for shelter without having an adverse effect on provisions for education.

In the face of such mixed effects from a combination of policies as having more provisions for shelter for some people at the expense of reducing below the Minimum Standards the provision for some of education, the Gains-Preservation Principle prescribes at least maintaining the present distribution of provisions for education so far as they can be, while the advances in provisions for shelter are to be seized. But again, this is something different from applying the Pareto Welfare Principle, since, as the Principle of Precedence demands, consistently with the Gains-Preservation Principle, resources may be transferred from people who have more than enough to meet all their needs, whether or not their preferences oppose the transfer.

For all its reliance on familiar ideas and familiar sorts of observations, how realistic would it be to claim that the construction just described can be made to work in everyday politics? Some features of the construction are realistic enough. The Criterion, for example, resting as it does on familiar social roles, invites ready assent at least to the most basic items on the List of Matters of Need – food, shelter, clothing, safety. If I were more interested in making a connection between the concept of needs and the philosophical literature on autonomy, I might follow Gillian Brock in making explicit room for personal autonomy in the Criterion for Matters of Need, along with other aspects of human agency that may not be covered transparently by the basic social roles of citizen, worker, parent, and householder. I would accept a variant Criterion of this kind as belonging to the same family of criteria.[5] I am so intently concerned, however, to demonstrate what can be made of the concept of needs as a practical and effective alternative to anything that the utility industry in philosophy and economics has made of the concept of utility, that I prefer a Criterion the ingredients of which everyone understands. Do even philosophers understand the concept of autonomy?

Moreover, I think that a Criterion resting on familiar social roles does markedly better in fixing for effective political use ideas about Minimum Standards of Provision. We may expect much more disagreement on the Minimum Standards than upon the basic List of Matters of Need. In both cases, however, we have the advantage of letting the basic Schema (List of Matters of Need taken together with Minimum Standards of Provision) contract or expand according to the extent to which ready agreement on the content to be ascribed to them can be achieved in a given Policy-Making Population. The arguments for contraction or expansion would continually appeal to the Criterion, which anchors the construction in firm if narrow ground in matters of fact.

What extent of agreement should we seek to achieve? To show that the basic Schema could be completely fixed for a time for use in a variety of applications it would help to argue that given a Schema contracted for this purpose, a consensus embracing pretty much the whole of a Policy-Making Population is not out of reach, especially if, as discussion ends for the time being, we set aside the irreducible disagreement of an intransigent minority of 5 per cent or 10 per cent. Arguments aiming at consensus upon the contracted Schema might invoke, sardonically, the Matters of Need and the Minimum Standards of Provision that would be appropriate for people being kept in prison. Should not the population out of prison, too, have provisions at least at this level? It might be said that the provisions should not be given them; they should in every case do work to get them. But this is not a question about what should be on the List and what the Minimum Standards of Provisions should be, in other words, not a question of principle to be settled by fixing the Criterion and appealing to it. What is to be in the Schema is one issue; what arrangements are to be made to give it effect is another (though no doubt people adjust their positions on one to accord with their positions on the other). The best arrangements for giving the Schema effect logically might be arrangements encouraging self-sufficiency (entailing in some places agrarian reform) or arrangements that left everything to the market.

I do not think, given this distinction, that widespread disinclination to accept the Principle of Precedence would stand in the way of an agreement fixing the Schema and guiding its use. The very people who might be most disinclined to make sacrifices to conform to the Principle may be people who think that the sacrifices will never come home to them – the best arrangements for self-sufficiency will make any sacrifices unnecessary. Moreover, there is a large amount of room in the process of expanding or contracting the Schema for discussion, in which people ready to make some sacrifices, but anxious not to make too many,[6] will be able to call for a shorter List of Matters of Need or less generous Minimum Standards of Provision. At the same time, if the discussion is open and free, people who would lose by the contraction can argue against it. Others can argue for expansion. Keeping to a List and Minimum Standards accepted for prisoners would not, after all, do more than provide for the bare beginnings of a commodious life for the general Population.

What will, much more often than not, make it difficult to fix upon one persistent, agreed-on schema is that contracting and expanding it will not go smoothly. Contracting the List, people may differ on which Matters to strike off in which order; they may differ also in being readier to accept more generous Minimum Standards of Provision for some needs than others – some, for example, will be more generous respecting provisions for safety, some more generous respecting provisions for education. Moreover, some people may be ready to subscribe to a longer List with less generous Minimum Standards of Provisions for all the Matters on it, while others would be more generous about Minimum Standards of Provision for the Matters, fewer in number, that they would have listed. In the face of considerations like these, advanced by Gillian Brock as criticisms of my account in *Meeting Needs*,[7] I think the best course to take is not to take a stand on the combination of strong conditions that by limiting variations in attitudes in the Policy-Making Population would guarantee smooth contraction or expansion of the Schema. The best course is to treat the Schema and the other features of the construction as offering so many dimensions in which discussion may be called for before we could make sure of any comprehensive use of the concept of needs giving SL-lexicographical priority to all Matters of Need taken together. For example, there will be discussion about which Matters of Need are to be included in the List and how each Matter of Need is to be defined; and discussion about what range of Minimum Standards of Provision is to be accepted under the head of any given Matter of Need.

Is this allowance enough for discussion of the Schema and variation in the interpretation of its features? It is consistent with the allowance, and, indeed, it is a point that I would insist upon, that we can predict from the familiar use of the concept of needs some Matters of Need that will be settled upon very quickly and some Minimum Standards of Provision below which discussion will not descend without becoming absurd. I would resist making so loose an allowance for discussion and intepretation as would risk losing the distinctive moral force of the concept of needs. The moral force depends in part, not only on there being some received agreement, extending across differences in social and economic position as well as in political beliefs, on the dimensions of discussion exhibited in the Schema, but also on there being some received agreement, likewise extended, on how to begin filling the Schema in. Food will be one of the Matters of Need; and more food than a thimbleful of rice will be required every week by every member of the Reference Population under the Minimum Standards of Provision for food.

Too much fashionable flapdoodle about the politics of interpretation in which the concept is no doubt involved will obscure the possibility of capitalizing on this agreement to bring about at least modest reforms. It will also be to a degree self-defeating. If you wish to convince people that facilities should be provided to battered wives, enabling them to live apart from their husbands, should you omit making the point that in their present households their needs for bodily, mental, and emotional security, including freedom from terror, are going starkly unmet? Even if you would prefer to make the case in terms of rights, you might think twice before disregarding the possibility of founding the women's rights on the narrow but firm ground of their minimal needs.

The force of the concept of needs can be carried beyond the bare minima where the force is strongest. In many cases, I would hope, even in the present circumstances of politics, it can be carried forward to more generous standards of provision than are now commonly adhered to. However, I think the concept should not be expanded so far as to risk making an approach to meeting needs indistinguishable from an approach to achieving all the good things in life that feminists, environ-mentalists, and activists for other causes seek, even when it is perfectly reasonable for them to seek these things. If it is to keep its distinctive force, the concept of needs, in my view, can go only part of the way to defining the common good and making sure of a commodious life, though it is a vital initial part of the way. Tragically, many people do not benefit from application of the concept even in respect to the bare beginnings of its application, where the concept is firmest and its force least deniable.

In practice, we should almost certainly not think of getting wide-spread agreement on all the dimensions of the Schema. So we should not think, in practice, of getting on to consensus on the Schema fixed at some level of contraction or expansion for persistent use applied to the whole variety of Matters of Need. We should expect to be getting consensus only for a moment, on one or two Matters of Need that have become salient issues and (equally transiently) on the associated Mini-mum Standards of Provision. Furthermore, the consensus may not be firm beyond a policy-making community (relevant bureaucrats, ex-perts, lobbyists, and legislators); even within the policy-making com-munity it may be undermined by a division of opinion about suitable arrangements. This picture goes hand in hand with a picture of fitful attention to policy questions about needs and fitful commitment to the Principle of Precedence. Matters of Need do make themselves felt in politics: people worry from time to time about safety of children in the central cities, about homelessness, about the proliferation of food banks, about the adequacy of public provisions for education. Seldom, how-ever, do any of these Matters get enough sustained attention to dispose of them by making sure of adequate provisions. Much farther away from characterizing real politics is anything like systematic combined use of the Principle of Precedence, the census-notion, and the Revision-ary Process (together with the Gains-Preservation Principle). But this is not (as is the case with the concept of utility) because people would not understand how to apply the Schema of needs, making systematic use of these things. It is because of the complications of politics – lots of issues, many of them not about needs, arising without coordination, distracting attention as they arise and aggravating the distraction al-ready present with the multiplicity of issues already present; lots of competing interests, some of them cherished more by the people who have them than any effective commitment that they might have to meeting the needs of other people.

In *Meeting Needs*, when I came to consider what it was realistic to expect in the way of application of the concept of needs in the complex democratic politics of a populous industrial society, I moved from SL-lexicographical priority for the Principle of Precedence, which only a thoroughly conscientious Policy-Making Population could be expected to press home, to what I called 'Role-Relative Precautionary Priority.' This allows for people being more attached to priority for Matters of Need when they are charged with working out policy proposals than they are when, as citizens, they must choose between the proposals; and more attached in their role as citizens (coming together to make decisions for the Common Good) than they are as consumers. Recognizing how people's addiction to tobacco runs counter to meeting their needs, the proponents of policy may seek to eliminate the tobacco industry; but, as citizens, they will divide on how long elimination should be put off, given the unsettling economic effects that eliminating the industry would have for many people; and, as consumers (some of them, in their capacities as proponents and citizens, strong adversaries of the tobacco industry), they will go on using tobacco so long as the industry feeds their habit. Yet even in such a situation the concept of needs counts for something: with the Principle of Precedence, it leads to agitation about the tobacco industry and to proposals that sooner or later, bit by bit, check its activities.

Role-Relative Precautionary Priority almost surely will not do as much justice as the concept of needs calls for. Having some people comfortably provided for while others are desperate for provisions to meet their needs is a spectacle that has always, for people with sensitive consciences, raised questions about justice. It at least seems to require some explanation as to why justice would not call for removing the discrepancy. A familiar explanation is that the discrepancy results from people being more industrious and productive in some cases than in others. The people who are not comfortable have no complaint; they should have worked harder and more productively. But this explanation does not seem relevant in situations (most situations) where the greater comforts of the comfortable classes originate in large part in riches accumulated by their ancestors. (Then the lesson to be drawn is perhaps the people who are not comfortable should have chosen ancestors who worked harder or more productively, or at least that the ancestors that they do have should have worked harder or more productively.) However, a philosopher famous for being willing to accept the results of honest industry and lawful transactions for generations on end has led the way in concluding that the appeal to the occurrence of these things in previous generations cannot justify present discrepancies. He is quite clear in his mind about how property is legitimately appropriated and transmitted; but he also feels compelled to admit that the pedigrees of present property holdings are tainted – significantly, though in ways that cannot in many cases be accurately specified – with past deviations from legitimate appropriation and transmittal. He recommends dealing with present discrepancies like the one assumed, between some people comfortable and some people desperate, by using Rawls's Difference Principle to give at least a rough measure of justice.[8] Then the people on top will be able to keep only so many comforts as are required to enable them to make a maximum contribution to the standard of living of the people on the bottom. In fortunate enough circumstances, this will assure the latter of meeting their needs.

The connection between needs and justice that I want to emphasize most here, however, is an indirect one. It goes by way of rights and the jeopardy that holding and exercising those rights comes, for some people, from other people accumulating extraordinary amounts of wealth and with it inordinate power both in economic relations and in political ones. Money talks in both connections. The power can be used in disregard of and in violation of the rights of poorer people. The rights so violated might be rights directly to having their needs met. Dasgupta for one talks as much about rights to have needs met as he does about the needs themselves, using to frame his discussion a distinction between 'positive rights' (to be given material benefits) of which he takes rights to basic provisions to be examples and 'negative rights'[9] (to be protected from harm). Yet even people ready to recognize such rights if they are useful may find direct resort to the Principle of Precedence and comparative uses of the census-notion more economical conceptually than setting up an apparatus of rights and more efficient in practice.

Furthermore, not everyone will be ready to recognize the rights. Libertarians, for example, incline to think that it suffices for people to have a right to personal liberty and rights to property acquired by honest industry and lawful transactions. How can it suffice to have those rights? For some people, in some circumstances, both rights are liable to disregard and violation by other people who have overweening power based on extraordinary wealth. Especially vulnerable are people whose needs will not be met if they do not give up their rights in submission to the designs of the extraordinarily wealthy. The pressure for submission may simply take the form of making the rightholders' positions economically untenable: desperate to meet their needs, they sell out at a nominal price when, if they could have bargained on equal terms, they would not have sold at all. Or – as has been very frequent in history – the wealthy arrange to override the rights in question altogether.

It may be said that, if those designs infringe some people's rights, they are morally objectionable and should be vigorously proceeded against as unlawful. But where is the vigorous proceeding to come from, when the police, the prosecutors, the judges, and the legislators have been corrupted? Overweening wealth had its way in reinstituting serfdom in Poland in the sixteenth century; it had its way in the Highland Clearances; it is having its way at this very moment as smallholders are pushed out of the way during the clearance of the Brazilian jungle. Justice, even justice on a libertarian definition, will not survive in practice if some people's provisions for their needs are put in jeopardy by an adverse distribution of wealth. Justice requires as a necessary condition – not in logic, but in practice – at least as much approach to equality of income as assures everyone of provisions for needs.[10]

If it were not rights to liberty and property but the Principle of Utility, as now commonly understood, that is to be invoked to safeguard justice by safeguarding the meeting of needs, one might fear that to get optimal overall results in meeting needs one would sometimes sacrifice meeting some people's needs to meeting the needs of others. Might this not mean introducing some injustices just to ward off others? But the Schema for needs opens up no room for such injustices. The Principle of Precedence is not an optimizing notion; it is, to use Herbert Simon's term, a satisficing one. As such, it falls silent when all the needs on the List have been met at the appropriate Minimum Standards of Provision for everyone in the Reference Population. Questions about what to do with resources not required to accomplish this will, of course, remain; but though they may have to do with a much larger quantity of resources, they will not be so urgent morally, because the neglect of them will not be so morally grievous as shortfalls in meeting needs.

During the advance to fulfilling the Principle of Precedence, the Gains-Preservation Principle stands against stopping or reducing (below the Minimum Standards) the provisions going to some to make sure of getting provisions to others. The census-notion itself stands against discarding anyone in the group surveyed in order to improve results. A policy that meets the needs of a greater proportion of a population because some people have been eliminated (who were present under the policy superseded) is not supported by a statistically relevant comparison. To compare the condition of a given group under one policy with its condition under another requires, as a basic consideration in statistics that is at the same time a basic consideration of justice, that the comparison not be rigged by tampering with the population surveyed. Natural changes in the number or composition of the population are another matter; but here, too, the claim that one policy does more over time than another would have (or did, in some other jurisdiction) requires that no subset of the population (e.g., people without health insurance) be set aside just to obtain an improved reading.

I am not sure that we can attribute the Gains-Preservation Principle to the teachings of the great figures in the history of utilitarianism – Bentham, Mill, Edgeworth, and Sidgwick – though I expect that they would give it a sympathetic hearing. I am tolerably sure that we can attribute to them the presupposition that a population to which the Principle of Utility is to be given comparative application is to remain the same for any comparative assertions about the happiness of that population.[11] To be sure, very early in the historical career of utilitarianism, thinking in terms of the felicific calculus seems to have moved on from thinking of the happiness of the people in a group to thinking sometimes of the aggregate, sometimes of the average happiness of the group. This led Sidgwick, a judicious thinker elsewhere, to license increasing the population of the Earth until the marginal net increment of happiness attainable by adding yet another person to the population vanished, though the appearance of this person would diminish, by crowding and other ill effects, the happiness of everyone else.[12] But it did not lead him, or any of the others, to suggest that to get a higher aggregate happiness score some people might be done away with. The closest any of them come to such a suggestion is Edgeworth's idea that especially morose people might be encouraged to emigrate;[13] but he was supposing that while the people at home would be happier for their absence, the morose people would be no less happy living abroad than before. He stopped there.

In their extended reviews of objections to utilitarianism, neither Mill nor Sidgwick considered defending, because they did not dream of having to defend, utilitarianism against being ready to tamper with a population to get better overall scores. Thus, utilitarianism, if it is not ready to be recast as an ethics giving SL-lexicographical priority to needs, and not content to operate with the concept of needs as a surrogate and source of surrogates, can at the very least make explicit the same safeguard against sacrificing people's lives as the Schema for needs – a safeguard that comes from the basic statistical consideration logically prior to using either the calculus or the census-notion to marshal statistics. It can also, to its great advantage, adopt the Gains-Preservation Principle. This will be more conservative in operation applied to happiness, unbounded in any individual case, than it is to needs, where it can license transfers of resources above and beyond what individual persons require to meet their needs. It would still not be so conservative as the Pareto Welfare Principle if it were not taken to imply (as it would not have to) that people could only be happy with just the combination of goods that they happen now to prefer.

It might be best for utilitarianism to abandon utility, though given the intellectual investment in the utility industry this will not be easy to bring about. Utilitarianism could recast itself as an ethics in two parts, the first part of which frankly champions, ultimately, SL-lexicographical priority for needs settled upon after due discussion under the Schema for basic needs, and the second part of which deals with the pursuit and mutual accommodation of preferences that do not express needs but that still must be heeded for people to have commodious lives. Should utility be brought back for service in this part? I do not think so, though I tend to be of two minds about this, more affirmative in *Utilitarianism: Restorations; Repairs; Renovations*, less so here. No one has yet drawn up a preference map or utility map for even one person, let alone the millions of people who compose in each case most current societies. No one ever will. It is much more fruitful to think directly of seeking, alongside the operation of a market in private goods, goods public relatively to one or another public that contribute to their happiness, and making institutional arrangements to minimize conflicts about which of these goods, football stadiums or opera houses, to have. But it is not my business here to work out how utilitarianism can dispense with utility, even when it goes on from needs to matters of preference only.

Finally, the light that making the concept of needs clear throws upon the theory of utilitarianism recast as the theory of a needs-based ethics extends to showing how the theory, even unrecast, can have had some effect on the choice of policies in spite of offering a principle incapable of direct application. It has not required direct application to be effective. For, one could assume, at least in a rough practical way, that providing for this or that Matter of Need would foster happiness. The need for sanitary housing, met by introducing a modern system of sewers, was a good, intelligible surrogate for utility or happiness. As Chadwick saw, those London tenements the courts of which were ankle-deep in human excrement generated diseases that stood in the way of fulfilling anything like the Principle of Utility, were one to find a way of applying it.[14]

2

Where Does the Moral Force of Needs Reside, and When?

Does the Moral Force Reside in a Systematic Schema? Not in Any Simple Way

My point of departure in the book *Meeting Needs*[1] was the conviction that the concept of needs has moral force, but the force has been dissipated and made hard to see by multiple complications including, but not confined to, multiple abuses. I now think that is only half the problem.

To help restore the moral force to view for systematic application, I worked out a philosophical construction – a Schema – designed to give a stable foundation for the concept of needs in the uses in which it carries moral force. It is this Schema on which I shall focus in the present chapter. If vanity, in addition to familiarity, plays any part in my decision to do so, the vanity is offset, I hope, by the fact that I shall be carrying out an exercise in self-correction, and by the reasonable expectation that what I say in correcting the view to be taken of my own schema will apply to other attempts to systematize the concept.

The Schema specified a List of Matters of Need and Minimum Standards of Provision for each need and each person. The Matters of Need were course-of-life needs, that is to say, needs (like the need for food and the need to be spared terrorization) that people have throughout their lives, or at least (like the need for sexual activity) in certain stages of their lives. The Minimum Standards of Provision varied with persons (some people really need more to eat than others). They varied with climates (in some climates shelter is needed more to reduce exposure to the sun than to keep warm). They varied with cultures (the forms of food acceptable as provisions differed from culture to culture in respect to the animals that people were ready to eat).

Both the List and the Minimum Standards were governed by a Criterion. The Criterion certified each Matter of Need on the List and – person by person – each of the associated Minimum Standards of Provision as something to be met as an indispensable condition of being able to perform four basic social roles: citizen, worker, householder, and parent.

Within this Schema, I allowed for discussion and negotiation to fix the content of the List and the level of the Minimum Standards of Provision. Negotiation (which I did not then distinguish, though it was allowed for) brings in bargaining, which discussion may not. Bargaining in the case of settling upon the features of the Schema consists, I suppose, mainly in someone's agreeing to a more exacting concept of needs on one point (say, recreation) in return for getting someone else's agreement on a less exacting concept of needs on another (say, shelter).

In the discussion and negotiation, the main issue would be what List and what Minimum Standards would be generally accepted by people of good will in a certain Policy-Making Population or community as having priority under a Principle of Precedence. The Principle consisted in giving needs precedence over matters less important both for themselves and for other people in their own community or in one or another population otherwise defined for which they were ready to take some responsibility.

The moral force of the concept of needs would thus be fixed – though subject to further discussion in future rounds of policy-making – by the combination of the other features of the Schema with the Principle of Precedence, when agreement was reached on how the Schema would be filled out.

It might seem that the Criterion, resting on empirical evidence, would not leave much room for discussion. And indeed, I think there is a tension in the Schema between what can be established by common sense or science as facts about needs and what is accepted as the meaning of needs by people ready to agree to being guided by considerations of needs in making policies. But this tension in the Schema reflects a real tension in the world of policy-making. Furthermore, it does leave a good deal of room for discussion: People may disagree, for example, on whether the indispensable conditions relate to being barely able to perform the basic social roles or being able to do so with some room to spare (and hence some energy for trying out new ways of performing the roles). They may disagree about how far the deliverances of science or other bodies of evidence are to be taken as well established or even relevant. They could disagree about what population or populations they would assume any responsibility for and about modifications to the List or modifications to the Minimum Standards of Provision as one population after another came into view. They may disagree about other things, as well: for example, the liberty to review, in a later round of discussion and negotiation, any agreement that they make about the Schema for this round.

This brief summary (reflected in chapter 1) shows how my thinking on the subject of needs once came to rest. I owe to a student in a graduate seminar at The University of Texas, Brandon Butler – or perhaps better, I owe to Brandon Butler's father and grandfather,[2] whose position in these matters was invoked by Brandon in discussion – the stimulus for thinking again about just how the concept of needs has moral force. If it does, does all or any of the force reside in a Schema of the sort that I constructed? Is there any force in the Schema abstracted from the urgency of specific occasions? How and in what terms does the urgency manifest itself?

In use, the concept of needs is infected by non-motivating aspects of the concept of neediness. Neediness is a tiresome subject, of which bleeding hearts, among whom I daresay I should count myself, may often make too much. Neediness also raises – directly, perhaps, but certainly in reaction to the bleeding hearts – a question about how the needy got that way. Was it through their own current shiftlessness? Or, ready to work as they now may be, did they fail in their grasshopper days to acquire marketable skills? Approaching needs in this way, through the concept of neediness, Brandon Butler's father and grandfather might well find, as Brandon reports, nothing particularly moving about the concept of needs.

Their position (as Brandon suggests) may be tied up with notions about deserts. Do the needy in this instance deserve to be helped? Short of bringing in an issue about deserts, the position might be, simply, that through their own improvidence the needy in question had created a difficulty about meeting their needs. Without going on to blame them for their improvidence or to treat their difficulty as a natural or divine punishment, one might hold that it was now up to them to get out of the difficulty as best they could. Even the feeling 'Serves them right!' might not go that far into blame; it might just mean, 'What did they expect, if they spent all that time dancing about and neglecting their crops?'

Yet I conjecture that for many people, without their necessarily subscribing to a Calvinist-like religion, in which divine punishment is a prominent feature, the improvident deserve blame and punishment.

Many people may look upon withholding help from the undeserving as a punishment, though they do not need to do this to feel justified in the withholding.

Up to a point, I sympathize. I want to be a grasshopper, as Isaiah Berlin's Tolstoy wanted to be a hedgehog, but I am an ant at heart, just as Berlin's Tolstoy was a fox. I think that there is a moral and practical issue about whether measures set on foot to meet needs benefit some shiftless people. At any rate, there is a moral and practical issue about whether this possibility is an important obstacle to supporting the measures or something that can be tolerated, like having an occasional man live with a welfare mother. It is an obstacle really present, and an obstacle difficult, perhaps, counterproductive, to root out.

It is, I suspect, frequently untimely to appeal to anything like a Schema for needs. For logically, as I point out, all the needs may currently be met, and so why ask for contributions? Let people go on taking care of themselves. If they do not succeed, it may be for reasons that do not deserve respect. The Schema thus should not be treated as if it continually entered into the policy-making process, even if it helps explain why shortfalls of personal resources in some connections turn out to be urgent issues and how the episodic use of 'needs,' which calls attention to the shortfalls, comes into play. If all the needs are currently met, though they certainly remain needs, there is no occasion for the episodic use.

Furthermore, I think that the moral force that I assumed is to be attributed to the concept of needs as exhibited in the Schema may as well be attributed to specific instances of needs, and perhaps better so attributed, to persuade more people to act helpfully. When I adopt the perspective of utilitarianism, I treat needs as surrogates for whatever directly falls under the concept of utility, which I regard as too abstract for practical use – so abstract that it has not yet been firmly associated, even in theory, with a calculus both wholly intelligible and wholly acceptable. But the concept of needs as systematically presented in the Schema may itself be too abstract, too far removed from the actual practices of policy-making, to be useful. When needs are appealed to during those practices, does the denomination 'needs' bear the moral force? Or does the denomination as a specific need? Is it denomination as a specific need only in the context of a shortfall in meeting the need? Is denomination as a need then even necessary?

Even more important, some respect should be given the fact that people may quite reasonably not want to be bound as private persons to meet the needs of other people, especially people outside their family circles. Would any of us be happy writing a blank cheque in this connection? Many of us would not be happy to write a blank cheque within our family circles. I do not think philosophers themselves would want to write blank cheques; so far, Brandon's father and grandfather and other philosophers will be allies.

What citizens might bind themselves to is another matter. Then the responsibility, even if it is blanket, is not so overwhelming, since it is shared and can be limited to taxes, which are not usually so burdensome as politicians vie to make out. However, citizens, too, will sooner or later want to know whether there is any limit to the number of needs that they are invited to attend to and what serious footing all the needs have. Moreover, to say the least, the moral obligations that people have as private persons do not neatly divide from the moral obligations that they have as citizens. We should also want to keep up certain parallels between the two sets of obligations. Bodies of citizens can squander resources just as private persons can; and neither bodies of citizens nor private persons should ignore the extent to which on occasion efforts to meet people's needs miscarry.

Needs vs Capabilities as Alternatives to Utility

In Britain, there is a sharp increase in mortality among old people during especially cold weeks in the winter. In Chicago and Texas, and in Paris, there is a sharp increase during especially hot weeks in the summer. In the one case, the old people do not have enough heat; in the other, they have too much, because they lack air conditioning. The consequences are morally horrifying. I do not entirely know why the horror seems not to be felt among those economists who incline to dismiss basic needs, when the needs can be agreed upon, as too trivial in their claims on the Gross National Product to be worth talking about.

Economists will not do any better with the concept of utility. The notion of utility, along with the project of getting from this notion exact optimal solutions to problems about the choices of policies affecting human welfare, has bewitched economists who are thoroughly alert to unmet needs and thoroughly committed to getting them met. The bewitchment survives, even in the case of Amartya Sen (at one point at least in his recent writings[3]), and Sen is an economist who could not be more fully aware of the theoretical disasters to which attempts to found social choices on utilities and preferences have led in welfare economics and social choice theory.

Sen, in the book that I have in mind, is reluctant (even though tempted) to endorse the concept of needs, in the absence, he intimates, of a demonstration that the concept of needs can meet the test of utility, that is to say, among other things, of the expectations of precision associated with utility.[4] I think that here he has got things just upside down. The concept of utility is nowhere in direct application in practical discussions of policy-making;[5] and though Sen has a lot to say, all of which I applaud, in objection to relying on the concept of utility for the evaluation of policies, its absence from practical policy discussions is not something that he makes any fuss about or even notes.[6] This omission is, I think, a predictable consequence of his approaching practical discussions from the viewpoint of an economist. Habituated to discussions with economists and philosophers in which utility is an ubiquitous concept, Sen has not looked to see whether it is in use in practical discussions, or at any rate in use by other people in such discussions. In sharp contrast to the concept of utility, the concept of needs is in application on every hand (though not always under that name, and in a complex pattern of representation and application that I am about to describe). If utility works out in a way that seems to conflict with the concept of needs, reflective equilibrium is not going to give so much weight to utility as to needs. Indeed, insofar as utility (as advanced by the utilitarians) has had any application in choices of social policies during a history now of two and a half centuries, it is by way of the concept of needs, with provisions for individual needs serving as surrogates for utilities. Utility is too refined a notion and, even so, too problematical in application for economists to deal with when they give advice about policies, and certainly for people generally and politicians.

Moving away from utility, notwithstanding any lingering bewitchment, Sen would have us deal with the 'capabilities' (or freedoms) that people enjoy, given appropriate resources.[7] These extend far beyond provisions for basic needs to include having the resources to take part in higher cultural activities and in politics and, indeed, extend to all the aspects of living largely and generously, attaining what Thomas Hobbes would call 'commodious living.' (Curiously, the functionings that Sen's capabilities serve are just what would be in the eyes of Karl Marx, young and old, needs in a rich and expanded sense.[8]) In writings later than the book that I have just cited, Sen clearly treats needs as I understand them, to imply conditions indispensable for having important freedoms, among which he includes the freedom to survive.[9] There is no disagreement between us on this point; even if I would use 'freedom' in a more restricted way, I am ready, indeed eager, to go along with him in advocating effective practical attention beyond needs to the whole range of capabilities. I do not hold that everything important in life or social policy is best covered by the concept of needs.[10]

We can try to expand the list of basic needs and raise the standards for meeting them, and this is plausible up to a point, but it risks diminishing the force of the appeal to needs. We can leave off expanding when the application of the concept is felt on every hand to have become tenuous; then we can build into our system of evaluation a level above needs to deal with personal values, which are to be taken seriously in the same way as needs, but perhaps in a lexicographically secondary place. Sen's 'capabilities' may be regarded as doing much the same work as a two-level construction of this kind. His concept of capabilities, I might say, focuses on the Criterion that figures in the sort of construction or schema that I associate with needs. That Criterion already takes some of what Sen calls 'functionings' into account: specifically, functionings in the roles of householder, parent, citizen, and worker. As it stands, moreover, with the role of 'citizen,' the Criterion already has implications for political liberty and justice, since no one can play the full role of citizen in the absence of these things. But, in effect, Sen generalizes the Criterion to embrace functioning in all the roles that people might want to have the freedom to play – to do 'one thing today and another tomorrow, to hunt in the morning, fish in the afternoon, rear cattle in the evening, criticize after dinner.'[11] It is having with the appropriate resources the capabilities of functioning in all these ways to which Sen wants to direct comprehensive attention in making social policies.

Sen's approach has the advantage (against the concept of needs, as stabilized in the construction) of giving more weight to agency, an effect of using the term 'capability,' which connects with agency more directly than the term 'needs.' Moreover, Sen, in his discussion of the approach, returning to the subject of agency repeatedly, gives more weight to it – weight that I welcome – than I have done in my discussions of the Schema for needs. Yet agency is already allowed for in the expectation that the details of the Schema will be fixed by negotiation and discussion among the agents who will act on the Schema. Again, agency is allowed for in the Schema, not only in the role of citizen, but also in the other roles that figure in the four-role Criterion, since the roles are to be played by agents. These roles may be the best place to make the allowance, given that in receiving and realizing the benefits that Sen wishes to capture, agency and capability do not always operate.[12] Meeting needs has no implication that they do so operate.

The 'capabilities' approach has the advantage, shared with the concept of needs on the first level of the construction, of not concentrating even on the second level on preferences. When I want to emphasize the distinctive weight to be given needs, I refer to a second level of 'matters of preference only,' but this makes the second level sound unduly frivolous. No doubt some things on that level are frivolous, but many of the added functionings are important aspects of good lives, personal fulfilment, and civilized societies. Of course, the added functionings would have a plausible place in a second level of construction only if the roles with which they are associated were roles that people choose to play, in choices expressing their preferences, but the same could be said of the functionings in the basic four-role Criterion. People's preferences operate in their choosing to be citizens and householders. Furthermore, whether or not the resources supporting the capabilities are used depends on people's preferences regarding taking them up; but this is true, too, of the provisions for basic needs: people sometimes refuse to eat, or prefer to sleep 'rough' in the streets. Yet the three-term relation between resources, capabilities, and functionings is an objective one, which does not depend on preferences. One will not have the capability to function as a pianist if one does not have access to a piano.

To all these advantages must be added the overarching one of being comprehensive in a way that it would be unwise (in spite of Karl Marx) to think of needs as being. The approach through 'capabilities' helps make sure that concerns stretching beyond needs will get due consideration; and thus lays to rest the misgivings of some thinkers that a preoccupation with needs will distract people from these other concerns, which include, for example, the concerns at stake with affirmative action. No one, in a cautious use, for purposes of social policy, of the concept of needs, needs to be a lawyer or a doctor, a university professor or an actress. To give people the capability – the freedom – to pursue such careers (given aptitude) is, notwithstanding, an important objective of social policy.

However, here we touch upon a limitation of the capabilities approach. It may have the opposite disadvantage from making too much of needs. Great strides in American social policies have been made with affirmative action (a feature of those policies that gives an advantage in present competitions for place to groups that have suffered discrimination in the past); but simultaneously, the basic needs of many people in the same country – for not too much heat and not too little, for food, for shelter, for provisions suited to their disabilities (something much in Sen's mind) – go unmet. The capabilities approach may distract policymakers from giving sufficient weight to needs.

I think Sen does not make as much as can (and should) be made of the concept of needs. The concept of needs, along with the term, is familiar to everyone and by everyone regarded as relevant, though with some uncertainty about how it is to be used if it is left unstabilized. Moreover, even with Brandon Butler's father and grandfather in mind, I expect that it will not only be easier to get people to commit themselves to providing for other people's needs than to get them to commit to heeding other people's preferences; it will also be easier than to get them to commit to enlarging other people's objective capabilities. It may be a fine thing for N to be able to play a musical instrument, but how compelling is the call to help him acquire this capability? The capabilities that do have some moral force get it from an extended argument showing how they figure in human welfare. Needs already have moral force, I want to say *prima facie* and by the very use of the term. That is one reason why the concept of needs is so much abused: it pulls, or at least tends to pull, on people's heartstrings. Caution about uses comes in, but only in second thoughts.

Part of the trouble with capabilities here is that in their upper range they are very diverse and are not capabilities that everyone has to have to lead a good life. Some people will want one; other people, another. People who go in for extreme sports are not likely to be the same people who want to play in string quartets. Needs, by contrast, in the first level of the Schema are, some of them, like food and freedom from harassment, universal; and others, like recreation and companionship, are at least presumptively so. I do not say that lack of universality puts any of the higher capabilities out of account morally. Yet it must complicate the argument for giving them moral force, since the argument may best go by way of citing universal human properties – shall I say universal needs – like having some, at least, of one's preferences heeded, or having heeded one's most heart-felt desires, if needing them is feasible. The complication is so serious that the argument is not likely to get off the ground with Brandon's father and grandfather.

I do not come away from this comparison of the capabilities approach with the needs approach with any sense that either approach has won the victory and displaced the other. On the contrary, I think that the two approaches should be combined. I can only speculate that the strategy of getting basic needs met first, before putting full moral effort into achieving the capabilities in the second level of construction, is more likely to be successful. Trying out capabilities first may be rejected out of hand, especially when people learn that affirmative action is one of the connections in which efforts to enlarge capabilities is most active.

Support for enlarging the higher capabilities may demand altruism of a sort that people cannot reasonably be expected to practise. Altruism is commonly defined as putting other people's preferences or interests (in which preferences are commonly and wrongly accorded a basic part) ahead of one's own. There is vanishingly little appeal in that. On the other hand, suitably presented, an altruism that to some extent puts other people's needs ahead of one's own preferences may well have widespread attraction. Concern with other people's needs, moreover, is something that can be more convincingly advanced by judicious moral education. (In a judicious moral education Economics 101 is postponed until the students' benevolence has been fully established.)

Needs as Surrogates and Surrogates for Needs

Needs (provisions for needs) are surrogates for utility. However unrefined our practical ideas about utility or even about the less recherché subject of happiness may be, we may, while we are waiting for the concept of utility to be perfected, assume that meeting the needs that people have for pure water, unpolluted air, heat neither too little nor too much, food, clothing, shelter, education, along with recreation, will favour their happiness. So we act to meet those needs, perhaps by establishing a truly competitive market, perhaps by setting up, along with the market, arrangements to correct the imperfections of its operations. The Schema shows how to keep the uses of the term and concept of needs in these connections under control. (So it is at least a barrier to losing the moral force of the concept by using it too loosely.)

But is it the term 'needs,' designating the concept as exhibited in the Schema, that we most commonly and effectively invoke? The term in its 'episodic' use, to designate a shortfall in meeting one of the Matters of Need on the List, may be more effective. Even so, is it as effective as simply describing as such people who are starving, or dying of exposure? To activate the good will of many people, I expect we commonly bypass the term 'needs' even in its episodic use to resort to surrogates for needs, or at least to surrogates for the term, namely, terms that alert people to specific instances where help is urgently called for: thirst, starvation, exposure, illiteracy.[13] We commonly also supply, along with these terms, disarming explanations of why they have come to apply. The wells and creeks have dried up, so people have run out of potable water; their crops have failed because of drought and they are starving; their homes have been demolished by tornadoes; their schools have been closed because rebel forces have trashed them, and anyway funds and teachers for them are not available. We do not – and the victims do not – have to use the term 'needs' to call for help; it would be idle or redundant in the immediately practical context to use the term; to insist on it would be puzzling.[14] That help (from some source) is called for is obvious; it goes without saying.

People may be moved by these terms whether or not they would be moved by our saying that here there is an unmet need and here another one. They may be moved whether or not they would be moved by our presenting to them a List of Needs and a schedule of Minimum Standards of Provision and calling upon them to support standby arrangements for meeting them should they ever be in danger of not being met. Yet, once being moved by more immediate terms is something acknowledged to occur, we can see more easily how the term 'needs' becomes ready for use for special purposes. The situation may compel us to recognize that any one of these shortfalls is a shortfall in meeting one need among others. We say, 'We have to do more than provide shelter; these people need education, too.' So considered, all of the shortfalls have some moral force, but some may require more urgent attention than others. Disaster comes more speedily with lack of water than with lack of education. We have to balance these matters just because we understand that they are needs. We do not have to balance them against the victims' preferences in the same way (even if, other things being equal, we are ready to arrange for provisions that they prefer instead of provisions that they do not).

Moreover, the force that they have in common can be exhibited in a systematic construction, for example, in a schema of the sort that I constructed. This, when there is occasion to bring it in, explains and justifies the moral force, besides showing how the force can be both limited and (by, among other things, being limited) kept alive.

The Practical Timing of Appeals to Needs

What I have just done is lay out the elements of a pattern of presentation for needs. The elements of the pattern are so many vehicles, operating on different occasions, for presenting the concept to attention. More specifically, the vehicles are utterances in which figure

the immediate descriptions of shortfalls;

or their descriptions by the episodic use of the term 'needs';

or the designations of individual standing (course-of-life) needs that lie behind each of the episodic uses;

or references (including references expansible into references of this kind) to the Schema in which standing needs and the Minimum Standards of Provision for them are marshalled under a Principle of Precedence.

All these things can be distinguished by reflecting on the use of the term 'needs' and testing the reflections dialectically in conversation with other theorists. So, concurrently, can some at least of the typical occasions for relying on one vehicle rather than another. What cannot be done without empirical non-philosophical research in social science – systematic survey research – is establish how far the distinctions are heeded (and recognized) by the general public. Empirical research of a specialized kind is also needed to establish firmly how often in practical discussions about public policy one or another of the vehicles distinguished is used, on what occasions, and in what sequences.

Research of this kind, though not yet specifically in application to needs, is notably carried on in the empirical investigations of practical discussions by my friends at the University of Amsterdam, who are advancing argumentation theory under the banner of pragma-dialectics.[15] I am not now in a position to conduct such investigations myself. I can say some things speculatively, which empirical investigations may confirm or disconfirm. In the book *Meeting Needs*, I allowed for some important complications in applying the Schema: the List of Matters of Need; the Minimum Standards of Provision; the Criterion; the Principle of Precedence. I distinguished between strict final priority and a looser sort of priority in which the priority given needs varied with different social roles that would figure in policy-making. Strict final priority means giving for a specified population lexicographical priority over mere preferences to the whole List of Matters of Need together with the whole schedule of settled Minimum Standards of Provision. In a real-world policy-making community, perhaps only experts working out ideal plans for public policy would heed strict final priority; people in other roles – as legislators, citizens, and consumers – would invoke needs less systematically and less trenchantly. As consumers they may go on smoking, while as citizens they support vigorous measures to curtail the sale of cigarettes.

I have allowed, more in the essay that I contributed to Gillian Brock's collection[16] (figuring in this book as chapter 1) than in my book *Meeting Needs*, for there being rounds of discussion and negotiation in which changes in the Schema or in any part of it could be introduced. I had in mind chiefly rounds of discussion within a given policy-making community, preoccupied with the needs of its own members. Furthermore, I made a beginning to allow for the untidiness of the practice of policy-making. The distinction just recalled from the book *Meeting Needs* between the two sorts of priority is already a beginning. In Gillian Brock's collection, I went further, opening the way to allow for discussions that, far from taking a systematic view of the whole range of basic needs, concerned just a few needs, maybe only one, and did not press the discussion even of them to the end, that is to say, to a settled conception of them of the kind called for in the Schema. Real-world discussions are continually being interrupted by other considerations, so an issue about a need may be resolved only in part before public attention shifts to something else entirely.

Much more has to be said, however, both to be more realistic about contexts of application and to explain where in bearing on any given occasion the moral force of needs resides. It certainly does not reside time after time in the Schema alone. I now think that it resides in the Schema, so far as guiding choices of actions and policies goes, only on specially suitable occasions for invoking it. On most occasions in real-world policy-making, I expect, nothing like the Schema is brought into view at all. If it is brought into view, it is more often brought in only part by part than as a systematic whole.

Let us imagine, however, an occasion on which it might be brought into view during the exploration of certain ramifications of an issue about needs. Civil war breaks out in a poor country, quickly depriving the population of security of life and limb. No one who wishes to help or to appeal for help has to say that their need for security is not being met, though this is as real as a need can be. It risks redundancy even to say they have an urgent need (the episodic use) for security. Yet suppose someone does say this. An expectable response is that they need food and shelter just about as urgently. The point made by bringing in the term 'needs' is to align the one shortfall with the others in the spectrum of needs – on the List of Matters of Need. Suppose someone now asserts that the population in view has a need for education that must not be overlooked. Other discussants question whether the shortfall in education is anything that needs immediate attention. 'Perhaps not this week or next,' says the discussant who brought up education, 'but in the long run, even over the next couple of years, if the need for education is not met, the people we are discussing will remain in a desperate condition. They will not be able to understand or apply the agricultural techniques that they must employ to prosper; they will miss opportunities to defend their interests as farmers; they will not do anything to reduce the birthrate.'

Someone may not see the connection with needs, or at least may be a little unsure about just what the connection amounts to. Is education more than a means to meeting the needs for security, food, or shelter – and a rather indirect means at that? The response might run on two tracks. On one path, it would be pointed out that even if it is no more than a means, it is a means to meeting a number of needs all of which will have to be dealt with urgently in the case of shortfall. On the second track, it might be argued that the need for education has the same footing as the need for food and shelter. This is just because, unless it is met, people will not be able to carry out their roles ('functions,' Sen would say) as householders or parents or workers or citizens as fully as can reasonably be demanded. Unless it is met, along with meeting the other needs, provisions for which have to be made if the community and its members are to thrive, there will be shortfalls that give rise to urgent needs – needs in the episodic sense. The Schema is here being drawn into the discussion, even if it is not laid out in full elaboration.

It may not require to be fully elaborated even if economists, or other people misled by economists to disdain the concept of needs, question whether the concept is not too fluid and too much compromised by expressions of wants – mere preferences – to be useful. For it may suffice to answer this question to show that the one or two needs that may be under discussion do satisfy a criterion that mere preferences do not; and call for arrangements for steady provision if the community or population in view is to thrive or at least survive.

What, however, is the status of the Schema? It is a philosophical construction that can be described as useful in answering questions about the footing that course-of-life needs share and in limiting the recognition of such needs to those that have this footing. Such questions may sometimes, if only rarely, arise in real-world policy-making processes; I have just outlined an illustration in which they do (or at least are on the point of arising). 'Rarely' here is perhaps too lightly conceded, under a presupposition narrow in its view of policy-making processes. On a broader view, books like Sen's *Development as Freedom* are contributions to real-world policy-making processes; that is precisely what Sen says he intends this book and his other writings on the same and related themes to be.[17] They are all writings at a level of discourse that invites presentation of a schema of needs, with which Sen's concept of capabilities intersects and has clear affinity.

The particular philosophical construction that I have offered contemplates having its features – the Schema with its List of Matters of Need, its schedules of Minimum Standards of Provision, its Criterion – settled by some sort of agreement among the people who are to apply it in conjunction with the Principle of Precedence. When and where was this agreement ever reached and who took part in reaching it?[18] Has it ever been anything more than a hypothetical topic in philosophical theorizing?

I give a three-part answer: (1) if the agreement has never been more than hypothetical, nevertheless, as a feature of the Schema it has a part to play in showing how the concept of needs is to be given a systematic basis; (2) agreement on something like the Schema, or at least the beginnings of it, if not often explicit in domestic politics, is present in the lists of basic needs adopted by agencies and advisers active in the business of the United Nations and other international organizations; (3) ad hoc agreements on parts of the Schema come about from time to time in real-world policy-making processes. Is it really no more than moonshine to suggest that there is something like this agreement at once on the standard provisions for housing offered by Habitat International and on the standard provisions for drinkable water? To be sure, most people leave action on the standards to others, or, making too much, among other things, of the ways in which appeals to the concept of needs may abuse the concept, may not support action on the standards by anybody.

I might say a little more about point (3), about ad hoc agreement on parts of the Schema. On occasion, an appeal to a need (say, to recreation, or even to education) is questioned as having to do with something dispensable, or maybe something with no firm basis distinguishing it from things that it would be nice to have, but that answer to nothing more than mere preferences.[19] Suppose the question – either question – is answered by bringing up a criterion (about survival, about thriving) that, at least in time, the needs in question satisfy just as much as the most obvious needs, like the need for food or (in some climates) the need for clothing. It is admitted that some discussion about Minimum Standards of Provision has to take place before the answer is entirely satisfactory; otherwise, the dimensions of provision that fall outside the criterion, into what in this connection may be tendentiously reckoned the realm of matters of preference only, will be given undue relevance. Suppose as one after another need comes up and on every occasion the same criterion (or at least a criterion belonging to the same family of criteria) comes up and the same discussion of Minimum Standards of Provision takes place, ending in tentative agreement. This is surely a plausible process. Does it not amount to building up, step by step, a comprehensive agreement of just the sort that the Schema calls for? The agreement at each step brings into operation an application of the Principle of Precedence; and every application is formally, even if imperfectly, coordinated in a schematic way with every other.

Epilogue

In the body of this chapter, I have relied for the most part on an intuitive understanding of moral force, except that at one point, where I identified a pattern of presentation of needs with a number of alternative vehicles for presentation, I said something that foreshadows what I am now about to offer as a sketch of how I think moral force may be explicated: 'The vehicles [of presentation] are utterances in which figure the immediate descriptions of shortfalls; [or, alternatively] their description by the episodic use of the term 'needs'; [or, alternatively] the designation of individual standing (course-of-life) needs that lie behind each of the episodic uses; [or, alternatively] references (or references expansible into references of this kind) to the Schema in which standing needs and the Minimum Standards of Provision for them are marshalled under a Principle of Precedence.'

I shall treat moral force as relativized to a certain population (which may be as large as all human beings of good will, but in practice may be much smaller). An utterance has moral force if it is accepted by the population in question in four respects. First, it is accepted as expressing an emotion favouring an action of some sort and capable of inducing a like emotion in other members of the population. Second, it is accepted as expressing in standard cases, where present time actions and policy-making are at issue, an imperative to settle the issue in one specified way, with action in accordance following. Third, the utterance, in both its emotive and its imperative aspects, expectably has the implied perlocutionary effects on other people. Fourth, it is accepted that all of these things can be associated with a convincing moral argument that itself is accepted. The argument may be simple or elaborate: simple, if it involves no more than saying something like 'We can't let people starve, can we?'; elaborate – the acme of 'elaborate' – if it brings forward a full-blown ethical theory, utilitarianism, contractarianism, or natural law theory.

On various occasions, all of these things will be present for any of the vehicles that I distinguish: for utterances describing shortfalls ('These people are starving'); for utterances describing the shortfalls by the episodic use of the term 'needs' ('These people have urgent need of food'); for utterances designating the individual course-of-life needs lying behind each of the episodic uses ('People cannot survive or thrive unless their need for food is met'[20]); for utterances embodying references (or expansible into references) to the Schema ('People not only have a need for food; they have a need for shelter and a need for education, among other things; and they must have a minimum of provisions for all these things if they are to thrive, even survive').

The moral force of the vehicles will vary not only with occasions, but also with the population to which the force is relativized. If we start with a diverse population, like the body of citizens in any one of the United States, say, Georgia, only a subset of that population may be moved by a given vehicle on a given occasion. No doubt there will often be efforts by moralists and politicians to enlarge the subset. The general picture, however, is one in which it cannot be safely expected that the whole of the initial population will be moved by any vehicle on every occasion. This does not seem to me to impair the notion of moral force. It is always an empirical question whether the force is felt by a given set of people in a given connection.[21]

SECTION B: RIGHTS

3

The Analysis of Rights

Here I set forth my basic analysis of rights as presented in my book Three Tests for Democracy[1] *(1968), with some revisions, I hope improvements, that occur to me, coming back to the text after thirty-six years.*

Rights, as I shall contend in the following chapter (4), are social and social in origin; they are not usually collective. There are such things as collective rights, which can be exercised only by collectivities. Graduates of the University of Oxford used to have, collectively, the right to elect a Member of Parliament. Most rights, however, are rights assigned individual persons – hence individualistic in application – and also individualistic in administration. There are, of course, social agencies that assist in the administration of rights – the police and the courts, for example – just as there are social agencies for undertaking other tasks of government. A good part of the administration of rights, however, is left to the individual persons who have them and who, having them, must decide whether or not to exercise them and when.

Rights encourage individual self-reliance in one's own defence. Every man and woman – or, at least, every man and woman and their lawyers – are their own administrators, capable and responsible under the concept of rights of initiating defensive action against other people – private persons or official ones. Thus, a man and woman, invoking their rights, defend their privacy; recover their property; obtain the use of public facilities. Every man and woman are likewise capable of being their own evaluators, putting the concept of rights to its secondary use of evaluating governments, by beginning with their own cases. How, they may ask, does the government do in respect to *our* rights? If it disregards any of *our* rights, it is thus far to be judged bad, never mind how it treats other people's rights. For attending to other people's rights is no excuse for ignoring *ours*.

Yet other people's rights as well as our own must be the concern of conscientious citizens. Conscientious citizens must hold governments accountable for respecting everybody's rights as a fundamental test of the governments' acceptability. But just what are rights that so much as this is to be made of them?

Rights as Combinations of Rules

Two-Part Combinations of Rules: Exercise and Status

To say that a person, N, 'has a right to *x*' or that she 'has a right to do *a*' is in both cases – though the latter formula does more to suggest the exercisable aspect that I shall attribute to every right – logically equivalent to asserting the existence of a combination of rules, with two main parts:

1. a rule according to which if N does a certain action (or falls into a certain condition[2]) then M, some other person or persons fulfilling certain conditions, are called upon to do or refrain from doing a certain other action or actions (in doing, to assist N; in refraining, to forbear from interfering or from penalizing);
2. a rule according to which the fact just set forth implies a certain status for N, vis-à-vis M, and perhaps vis-à-vis other people as well, which even should N fail to do any of the actions first mentioned requires M, and perhaps some other people, to do some actions or refrain from doing others.

Rules of sort (1) express the *exercisable* aspect of a right. Rules of sort (2) express the *status* aspect. The existence of N's right in its status aspect is a necessary condition of the existence of her right in its exercisable aspect. Having a right typically requires other people to do or refrain from doing various things, whether or not the person holding the right exercises it, invokes it, thinks about it, or even knows of its existence. If N has a right to certain movable items of property, the items are not to be appropriated by other people even if N herself is not using them. Similarly, if a person has a right to free speech, other people are not to interfere with her opportunities for free speech, even if there is no prospect of N's making use of any of these opportunities. Moreover, in both these cases, other people may be required to render concrete assistance in the protection of N's status.

N's status (as an aspect of a given right) may, in the case of some rights, be accorded her without her having to do anything to earn it. She may have the status accorded her because she has inherited a certain social position, or because she is a member of a certain social class; or because she is a fellow citizen; or simply because she is a human being. In the case of some rights, however, the status may be something that everyone qualifies for by performing some previous actions: by N's doing work on her own account, or by N's doing some work for M, or by N's paying M some money. N's right to a specific item of private property may derive from either class of rights – for example, as being inherited or as being earned. The status associated with this right, whether earned or unearned, is susceptible to being extinguished and with it the right, sometimes without N's voluntary participation (e.g., when a court seizes her assets to pay off her creditors), and even without compensating her for its extinction.

What people are called upon to do or refrain from doing in respecting the exercise of a right is in every case something that they are obliged to do. Hence, to every right there are corresponding obligations, an obligation not to interfere if nothing else. It is not the case that to every obligation there corresponds a right, since some obligations are imperfect, like the obligation to give alms to the poor. No specific poor person has a right to the alms. However, if we have in mind only obligations that are owed to specific persons, then the correlativity does run from the obligations to the rights. It has been suggested that there are rights, like the right to revolution and the right to self-defence, which have no correlative obligations,[3] but this seems to me to be a mistake. The right to self-defence has the correlative obligations of not interfering with the exercise status of this right and not penalizing anyone for exercising it. The right to revolution, if there is such a right (perhaps ascribed, following Locke, to a civil society affronted by the government that it established), would imply an obligation of not penalizing anyone who revolted for good reason under it.

Third Part Added to the Combination Making Up a Rule: Conditions for Status

The conditions, such as they may be, surrounding the status referred to in part (2) of a right, considered as a combination of rules, are perhaps best formulated by recognizing a third part in the combination, a rule

(3), to the effect that N's having the status referred to in part (2) implies (in its turn) the fulfilment of various conditions by N and other people, conditions that together are both necessary and sufficient for N's having the relevant status.

These conditions, which will be spelled out when the combination of rules corresponding to a given right is spelled out, vary enormously from one right to another. In some cases, the conditions would very easily, even automatically, be fulfilled, without action on N's part or anybody else's; in other cases, only by a concatenation of contingencies, each requiring the consent and action of a number of people. Any person N failing to fulfil the conditions would fail, of course, to have the status, and if he did not have the status, he would not have the right in its exercisable aspect either. Whether N's right contingently originated in a grant from other people, and whether – contingently originating in this way or not – the right is extinguishable, and by whom, would be shown by spelling out the conditions mentioned in part (3) of the right. Similarly, part (3) would show whether or not, and by what procedures, N can alienate the right.

The right to a specific item of private property is an example, indeed the leading example, of an alienable right. The status connected with it, acquired in various ways, can be given up, and when it is given up, the exercisable aspect of the right disappears. Acquiring the status implies that the item in question was acquired by finding, or earning, or purchase, or by gift or inheritance; continuing to have the status implies that the item has not been sold or given away or forfeited.

Inalienable Rights

Are there any *inalienable* rights? Pretty clearly there are , and since these are (it seems) also rights that cannot be extinguished (alienable in N's case by someone else), the traditional extension of 'inalienable' to cover what would otherwise have to be called the 'inextinguishable' feature of certain rights can be decently excused.

Some rights are inalienable because it would not make sense for anyone to give them up; any attempt to do so would betray an inadequate understanding of the rights in question. They are inextinguishable because no procedure exists that accords other people the authority to extinguish them.

Indeed, it is typical of rights that they cannot properly be extinguished or even abridged without the consent, or at least the legislative participation, of the person or persons holding the rights. Rights that exist only on the sufferance of other people (e.g., the people who have granted them) are exceptional cases, even when they are important ones, such as the right of a member of the President's cabinet to take various actions so long as the President continues to accept him as a member of the cabinet. In such cases, even when the rights have to do with relatively unimportant actions (like looking up, with permission, something in someone else's diary) to say, 'N has a right to x,' or 'N has a right to do a,' means more than that it would not be wrong for N to do certain things; for now servants and policemen and neighbours, for example, are called on to respect successful exercise and to assist in protecting N against being interfered with in the exercise. N, for her part, has certain expectations on which she can base definite plans; the others concede the legitimacy of the expectations.

Some rights cannot be abridged even with N's consent. Consider the right to a fair trial (in the United States, also the larger right to due process of law); or the right to free speech. A person of a specially servile or masochistic disposition, or maybe a perfectly normal person in a threatening situation, might perhaps on some occasion feel ready to say, 'I abrogate my right to a fair trial' or 'I abrogate my right to free speech.' But what sense would there be in her saying either of these things? They go much further than not invoking the right in a particular instance.

Saying them would make no more sense than your saying or my saying, 'I declare the currency of the United States worthless' or 'I declare Nova Scotia to be French-speaking.' There are some things that one can do by words: appoint somebody to take one's place for certain purposes; agree in our person to buy a house; renounce citizenship in a particular country. Such verbal performances change the world, but their scope is understood to be defined by prior provisions for correct procedures and suitable occasions. Without such acknowledged provisions the performances would be conceptually out of place. They are out of place in the case of rights that are understood to be inalienable. No person, on any occasion, ever has the acknowledged power necessary to abrogate his right to a fair trial or his right to free speech.

By emigrating to one or another less than charming country, a person bent on making as little as possible of his rights might put himself in the hands of people who could be counted on to infringe his right to a fair trial or his right to free speech. Likewise, a government might, by decree or by some form of legislation, instruct its minions to hold bloody assizes rather than fair trials and to suppress free speech rather than protect free speakers. But this is similarly beside the point. As the rights to a fair trial and to free speech are understood by people using our language, no government has or could have the acknowledged power to extinguish those rights. They are understood to be inextinguishable. So long as this understanding continues, any laws or decrees purporting to do so would be conceptually *ultra vires* and therefore void.

Rights that people have put beyond the powers of government to extinguish are rights that they have often conceived of putting beyond their own powers, too, whether to extinguish or to alienate. Historically, they have regarded these rights as somehow inherent in the nature of man and of human society, or they have (maybe simultaneously) regarded the rights as conferred on human beings by God. The latter position, looking to divine authority and decree, begs fewer questions about confusing moral notions with descriptive ones, though it has the weakness of depending on religious belief. However, even the former position may well attract some convictions; for it may be argued that unless various rights are maintained, a human society will not succeed, or will not have certain widely desired properties.

Rules for Rights Distinguished from Other Rules

The rules that define social activities and the roles that people play in them concern relations between different persons and reciprocal actions (or inactions). When one person does certain actions, he looks to others to respond by doing appropriate actions of their own, or at least by refraining from doing inappropriate ones. Are these other people, then, always being 'called upon' in the same sense as the people called upon by setting forth a rule under the concept of rights? The notion of calling upon demands more careful consideration; once we have met the demand, we shall be in a position to clear up the notion of setting forth, too.

Consider the following cases: (1) N is a concert-goer, and M is a member of the orchestra, indeed, the first trumpet. N may expect M to play the right note in a certain passage of the overture; he has paid for his ticket and come to hear the music accurately played. Does he have a right to have M play the right note? (2) J is a player in the orchestra, say, the percussionist; a drum tap from her gives M the cue to play a certain flourish on the trumpet. Does N (again the concert-goer) have a right to have M sound this flourish, once the cue has been given? Here, as in the first case, M is surely called upon to play as expected, though here, the calling upon is directly signified by an action of J's. (3) N, a sergeant, orders a platoon of infantry, to which M belongs, to present arms. M may fail to do so. Does N, who by her command has certainly and quite explicitly called upon M to present arms, have a right to have M do so? (4) Two men pick up baseball gloves, and one of them, N, picks up a ball; they separate to a distance of forty feet and face one another; N then throws the ball to the other man, M. M is called upon to catch it (if he can) and (at any rate) to throw it back. If he steps aside, however, has any right of N been violated? (5) N sets herself up on a street corner to hawk wind-up toys to passers-by. As her spiel begins, a small audience gathers. The people in the audience, who include M, are certainly being called on to buy the toys. Does the hawker, N, have a right that requires M or anyone else in the audience to respond? (6) N and M are introduced to one another. N offers M his hand. Does he have a right to a handshake? (7) N and J know each other and have not hitherto been on hostile terms. N encounters J on the street and greets her. Can J snub him without violating one of his rights?

In all of these cases, N acts so as to establish a context of action, in which a reciprocal action is called for and may reasonably be expected to occur, as everyone participating in the context understands. Yet I hold that the callings upon in none of these cases have the force of rights. In some cases, I suggest, they fail to have the force of rights because the one doing the calling upon cannot compel the other to reciprocate; nor will other people help to compel M. Compulsion does not enter the picture. Clearly, it does not in the streethawker's case; I hold that it does not, in any relevant strength, in the pitch-and-catch case either, or the cases in which M or J may spurn N's hand or fail to acknowledge his greeting. In these cases, N and the onlookers may reproach M or J for their disappointing behaviour. When M, supposing he tentatively moved to buy a toy from the street hawker, makes it clear that he has decided against doing so, the reproaches stop, if they have even begun; when it is clear that M really does not want to play pitch-and-catch, the reproaches will cease. M's discourtesy regarding the handshake and J's regarding the greeting may be taken more seriously; in some special contexts N and other people may follow them up by demanding that M or J apologize. I am not sure that something like a right does not begin to be visible then, at least to the people demanding the apology, though the language of rights may not be used. Normally, however, M's and J's discourtesies will not be redressed. They may have lost possible friends in consequence, since what they did in discourtesy was significant, but they will not be compelled to shake hands or return the greeting, much less compensate N for their having omitted to do these things.

If M, as a trumpeter, plays the wrong note, it may be that he cannot help doing so; if he is an able and conscientious trumpeter otherwise, no question of punishment may arise, and neither N nor anyone else (including M's employer) might be said to have a right that has been violated. If he deliberately plays the wrong note, however, compulsion enters the picture; the management will not keep a player who deliberately ruins a performance. It has a right to have the player do the job that he was hired to do. Likewise, compulsion enters relevantly into the other orchestral case and into the military example.

In the orchestral cases, however, N does not have a right that M violates if M fails to respond. (Perhaps the audience as a whole has a right to have the performance occur, having bought tickets, but they have no right to have it occur flawlessly.) The compulsion will not be exerted to enforce a right of N's (though he may benefit) but to enforce a right of management's; the option of invoking compulsion lies with the management, not with N.

The military example requires more elaborate treatment. It shows that we cannot simply say rights are distinguished by systematic compulsion, even though – as the other examples show – many callings upon differ from the callings upon brought to bear with rights in not being so backed. In the military example, a great deal – perhaps a maximum – of systematic compulsion is present. If M fails to present arms, to be sure, he is defying discipline – the organizational hierarchy of the army, not just the particular sergeant confronting him – but he is defying N, the sergeant, too, and N may invoke compulsion (e.g., order a couple of other members of the platoon to escort M to be confronted by the company commander).

We cannot say that the sergeant does not have a right in the matter because superiors do not have rights in relation to inferiors; for though this comment has some value, it is not strictly true: parents have rights in relation to their children even while the children are inferior in strength. Does N, the sergeant, have no right because she has no option? She cannot let M's defiance pass. If the company commander is watching, he will not let N let it pass. But though rights typically are optional in respect to exercise, not all rights are; people do not have an option about exercising their right to a fair trial, or at least to a fair hearing at which they are told that they have such a right, and the right covers their choosing, aware of what they are giving up, to plead guilty.[4]

I suggest that the reason why we do not normally or naturally speak of a 'right' in the sergeant's case is that we cannot easily imagine anyone's interfering with the sergeant from outside. Assuming that N's command 'Present arms!' itself is not an act of disobedience, the whole army – a formidable self-contained bureaucracy – backs N in the execution of her duties and in the maintenance of discipline. Suppose, however, that some conflict arises between the military and the civil authorities. N and her platoon have been sent to garrison a small town and the civil authorities there try to prevent her giving orders and having them carried out. Then, I think, we would begin to speak of N's right to give the command 'Present arms!' and other, more important commands and simultaneously imply that compulsion beyond the normal military regime might legitimately be employed to enforce N's right. Proceedings of some sort might be taken against the town authorities.

So extended, I think the military example throws light on how rights first come to be spoken of when they are added to practices already established and familiar. It also throws light on the general relation of rights to compulsion. We speak of a right, I suggest, only when there is (or has been) a real prospect of N's being obstructed by other people in doing whatever the rights would entitle her to do – which is typically something quite definitely circumscribed. According N various rights amounts to according her, piecemeal, in various particular connections where there is (or has been) a genuine need on her part for such devices, the means of invoking systematic compulsion against people otherwise expectably equal or superior in power. Where comprehensive social provisions for superordination and subordination exist, as in the army, N normally has no need for for the piecemeal help of such devices when she is acting within the authority conferred upon her by these other provisions.

The callings upon associated with rights differ, then, from many other callings upon by being connected (as they are not) with systematic compulsion exercised on behalf of the holder of the right for his benefit or (as with a parent) in the execution of his functions. They differ from other callings upon, which are connected with systematic compulsion, in not having the support of a comprehensive system of superordination and subordination among agents, which would make piecemeal devices for invoking compulsion superfluous. Whether the compulsion will actually be exercised or not depends typically (though not always) on the holder's initiative in exercising her right and in calling for enforcement if the exercise runs into interference. More precisely, to say that N has a right implies that the right is or ought to be enforceable by systematic compulsion if compulsion of this sort would be effective in cases of this kind.

Double Variation: Legal or Not-Legal; Morally Endorsed or Not Morally Endorsed

The means of invoking systematic compulsion contemplated in assertions of rights are normally legal means, and the implied systematic nature of the compulsion behind rights is the systematic nature of ordinary legal processes. Either the compulsion is now available in the law or it ought to be. The callings upon associated with rights are further distinguishable from other callings upon by their complex relationship to the law and to moral endorsement.

This complex relationship consists in rights and their callings upon being subject to a double variation. A right, and thus its callings upon, may or may not be morally endorsed, and they are either asserted as already matters of law or championed as deserving recognition with the force of law.

Of the four possible joint cases that result from this double variation, only three require to be considered. A right championed as an addition to the law without being morally endorsed, at least by the person championing it, would awaken at most only technical interest; if any substantial benefits or drawbacks hung upon it, the question of moral endorsement would stand in the way, and have to be entered upon, before the addition could be rationally approved. The three important cases of the double variation all concern either moral endorsement or an assertion of fact about present law, or both together; and the case of both together, when the right is both a matter of current law and morally endorsed, overshadows the other two. This is the paradigm of rights, though it does not represent all of them.

When a right no longer commands moral endorsement, either it becomes a dead letter or its exercise begins to invite disputation. Why should it be exercised or respected if it no longer has moral backing? On the other hand, a right that has not yet made its way into the law invites disputation by coming forward as a proposal, legal-in-intention, demanding assessment on both moral and legal grounds before it becomes legal-in-fact. By contrast, a right that has both moral endorsement and legal recognition has (at least for the time being) settled into place: it is fully a right, currently unshaken by disputes.

I hold that saying N has a certain right is logically equivalent to setting forth a combination of rules, bearing upon various matters and expressing various callings upon. These rules have parallels in the sort of propositions that von Wright calls 'normative statements.'[5] Such statements assert the current existence of the rights in the combination and, as statements, they have truth values. However, a declaration that N (or others) has a certain right does not imply such parallel statements when the declaration appears in a bill proposing the enactment.

The thesis that a right is always either legal-in-fact or legal-in-intention needs to be qualified, but not so qualified as to give any credit to the view that sometimes 'N has a right to do a' means no more than 'It would not be wrong for N to do a,' which lends some support to the familiar position that there are two corpuses (corpora?) of rights, one corpus moral, one corpus (to an extent parallel) legal. This position itself is something that I want to reject.

It is, I hold, never the case that 'N has a right to do a' means no more than 'It would not be wrong for N to do a.' If the latter statement is all that is meant, then uttering the former sentence is a mistake (even if it happens fairly frequently, since it can always be effectively challenged). Changing from asserting a right to saying that it is not wrong always involves stepping down, waiving the callings upon specially directed at M and other people. Changing from saying that it is not wrong to asserting a right to do a always involves stepping up, bringing on the scene special callings upon not previously given attention, though these may still have to be spelled out.

One can feel the force of the changes everywhere. N has lent his car to M for the day now over. It would not be wrong for N to take the car back; but if only this could be said, it would not be wrong, either, for M to keep it. N has a *right* to take the car back. N has a right to a fair trial; having it, he would be remarkably unwise to settle for the concession that it would not be wrong for him to have a fair trial. N has (from M) a right to look at M's diary, and so may expect M's secretary to make it available; if it were merely a case of its not being wrong for him to look, given that he has a good reason to, everything would depend on the secretary's goodwill. It would not, perhaps, be wrong for N to attend classes at X, a school for Catholic children; but that is a far cry from his having a right to attend classes there.

Not only does its not being wrong for N to do a fail to imply that N has a right to do a; N's having a right to do a does not imply its not being wrong for N to do a. Having a right amounts to having in hand a special social device. However, it cannot be guaranteed that the device will never be used in ways that are morally objectionable. Human knowledge and foresight, as embodied in the construction of social devices, do not extend so far. N may have a right to marry a certain girl – he is not married; she is not; both are healthy; both are of age; she has freely given her consent – yet it may transpire that it is wrong for him to exercise his right in this case. Perhaps a discrepancy in their ages is objectionable; perhaps marriage will prevent either or both of them from pursuing careers of great benefit to the community.

Probably there are several ways of distinguishing even highly generalized assertions of rights from denials of wrongdoing. One way follows from distinguishing in matters of skill and in competitive situations between attempting and achieving. 'It is not wrong to do a' applies equally well to attempts and to achievements: it is equally not wrong to cry up one's goods and to sell the whole lot of them; to study German and to master it; to work on brake design and to invent an improved braking system; to enter a race and to win it; to try to prevent a hurricane from occurring and to prevent it. In such cases, however, one can have rights only to attempt, not to achieve. (Sometimes the crucial verbs are ambiguous between attempting and achieving; the street hawker has a right to sell her toys – if she can.) The reason is not far to seek: to require the actions of other people that would defend and guarantee N's achieving such things either would be absurd, as beyond human capacity, or would destroy the species of interaction in question: bring the game to an end, spoil the race as a competitive sport, or close off opportunities for economic competition.

There is frequently a discrepancy between rights morally endorsed and rights legally recognized, but this occurs in two sorts of cases: the cases where people affirm certain rights as matters of law, without meaning to endorse them morally; and the cases where people endorse certain rights morally without meaning to imply that they are already matters of law. There is, of course, no discrepancy in the central cases where the rights are both matters of law and morally endorsed.

Is it to be supposed that in such central cases there are two sets of rights, moral rights and legal rights, which here fortunately happen to match? The two corpuses (two corpora!) view is not an economical explanation. Moreover, it leaves one to grope in separate spheres for moral rights as against legal rights without furnishing any instructions about where the sphere of moral rights might be looked for. Turning away from the two corpuses view to the view adopted above, one beholds rights ascending from championship to full recognition, at once moral and legal; and then, in some cases, with the passage of time losing their moral force while they retain a foothold in the letter of the law. This conception dispenses with dispensable mysteries and stimulates inquiries correctly aimed at historical processes of debate, innovation, and decay.

The thesis that a right is always legal-in-fact or legal-in-intention nevertheless requires qualification in at least two connections.

In the first place, the law in question may be not the law of government and the courts of justice, but the law of other institutions – of the church, for example, or of a university, relating either to its faculty or to its students. The law in some of these institutions has provisions for testimony and adjudication as elaborate and continuous as in the courts of justice. The parallels, of course, vary from firm to faint. A grievance procedure, voluntarily conceded by management to non-union employeees, will be less law-like than canon law, which is enforced by ecclesiastical courts; though grievance procedures established in a union contract might not suffer from the comparison. The rules of a private club may be very informal; the customs of a family would in most families hardly be codified at all. Yet even in a family there may be something enough like a legal system for parents and children to have mutually acknowledged rights within their own household. (Perhaps, for instance, they have a right, day by day, turn by turn, to choose dessert.)

In the second place, there are some cases of rights that are championed, even acknowledged as fully as they ever are going to be, without there being any intention of making them matters of law, whatever kind of law or institution might be in question. Such, for example, is the right of a friend, about whom you have expressed suspicions, to obtain a hearing from you. More, certainly, is at issue here than its not being wrong for her to have a hearing; it would be absurd to suggest that there is not more. Yet, almost equally clearly, people would be reluctant to make such a right a matter of law, to be enforced in procedures for formal hearings, with compulsory process for witnesses, ending in adjudication ignored only on the pain of incurring the judges' displeasure. Litigation would kill the friendship more surely than the suspicions.

Both these qualifications, sized up too quickly, tend to give new life to the two corpuses (corpora?) view. Are not rights that are never meant to be law members of another corpus? Are not rights connected with systems of rules not legal in the full, general, public sense best thought of in the same way? The two corpuses (corpora?) view, however, simplifies matters in a complex field of topics without anything like due regard for the structure of the field. In that structure rights simultaneously morally endorsed and legally affirmed are central. All other rights are to be understood as approximations of these. When I say 'Your friend has a right to a hearing from you,' I mean that you, though not in fact under legal compulsion in this connection, should accord her something like the same serious attention to the right as if it had the force of a law that you respect.[6]

All of the examples of callings upon mentioned above as not having the force of rights could be recast by innovation so as to have that force. One might imagine a society taking pitch-and-catch so seriously that the man who stepped aside instead of trying to catch the ball would be taken to court in disgrace. There are societies where what might seem to us mere failures of courtesy would be treated as violations of rights: there the spurned hand would turn to litigation, or to the sword. The hawker might be given the right not merely to sell her toys – if she can – but to force sales of them on each of her auditors.

Innovation has not, in fact, gone to such lengths. There are plenty of social rules that fall outside the concept of rights. It is lucky that there are, because not only would it dilute the force of the concept of rights, it would turn out to be extremely inconvenient, if innovation were carried to the limits of what might be treated as rights. The resulting system of interaction would be rigid beyond anything yet dreamed of in human societies. If people insisted on all their rights – and what point would there be in giving them all these rights if they could not insist, directly or through their guardians? – no discretion would any longer be left to expected or hoped-for respondents; law would ordain the reciprocal roles of people interacting with one another, without any room for mercy or charity or even kindness. (Would we ever say, except mockingly, that it was 'kind' of a man to respect the rights of others?) Where it was not desired to have the reciprocation exacted from M as a matter of right – as it would not be in the case of the street hawker; as it would not be, one supposes, in the case of every possible suitor for a given lady's favours – the possibility of N's initiating interaction would have to be cut off. The result would drastically impoverish social life on the side of interpersonal initiatives and stifle any chance of freedom or discretion on the side of interpersonal responses.

The Justification of Rights

Forestalling Considerations of Consequences Pending New Legislation

The person holding a right is the person (normally) entrusted with deciding whether or not it shall be exercised. If it is an alienable right, and he has not forfeited in any way the status associated with it, he is the person to decide whether or not it shall be alienated. Rights function like moral or legal instruments, distributed to the people (normally) most concerned with invoking them, whether to protect themselves in the exercise of the rights or in the associated status.

The valid assertion of a right is (normally) conclusive against speculation about the possible consequences of heeding or not heeding the right asserted. It is also normally conclusive against general consideration of such consequences, even when the consideration is *not* speculative. An agent, faced with an assertion of right calling for a facilitating response from her, cannot excuse herself by saying that the general happiness might possibly be advanced by disregarding the right. She cannot even excuse herself from honouring the right by saying truthfully that several unfortunate things are likely to happen if the right is not disregarded in this case, so unfortunate that the consequences of disregarding it will probably be better than the consequences of respecting it.

Like other remarks that I have just been making, this remark rejecting excuses needs to be qualified with the word 'normally.' If the consequences of disregarding a right would be a final and irremediable disaster, obviously not anticipated when the right was established, the agent would be excused for disregarding it in that particular case.

However, one of the basic purposes behind the practice of establishing rights, asserting them, and heeding them is precisely to forestall general considerations of happiness or well-being and the like from being freely invoked to decide the particular cases embraced by rights. Neither the person asserting the right nor the agent or agents called upon to respect it would normally be able in a particular case to review thoroughly the alternative possibilities and their consequences. It would be dangerous to empower agents to act on such reviews as they can make: dangerous not only because the agents are liable to bias by their own interests (or the interests of any group to which they owe special allegiance), and with the bias deviating from a balanced view of the demands of the asserted right in making their reviews, but dangerous also because the agents involved are out of communication with one another and do not have the information necessary to coordinate their actions. Hence, some gains obtained by individual agents' disregarding a certain right, taking these violations one by one, may be cancelled out by the aggregate losses sustained by the persons holding the right (and by other people).[7]

As devices for protecting personal interests rights are imperfect, because, as it turns out, they conflict with one another in unanticipated instances; and because, perhaps without such a conflict occurring, they sometimes turn out to do less than they were expected to do to protect interests, and possibly turn out, in fact, to do more harm than good (e.g., by generating a lot of vexatious litigation). This eventuality may be discovered either simply from the succession of events, or by reconsidering the supposedly beneficial features of the devices. What seemed to be net benefits may not be found to be so when a correct view is taken of the relevant consequences. (For a utilitarian, rights are rule-utilitarian devices, subject, in the appropriate circumstances, to revision on an act-utilitarian review.[8])

One might imagine such imperfections – conflicts of rights with rights, conflicts of rights with welfare – being dealt with by periodic general legislative sessions embracing or representing the whole community to which the individual persons, holding rights and called upon to heed rights, belong. Those persons are forestalled from acting independently to correct the imperfections, but they may act together and legislate. General consideration of the net benefits of consequences, ruled out in individual cases, would then be postponed only until the next legislative session. In that session the rights in question would be modified for future use, and perhaps some sort of compensation would be arranged for those who had unexpectedly suffered from the past exercise of the unmodified rights.

This imaginary picture is, of course, much too tidy. Legislation does visibly occur and visibly affect the existence or the scope of particular rights. Overshadowing the formalities of legislation, however, are larger historical processes of debate, fashion, obsolesence, piecemeal variation. Much about these processes is obscure. Such debate as people carry on about rights is intermittent. Favour or disfavour for given rights may depend not so much on debate anyway as on motivations unacknowledged or unperceived.

Whatever their nature, historical processes gradually raise up new rights to fixed positions and at the same time undermine the position of the old ones (though not of all the old ones). Meanwhile, however, the chief way out of the rigidity of current rights lies in the discretion accorded to the rightholder in respect to exercising it or forbearing to exercise it. Besides pointing out to rightholders that they have this discretion and responsibility, the instructions about exercising rights should stress that it is not always good to exercise one's rights. Doing so frequently exemplifies priggish, selfish, even callous conduct.

Inalienable Rights Again

The justification of particular rights requires empirical evidence about effects promoting human interests. This evidence is fallible; it therefore invites periodic review. How, then, can there be inalienable or inextinguishable rights? True, some rights might pass every test again and again. Yet logically, what may have been a justified right a generation ago might in every case no longer be justified. Would it not be perverse to safeguard any right from all attempts at relegislation? Perverse, one would think, and very likely often futile, because the long-term, large-scale historical processes that raise up certain rights and wear away others will go on, notwithstanding, and may affect, ultimately through legislative proposals, almost any right that one cares to name.

A right is inalienable or inextinguishable because people understand it to be so. Reflecting carefully on such a right, they would reject identifying it with any combination of rules that contained provisions for alienation or extinction as not offering a correct analysis. But why should people, choosing to understand certain rights in this fashion, put the rights out of reach of themselves or their successors, as regards giving them up or abolishing them? Historically, no doubt, the chief reason has been the conviction, already mentioned, that the rights in question originate with God or in nature. Even without this conviction operating, however, people may regard certain rights as inalienable, considering that the rights in question have emerged from profound social processes worth continuing respect. If the rights themselves are morally enlightened, this respect may not be misplaced; the rights may be touchstones for moral enlightenment. The fact that they are inalienable rights does not perhaps entail that they are enlightened (they might be priestly prerogatives); but the fact that they are enlightened (to be treated humanely when in the hands of the police) may reconcile people to their being inalienable.

There is, furthermore, an impressive empirical consideration that offers a strong defence, indefinitely continuing, for the inalienability or inextinguishability of certain rights. Mindful of the weaknesses of human nature and aware of the imperfections of provisions for legislation, people believe they will be safer if certain rights, like the rights of free speech and free association, are kept out of reach. They choose to regard some rights as inalienable, perhaps because they know that on almost any issue people can be frightened or deceived into giving oppressors a show of consent. They choose to regard some rights as inextinguishable, because they do not entirely trust the motives of people in power or their own capacity to control legislation. They may be very uncertain about some of these matters; but this uncertainty itself might be a reason for taking precautions.

Some rights, it might be said, are inalienable and inextinguishable for reasons that no empirical evidence could upset. Could the alienation or extinction of a right to a fair trial be accepted under some social conditions? It is misleading to answer 'Yes' too quickly to this question. One may point out that it would be possible for a society not to have trials at all, either because it had to its own satisfaction eliminated crime and conflict or because it depended entirely on other methods for dealing with them. One can argue that societies are imaginable – hard, but not impossible for us to describe – which may have provisions for trial and other familiar features of our own society, but which do not have any concept of rights. (The scholarship that argues that rights in the modern sense were first thought of in the thirteenth century[9] implies that preceding societies – the Roman Republic and the Greek city-states, for instance, are examples of highly civilized societies that got along without rights, though not without laws.) Yet it seems to be true, nevertheless, that if a society makes any use of the concept of rights to regulate its affairs, then in that society there must be a right to a fair trial (or at least to a fair hearing) in controversies about other rights, a right inalienable and inextinguishable. There must also be any other rights logically indispensable to the just administration of any scheme of rights whatever.

Even in making these last points I have relied, as grounds for inalienable and inextinguishable rights, on empirical considerations about how people understand the rights in question; there are logical connections within any system of rights, but whether there is any system, or any rights, depends on what people believe and do. Such considerations, though not always going so far as to support a system of rights, are grounds for identifying any rights.

I am inclined to take grounds of the sorts that I have mentioned – straightforwardly empirical in some cases, at once logical and empirical in others – as sufficient for understanding rights and conscientious practice with them. It is possible to take what people understand in a more rigorous sense, following Fichte,[10] in holding that philosophers, when they raise questions about what warrants our knowing anything, must ackowledge rights when they identify the conditions (the transcendental conditions) of our understanding anything. If you take up (which I myself am disinclined to do) the project with which, since Descartes, generations of philosophers have been preoccupied, of finding convincing philosophical reasons that lay to rest doubts which philosophers have raised about our capacity to understand anything about ourselves, about the world, and about our position in the world, Fichte's way of carrying out the project seems to me as good as any, better than most.

I have in mind the younger Fichte, as interpreted with great impact on recent French philosophy by Alexis Philonenko;[11] and in the younger Fichte, I set aside the teachings that presage the absolute, all-encompassing Ego of the older Fichte. The fundamental principle of Fichte's approach is that I cannot realize what I am myself – most significantly, an embodied rational agent – except by distinguishing myself from other embodied rational agents (who, identifying themselves, have, at least in some cases, me in mind as distinguished from them). When I do this, I am bound to recognize them as having rights against me, the most important being the right not to be denied scope for exercising their powers of creation, just as I have rights against them. Rights are thus basic features of intelligible experience. Fichte quite realizes that there is some way to go from these basic rights to specifying the full content of rights in ethical or legal theory or in the practice of rights in a specific society; and he applies himself in argument to go that distance. However, it is already an arresting accomplishment to make a convincing case that rights come up simultaneously with each of us recognizing that we are present in the world with other rational agents, engaged in the same sorts of activities and inquiries.

Can Rights Be Bundles of Rules and Still, in Some Cases, Natural?

A distinction is often made in philosophy between 'conventional' and 'natural'; and rights treated, as I treat them, as being composed of rules may seem to fall on the 'conventional' side of this distinction and hence not qualify as 'natural.'[12] If we do not make a hard and fast distinction between 'conventional' and 'natural,' however, we can ask whether some sets of rules might be more natural than others.

Consider a set of rules *R* that, given constant basic features of human nature and a wide range of circumstances – perhaps the whole range in which human beings can live and reproduce – is indispensable to the thriving of a society and of its members (with a little luck in respect to war and natural disasters, all its members). Now suppose that an indispensable subset of *R* consists of rules combined as rights. Would they not be rights that in a reasonably convincing sense invite being called 'natural'? Let the indispensable subset be called [NR1].

Relax the second assumption. The subset of *R* consisting of rights is not indispensable, but it plays an impressively substantial part in *R*'s contribution to the thriving of society and its members. The case for calling them 'natural,' even if it turns out to be wise to make them inalienable and inextinguishable, weakens. But does it disappear? If it does not, then we have a second worthwhile sense of 'natural rights,' holding for the set [NR2].

Now relax the first assumption. *R* is not indispensable, but it belongs to a set of sets of rules from which it is indispensable to the thriving of society and its members to select a set. Now, in the set of sets every set might be such that the rules about rights would be indispensable; that would give us a sense of 'natural rights' almost as strong as the one holding for [NR1]: call it [NR1prime].

Further variations in assumption are possible that would preserve some claim to being natural for some rights. Moreover, some rights might be such that they would indispensably figure in any set of rights. For example, how could there be a robust practice of rights without a right to a fair trial of any disputes about rights? (This point was very important to John Locke.) Whichever of the above possibilities is realized, if this additional condition is met by a given right, it will have an enhanced title to being called 'natural.' Moreover, if a set of rules about rights is to carry really substantial weight in keeping up arrangements indispensable to the thriving of a society and of its members, rights against being harmed bodily or threatened with death might claim a place in every acceptable set. Again, that would give such rights an enhanced title to being called 'natural.'[13]

Rights Serving as Tests of Government Performance

Examples of Rights So Serving, in Particular Locke's Right of Private Property

It will help to understand how rights serve, not only to protect individual persons (and, exceptionally, private collectivities), but as tests of government performance, to consider some examples. When governments fail to respect the rights to freedom of expression or freedom of movement, they fail an important test. Likewise, they fail an important test when they fail to respect civil rights, like equal access to schools or other public facilities or equal opportunity for employment, private or public. The use of the concept of rights in such tests is an unsurpassably important one, and the examples I have given are important instances of rights that figure in the tests. However, they all have been elaborately discussed elsewhere by other authors. I shall take up another right, not perhaps so widely discussed as a test nowadays, though it has its fervent adherents, Nozick and others: the right to private property. After saying something about its importance in the past, in both theory and practice, I shall consider how present conditions favour attention, in respect to doing the same sort of work, to a second specific right, a new right: the right to a livelihood.

Whether a particular government is acceptable or not depends, for John Locke, whose view in this connection was long a model especially for American beliefs, on how well it passes the test of maintaining and protecting the right of private property. Robert Nozick followed Locke on this point – indeed, held it more adamantly – and did not include under the right, as Locke did, one's life and liberty as well, though Nozick favoured rights to these things, too. I shall here treat the right as if it concerned material goods only, chiefly farmland and the material assets of business enterprises. The right to private property, Locke held, citizens had anyway, without government. Government offers citizens no advantages over a state of nature in which these rights are recognized if government does not make the recognition and the defence of the right more assured.

One might wonder whether governments do not offer many other advantages: institutional support for enterprises of all kinds – irrigation; emergency measures organizations; schools; highways; national parks. But one must not foist on Locke our modern tendency to think of any social enterprise as an instance of government if it is carried on by the same institutions that exercise police powers. One must also remember Locke's near silence on the general subject of organized forms of social cooperation. For Locke, a government properly has the strictly limited function of protecting the property of citizens (though again, he includes under this head their lives and liberties). Government, in Locke's conception (and in Nozick's), tends to reduce to nothing more or less than a property owners' mutual protection association, and its job (apart from defence against external enemies) is confined to the work of the police and the courts.

This conception of government was already deeply entrenched in American thought before laissez-faire theories limiting government interventions in the economy appeared to reinforce it. It has had, and continues to have, a remarkably strong grip on North America, which was the part of the world to which Locke's conception best applied. North America was a part of the world in which self-supporting subsistence farmers could be reckoned to be typical citizens; and so long as a surplus of natural resources remained free for the taking on the frontier, an opportunity remained for other people to make themselves into independent subsistence farmers.

Given such circumstances, Locke shows how to obtain concrete safeguards for personal liberty without launching into abstract perplexities about a universal and generalized right to liberty. He also shows how sensible and far-reaching a case can be made for an unqualified stress upon the instrumental nature of government. Where, as in the given circumstances, a comparison with the state of nature makes some sense, government is not merely an instrument; it is an optional instrument for achieving limited purposes.

In the given circumstances, the right to private property – let us mean, here, just land – does most of the work of the right to liberty. The chief things that one would wish to demand under the heading of liberty – respect for one's person and for the peaceful enjoyment of one's livelihood; political liberty and freedom of expression – are taken care of by recognizing the right to private property. Freedom of expression, without fear of reprisals that would take away one's life or livelihood, is assured to those who wish to use it; they may become unpopular by speaking out, but they can continue to live and prosper despite the unpopularity.

The things that were achieved – or, not to beg questions about its actual diffusion and effect, that could have been achieved – by the use, following Locke, of the right to private property may inspire similar achievements in our own day, when the right to private property is not suited to current circumstances. No one, of course, could plausibly hold that the right to private property has become obsolete. The skeleton-right – under which N establishes her status as rightful possessor by doing work in her own time upon resources free for the taking – survives as an object of vivid intuitive appeal, though it is not often invoked. So does the highly elaborated right familiar in capitalist societies under which N may become the rightful possessor in multifarious ways, involving little or no effort on her part, for instance, by inheritance or by windfalls in the stock market. (One must bear in mind that Locke's argument about the skeleton-right does not really extend to justifying the elaborated right. Present-day disciples of Locke pass over the gap with scandalous negligence.)

Nowadays, however, in America as in Britain, the typical member of society is very far from being a self-supporting subsistence farmer. It was not unreasonable for Americans of the generation of 1776 and 1789 to think of typical citizens as such, either actually or with some hope of being so; but they are not today and they have no prospect of becoming so. The typical member of modern society, in America and elsewhere, is an employee who depends for his livelihood on the continuing receipt, week by week or month by month, of a pay cheque. He may own property, but only rarely does this consist of property under his control in the means of production, and only more rarely still does the property amount to enough for him to live on the income from it.

An employee in the United States enjoys under the Bill of Rights the same protection against action by the government as did the self-supporting farmer of earlier days; but the rights do not give him the same security. In the first place, he must please his employer; and employers vary greatly in the amount of liberty that they are willing to grant employees on or off the job. In the second place, an employee must be careful, even if he satisfies his employer in other ways, not to become conspicuously unpopular with other people. In one disgraceful episode of American history, a matter of living memory to many still besides the present author, something called the House Un-American Activities Committee steadily played upon this consideration to bypass the Bill of Rights. Its subcommittees swept through the country, calling people into the limelight of unfavourable publicity, and leaving employers to deal with these people afterwards. The employers (sometimes universities that on other occasions had made resounding declarations in favour of academic freedom) were often willing enough to oblige. The result was a trail of dismissed employees and, one conjectures, for every dismissed employee thousands of people shut up by intimidation.

Was it much consolation to these people that the intimidation was practised without ever violating the right to private property, or even, strictly speaking, the rights enshrined in the Constitution? Liberty no longer derives the effective protection that it used to have (at least in principle) from the right to private property; and no other right has risen to firm recognition that can serve it in the same way.

The Right to a Livelihood: Bringing Locke Up to Date

Can such a right be found? Something with a reasonable chance of becoming fully established, as a right not merely legal-in-intention, but legal-in-fact as well, morally supported as nearly universally and strongly as any right could be expected to be? I think such a right can be found: the right to a livelihood.

Before I consider how (in principle) it might work, I should point out that every right comes with costs. People have to bear the burden of acting to keep the right up when violation occurs or is impending. In a complex society this cannot most of the time be left to public-spirited people engaging on their own in resistance to violations. It will entail having courts, judges, and lawyers. When sanctions have to be imposed, it will entail having prisons and warders. All these things will have to be paid for, and desirable alternatives given up. When an additional right is proposed, a well-run political society ought to investigate what it will cost in these ways to enact the right and keep it up. The investigation ought to consider what the costs of present rights are and what the proportionate increase in the burdens from adding the proposed one would be.

Some of the costs – the ones that I have just mentioned – might, even so, lend themselves to reasonably straightforward assessment. But not all. Some writers have suggested, quite plausibly, that rights are confrontational, setting people at odds in ways and to a degree that they would not otherwise be;[14] and that they encourage rigid individualistic stands on matters that would be better approached in a spirit of amiable cooperation.[15] I think that these, along with the impairment of being and feeling personally free that come from being beset by rights on every hand, are real costs to be weighed among the burdens of having rights, but I think that trying to measure them would tax the techniques of social science.

In the following discussion, I shall simply assume that the extra net costs of bringing in the right to a livelihood would be either negligible or at least not so great as to be an obstacle. [16]

The right to a livelihood would do approximately the same work that the right of private property does in the kinds of society which Locke's doctrine fits best. It would also do this work in kinds of society that his doctrine does not suit. It would, of course, leave some things to be safeguarded by other particular rights, or advanced by evaluative considerations outside the concept of rights, but the right to private property in Locke's doctrine is less than comprehensive in the same ways.

A right of the kind now sought may be found by modernizing Locke's doctrine. Following Locke's example and preserving what is still relevant and useful in his right to private property, we wish to identify a concrete and particularized right, relatively easy to comprehend and relatively easy to administer on a decentralized plan. The right should be effective against interferences, both on the part of government and on the part of private persons, with the most vital aspects of people's freedom – for example, freedom of speech, of association, of movement from town to town, from job to job. The range of governments to be subject to the test of the new right will be governments in various highly industrialized societies in which the population consists predominantly of employees of large bureaucratic organizations. Both societies in which these organizations are all public ones and societies in which some of them, perhaps most of them, are private, and many or most of these are profit making, need to be covered if we are to compare, say, the governments of the United States and Canada with the most relevant alternatives.

The clue to the necessary modifications has become manifest in the success in the past of Locke's doctrine of private property. The reason why the right to private property at one time offered a robust means of defending liberty was that in the past respecting this right accorded typical citizens protection in their livelihood. Should not typical citizens be accorded the protection today? Liberty and democracy would be well served by elevating livelihood to a central place in a right that is to embrace and carry on the work of the right to private property and by transforming the right explicitly into a right to a livelihood.

Simply by being a member of the society falling within the embrace of a certain government, N would be entitled, if he needed training, to training that would qualify him for employment. By being a member of the society and having qualifications for employment, he would have a status, either as a job holder or as a job seeker, calling upon other members of the society, M et al., in both private and public positions, to do or refrain from doing various relevant actions, like publishing information about job vacancies and abolishing arbitrary disqualifications generally; refraining from racial or religious discrimination in particular.

As a job seeker, N would be exercising his right to a livelihood by calling upon various people, M et al., to try him out (or at least give trying him out serious consideration) in suitable vacancies; perhaps he would be calling on various responsible officials, M et al., to assist him with economic policies that create jobs. If he is a job holder, N would exercise his right to a livelihood by continuing to perform the job and resisting attempts to dislodge him from it. For those relatively rare people with enough property to live on and for people with pensions, the right would extend to protecting those sources of their income and, in the case of pensions, to making sure that the pensions are adequate.

I am deliberately using 'livelihood' to range over ways of obtaining the means of maintaining life (perhaps, life in a decent style) rather than to refer to the means of maintenance themselves: food, shelter, clothing, and so on. Hence by a 'right to a livelihood' I mean a 'right to having some way of obtaining the means of life.' I am not sure that I am thereby extending the ordinary use of 'livelihood.' Getting their livelihoods from the sea or forest or farm or factory, people receive either money income from employment there or goods that they sell for income, sometimes goods that they themselves consume. Even in these connections, however, to 'lose one's livelihood' would mean more than to lose some stock of goods or money; it would at the very least mean to stop receiving a flow of such things, and, by implication, the flow would have stopped because the way in which the flow had been obtained no longer served. Hence, people do not merely think of themselves as 'depending for their livelihood' on their properties or their professions. Speaking with at most only a little liberty, they identify their livelihoods with these things. A doctor may speak of medicine as his livelihood; a storekeeper, of his grocery. (Compare, 'medicine' or 'the store' ... 'is his whole life.')

It seems to me that the present use of the term 'livelihood' is complex enough to sustain thinking of the right to a livelihood as amounting to the right to obtain one's income in the way one is now obtaining it, or in some other way for which there is a present opportunity, supposing that it is not criminally obtained. I want to leave it open whether the right guarantees obtaining an income when one's present way fails. (Other social institutions or devices may make such a guarantee redundant.) Without extending so far, the right serves to exact compensation for interferences with one's present way and prevent interferences with seeking new ways.

If such a right were fully established – morally endorsed not merely as a matter of recommendation, but morally endorsed along with being established in law – the chief extant means for intimidating people in the exercise of freedom, including their freedom to exercise other rights, would disappear. Whatever success Locke's doctrine has had in defending liberty would thus be regained, by means conceptually continuous with Locke's own. The right to a livelihood would carry on the right to private property, so far as such property is for some people still indispensable to their livelihoods; and extend similar protection to people dependent for their livelihoods upon employment.

The comparison with a state of nature remains relevant. Admittedly, it is now impossible for a population as large relative to resources as that of the United States to support itself in the absence of government and intermediate forms of organized cooperation (like food wholesalers; transportation systems; retail chains). Nevertheless, reference to such self-support's being possible in the past justifies the view that government was an instrument of people's purposes then. It has not ceased to be an instrument. What has happened is that it has become an indispensable instrument. But the reason that it is indispensable is still founded upon its being an instrument for helping men gain a livelihood. Government is, we may say, an instrument for maintaining everyone's right to a livelihood. A government that does not maintain this right does less well for its citizens than they could do for themselves, given a state of nature and sufficient resources for them to be self-supporting therein.

How near are we to having such a right? One might claim that, fully expressed, the right has no settled authority either in Canada or in the United States, though there are various legal provisions (stronger perhaps in Canada than in the United States) checking employers from arbitrarily refusing to give jobs to qualified applicants or arbitrarily dismissing them. Moreover, some steps have already been taken to extend to employees rights that would be subfeatures, at least, of a right to a livelihood. The right to a livelihood in a society of employees would not, it may be conceded, be so easy to administer as the right to private property in a society of subsistence farmers. A livelihood is not, in general, such a tangible consideration as this or that particular farm. The criteria for determining whether the right to a livelihood has been respected are liable to be extremely complex – for example, as regards the question whether a given woman is qualified for a certain job, or the one best qualified. The criteria for determining whether the right to private property has been respected are by comparison simple and straightforward – at least in societies of subsistence farmers, with just their sorts of private property to consider.

Nevertheless, what constitutes good reasons for denying a person a given job has been defined in part by judicial and administrative experience with fair employment practices acts. What are to be counted good reasons for dismissing someone from a job already held have, in part, emerged during the vicissitudes of administering acts protecting workers in their attempts to unionize. Unemployment insurance exists as if called into being by the right to a livelihood (although it can be argued for on other grounds). Administering the rule against paying unemployment insurance to persons who refuse suitable employment has helped to clarify notions about when jobs and qualifications match each other.

Moreover, as Cass Sunstein reminds us in *The Second Bill of Rights* (see n. 16), Franklin Delano Roosevelt, in his eleventh State of the Union Address (January 1944), argued, 'In our day, [certain] economic truths have become ... self-evident. We have accepted, so to speak, a second Bill of Rights'; and among those rights there are four that combine to correspond to a right to a livelihood:

The right to a useful and remunerative job in the industries or shops or farms or mines of the nation.

The right to earn enough to provide adequate food and clothing and recreation.

The right of every farmer to raise and sell his products at a return which will give him and his family a decent living.

The right to adequate protection from the economic fears of old age, sickness, accident, and unemployment.

Taken together, these approximate a right to a livelihood. Perhaps one should add, drawing again on Roosevelt's list, 'the right of every family to a decent home.' A livelihood without a decent home would certainly be incomplete.

These rights have not perhaps been very frequently invoked by particular individuals or even (as rights) guided point by point public debate and social policy (as Roosevelt no doubt hoped and intended). However, as Sunstein shows, they have been asserted quite comprehensively in the United Nations' Universal Declaration of Human Rights of 1948; reflected in United States Supreme Court decisions (until Nixon changed the complexion of the Court); and embodied as late as March 2003 in a resolution proposed in the United States House of Representatives for a constitutional amendment.[17] There is enough accumulated force behind these ideas, force behind the right to a livelihood, too, to arrest the attention of anyone concerned with the rights and liberties of typical members of current industrialized societies. Especially if the right to a livelihood is brought up, as I have brought it up, in a historically critical discussion of the right to private property, proposing it can be seen to be in order, a timely challenge to existing institutions.

Roosevelt and his advisers, including his wife, Eleanor (who carried the ideas to the United Nations), arrived at the ideas collected in the Second Bill of Rights by reflections, beginning in the 1920s and intensified during the depression years of the 1930s and the war years following, on the position of workers and farmers in contemporary American society. They did not follow the route that I have followed, tracing the contribution to personal liberty of the right of private property from Locke through the Bill of Rights of the 1790s and the subsequent industrialization of American society to a proposal for renewing the protection to liberty once given by the right of private property. However, my philosophy has ended up in the same place as their practical politics.[18]

4

Our Natural Bodies, Our Social Rights

This chapter originally appeared in Noûs as a comment on a paper by Samuel Wheeler, a philosopher whose good judgment I respect and who has gone on to other, soberer accomplishments. He wrote the paper in question during the high tide of Nozick's influence, daring to go, beyond Nozick, wherever Nozick's style of thinking led him. In the case of rights the style led him far astray from sober consideration of the social origin of rights and the rules for rights. Nozick's own intuitions about rights were astray in this way, too, and with this comment I enlarge the argument in the preceding chapter designed to bring rights back to earth as observable combinations of social rules.

Samuel Wheeler's amusing paper[1] demonstrates, wittingly or unwittingly, that it is as feasible in philosophy as in modern art to produce an undetectable spoof. Are the absurdities that it perpetrates in the course of assimilating every possible item of property to parts of the body, to be brought under the same right, meant to be taken seriously? If they are not, to proceed gravely against them with reasoned objections is ludicrous pedantry, like trying to put a ripple of laughter through a tea strainer. On the other hand, if they are to be taken as seriously intended – which, given Wheeler's evident intelligence and remarkable sense of humour, I hesitate to do – they suffice to send up, in a puff of lurid smoke, the argument in which they appear. How could I – how could anyone – outmatch in the way of *reductio* what the paper already incorporates? For example, the inference that if someone owns the whole world's supply of food, to coerce him into parting with any is 'on a par with taking the flesh of the only robust person against his will to feed the starving' (186)? Or the conclusion that 'theft, taxation, and disembowelment are different forms of the same kind of violation of rights' (189)?

One is tempted to declare one's own holiday from straight-laced convention and join in the fun. Why not run Wheeler's arguments the other way? Moving one way, there is, Wheeler claims, no line to stop us from treating virtually anything that can be included in a person's property as something that he has incorporated in his body and holds by right like any other bodily part. Moving the other way, is there any line to stop us from treating virtually any part of a person's body as something of which social policy can as easily, and with as little moral objection, divest him as it can of an oil refinery? (We might pay him compensation; if he had operated in flagrant disregard of the public interest, perhaps we would not.) Surely, it adds to the interest of the game to grant that we might have strong intuitions at both ends of the continuum.

But why should the game be confined to running over the ground that Wheeler has thought of? Wheeler concentrates upon the classic example of a single producer, working, whether for a market or not, without collaborators. Imagine, however, some primitive form of collaboration – say, two men working together to make a dugout canoe. If Wheeler's theory of bodily incorporation applies, would not each have a claim to the canoe – or at least to part of the canoe – as a new bodily part? Where, however, does a claim of the one stop and the claim of the other begin? If no line can be drawn, will not the finished canoe be part of both their bodies? When full account has been taken of collaborative production, original and derived, body rights may turn out to be a good deal less individualistic than Wheeler anticipates. We may have to regard ourselves as so entangled with one another's bodies that we literally cannot dissociate ourselves from the common good. United we'd stand – divided we'd, well, be not only divided, but considerably mutilated.

The theory of bodily incorporation goes up in smoke. Yet it may be worthwhile poking about in the ashes for a moment or two to see how it was contrived. Part of the contrivance is treating a right as an all-or-nothing matter. Having a right is never, in Wheeler's view, a matter of degree; the concept of having a right, unlike the concept of being good, has 'no underlying dimension' (182). Wheeler does, it is true, associate the right that most intrigues him, the right of each of us to move and use his or her body, with an object that turns out, as he sees it, to be amazingly variable. His own account of his discussion of this variation, moreover, invites us to think of the variation as running over something like a continuum, at one end of which the body has only natural parts firmly attached, while at the other extreme it has a great number of artificial parts, of the most unexpected kinds, wholly detached. However, just because a right is not itself subject to variation in degree, it must be wholly present everywhere in this range if it is present anywhere.

The continuum is – shall we say? – too contrived to survive testing. Quite apart, however, from the fast and loose play with fictions and possibilities that was required to tack the continuum together, does not the argument misrepresent the nature of rights? One might concede that having a right is not a matter of degree. We do speak of one person's having more right to do something or to have more of something than another person. This way of speaking could be explained, however, as equivalent sometimes to saying that the one person had a stronger case for being accorded a full right and sometimes to saying that the one person had a right to a greater share than the other. (Perhaps the two had collaborated in making something – the dugout canoe, for instance – but one had worked much longer and harder.) Once these cases have been sorted out, one would end up speaking without qualification of the person's right, revising as necessary the specification of what it is a right to.

Would we then have established a right free from any consideration of variation? Sometimes not. The right itself, though now specified without qualification, may remain to be established, and establishing it may require us to consider matters subject to variation. Do I have a property right in the design of this newly produced stereo phonograph? There may be no other claimant. Then the answer depends on how far the design was my invention rather than a conception, already commonplace, in the public domain; and we may not have settled in advance how such questions are to be decided in every case.

Moreover, the right, once established as mine, may have to be exercised, if it is to be exercised at all, again in matters subject to variation. Thus it is with my right – a clear historical case of an undoubted though not unqualified right, now obsolescent – to administer corporal punishment to my child; thus it is, too, with my right to use the phonograph that is my property whether or not I invented it. My neighbours might be electrified, and edified, to hear the 'Dies Irae' from Berlioz's *Requiem* one Sunday afternoon, especially if it comes to them without warning, but will I be acting within my right in turning the sound up to full power, 75 watts in each channel? That depends on how close they live to me. If they live at all close, my right to play the phonograph covers only the use of part of the power range; use of the power range at the maximum end falls outside the right.

Wheeler may believe that he has allowed for such cases in acknowledging that one person's rights stop short of infringing other people's (e.g., to peace and quiet, untroubled secular repose). So he has – but has he recognized that scope and infringement are jointly matters of continuous variation, involving doubtful cases?

Some rights are certainly less prone to variable complications than others. If one had to produce an example of a right at present as little afflicted with variation and doubtful cases as one could find, could one do better than cite the right to move and use one's body, in respect at least to what is to count as parts of the body? Nature, in her solicitude for the preservation of natural kinds, supplies in almost all cases the same natural parts and fixes them in the same places. Setting aside grotesque fantasies, which may defeat our intuitions, or delude them, we even have a pretty firm idea about what may count as an artificial part: it is something (unlike an oil refinery, or even a kidney machine) that fits within the bounds of our natural bodies. Moreover, except perhaps when the question is one of replacing esoteric parts like endocrine glands, it is something that fits into the body at the right place, occupying approximately the same space as the part replaced. How very odd that Wheeler should choose just this right, in just this respect, to complicate with fictitious variation!

At the end of Wheeler's paper, in a supplementary argument that goes to extraordinary lengths to separate rights from social life, the theory of reference puts in a brief appearance. I think it would be unwise for me to venture any distance into the theory of reference. Much more zealous semanticists have returned from expeditions there with their powers of discrimination apparently paralysed, uttering sometimes banalities, sometimes wildly improbable things, like the supposed antithesis, 'Reference depends on what is in the world, what kinds there actually are, not on what sets of things our response-patterns would pick out' (192). Fortunately, I do not need to venture very far to restore to the concept of rights some of their more important social connections.

One might ask, to begin with, does Wheeler keep in steady view the fact that in application rights always concern other persons besides the person having the right? That is to say, every right, at the same time as it implies a certain status and confers certain powers upon the person holding the right, implies obligations that fall selectively upon other persons with other statuses and roles when such persons are present: obligations, always, to refrain from impairing the right and from interfering with its exercise; obligations, always, to assist in gaining redress when the right has been violated; obligations, with some rights at least, to carry out certain actions when the rights are exercised. If it is my dugout, and I ask for it, you must get out of it and give it back to me.

Wheeler admits in one place, 'Property rights *are* social in the sense that an agent in isolation has in fact exclusive use of everything and so has no call to enforce any rights' (189). But does this amount to admitting, even to begin with, that the explication of any right must refer to multiple social roles, to be occupied by different persons? What he says later suggests that this point at least does not stay in view: 'A rational agent is necessarily such that, if he's in contact with other rational agents, he should be treated by them in certain ways. This feature gives him his right. But this no more shows that he or his rights depend on other agents than ... that a brontosaurus' weight depends on chipmunks' (191). 'Depend on' is equivocal. I am not arguing here for any dependence on other agents' say-so. In the sense of dependence directly at issue, however, the analogy with a brontosaurus breaks down. Rights cannot be defined (explicated) without referring to other (possible) agents and what they are severally to do or not to do.

Rights cannot be explicated, however, with a mere reference to other possible agents; persons who will occupy social roles different from the role of the person having the right if the right or its exercise comes into question must be mentioned. A right is a complex relation with places to be filled in by persons. Wheeler holds that '"person *qua* person" is a notion which is metaphysically independent of "society"'(190). Does he have in mind animated human bodies, capable of learning? No doubt it is beneath our notice when we are doing metaphysics to observe that the various capacities of such beings wither away if the beings are not appropriately stimulated and encouraged at different stages of their development. Even in metaphysics, however, may one not insist that persons are more than animated bodies with capacities for learning?

At this point metaphysics intersects with sociology, which many people will regret and which certainly makes things less amusing, though I am afraid there is no help for it. Persons are beings with socially established characters, who have already done a good deal of learning. What they have learned – what now makes up their characters – reflects their experience of interacting with other persons in various systems of roles (one system at home; another, perhaps several, at work; another at church; etc.). Changing from one system to another, they have learned to change roles and, with each such change, to suit their actions to a different set of rules. Changing roles within systems, they perhaps may regard themselves as acting under the same sets of rules, but they understand that the rules ask different things of them in different roles.

This social metaphysics does not describe the whole of life, or even the whole of social life, but it describes the part in which rights crop up. The agents envisaged in the conceptions of particular rights are persons with the social skills that come from taking up different roles in different contexts, discerning as they do enough about the applicable rules to act appropriately.

Inevitably, that means acting, not with mechanical regularity, but with discretion and judgment. Rules actually institutionalized, even when they have been formally legislated and set down in statute books, are never perfectly definite. They have to be adapted, by people who aim to conform to them, to novel cases. Even when the cases are not novel, the rules rely on the fact that the people following them fall in reasonably closely with a social consensus in action and comment as to what are to be treated as like cases. If the rules in question are not formally legislated ones, furthermore, just what the rules are is something that the people following them, and others, learn from the social consensus. Various processes shift the locus of this consensus about. 'Reference is up to us when we're baptizing, but reference of general terms is to kinds, and what is another element of the same kind is not up to us or to the contents of our concepts, but rather up to nature' (192–3). If the kinds at issue include, however, the sets of rules about status, exercise, assistance, non-interference, and redress in which rights are actually institutionalized, 'nature' itself, presenting us with variable social institutions, presents us with variable kinds. If the right of a vassal to the land he held from his feudal lord belongs to the same kind as the right of a homesteader to the land that he himself has cleared and farmed, is it not a kind that is remarkably subject to change?

Moreover, how did that 'baptizing' occur? Was it an act of fiat by one person who hit upon the concept of rights in advance of any institutionalization? Or was it a long social process, going on from precedent to precedent in the course of institutionalization, with consensus at every stage resting on particular institutional developments beforehand? We must not suppose that even now the consensus is perfectly settled. Patterns of action, with the language used to describe them and to assist in regulating them, will develop further – under constraints furnished by the patterns and language themselves.

The capacity of rights to figure thus in such developments, which is a capacity based on their open texture, may be one of their most useful and characteristic features.[2] However, once some stability had been reached in the language of rights and in their institutionalization, it was certainly possible for philosophers to reflect that certain rights – some of them, perhaps, idealized generalizations of rights actually institutionalized hitherto – were more valuable than others. In the course of their reflections, moreover, philosophers may have worked out theories systematically justifying these more valuable rights as answering to the nature of man or to the nature of moral agents better than any other set. They may thus have proved these rights indispensable to civilized life and moral community. Then they might criticize – as convincingly as the nature of such criticism allows – existing societies, including their own, for failing to institutionalize these rights, or for institutionalizing them imperfectly. They might even convincingly hold that the rights that they had identified were not subject to compromise, and hence (in that sense) not subject to modification.

The right to move and use one's body may be among those rights. There may be more doubt about whether the right to property in other items is among them; or, if it is, whether it is in any sense that embraces oil refineries. Whether it is or is not, however, is it not – like the right to move and use one's body, and all other rights – social in all the senses that I have touched on? Social, because to explicate it, multiple places must be opened for different persons? Social, because the persons who are to fill those places are social beings? Social, because it can be realized only in social institutions, amid variable social processes? Social, because even an idealized version originates in reflection on such institutions.[3]

SECTION C: RULES

5

The Representation of Rules in Logic and Their Definition

The concept of rules joins the concept of needs and the concept of rights as the third tool in my kit for dealing with questions of public policy. I have already brought in the concept of rules to explain what I hold rights to be. There, however, I used the concept of rules without analysing it. Analysing it is the purpose of the present chapter. I shall start up the analysis by considering what aspects of rules come to light in a formal logic of rules, first, the logic of norms or rules offered by von Wright, then the logic of rules offered by the Dalhousie University team that produced *Logic on the Track of Social Change*. Readers averse to formal logic, of which there are all too many, even in the ranks of philosophers, can leaf through this part of the chapter, or skip it entirely, though with some loss of benefits. The heart of the chapter lies in the definition of rules given in part 2, which with the Dalhousie team I arrived at in the course of working on the logic of rules, but which can be expounded, as it is here, without formalism, as is the account of the uses for the definition and the logic in social science and history, which follows in part 3. In part 4, the formalism returns, to show what the logic of rules makes of rights, in particular the right of private property and the right to a livelihood, which figured so prominently in the discussion of rights in chapters 3 and 4.

I shall be occupied with settled social rules. Given that they are settled, they imply regularities of conformity and are often accompanied by regularities of enforcement in deviant cases (even if neither of the regularities is perfect). Paying one's taxes or refraining from incest are not settled social rules if most people most of the time do neither – do not pay, or do not refrain – and escape punishment for the omissions.

Starting up closer to the concerns that ethnographers have with settled social rules than to the concerns of economists or decision-theorists, some philosophers have asked what distinguishes rules from other social phenomena, in particular, from other phenomena that involve expressions in language. Though this will not do in the end as an accurate picture of rules, we may go some distance towards the distinction demanded – most, if not all, the distance to a logic of rules – by thinking of a rule as standing to its linguistic expressions in a relation parallel to that in which a statement stands to the sentences that express it. We would thus make no more in either case of a rule or a statement than a device for talking about a variety of linguistic expressions and the social practices to which they contribute. How do rules so treated differ from statements (singular, existentially quantified, or universally quantified), value-judgments, optatives ('Would that x were the case!')?

Work on this question has been overshadowed recently by discussions of rules as solutions to game-theoretical problems of coordination. An issue of *Ethics* specially devoted to the discussion of rules (norms) is typical in having contributors preoccupied mainly by such considerations.[1] Work has also been deflected year after year by a preoccupation, inspired by Wittgenstein, with what following a rule amounts to, taken up as a problem in the philosophy of mind. How does the person following a rule know 'how to go on'? How do we tell that he knows? There is perhaps some consensus on Wittgenstein's position that the problem cannot be resolved without invoking, in every case, public criteria for identifying any rule in question, even an idiosyncratic personal one.[2] But this still leaves open the questions about how rules differ from other phenomena in which language and behaviour intersect.

More in keeping with the aim of answering these questions than the preoccupation with the following of a rule has been the general project of deontic logic, which consists in trying to specify the features of rules crucial to their directive aims and effects on the one hand and to making visible their logical relations on the other. The chief contributor to deontic logic – several times over, producing a variety of analyses and logical formulations – has been G.H. von Wright.[3] It is remarkable that in the special issue of *Ethics* mentioned earlier there is no reference to his work. That omission, however, is evidence of a shift of fashion in the direction of game-theoretical considerations rather than of the work's having been superseded in the line of thought to which it contributed. There, it remains the richest contribution so far.

The Logic of Rules (Deontic Logic)

von Wright's Version (in Norm and Action*) of the Logic of Rules*

In his book *Norm and Action*,[4] von Wright arrives at a logic of norms – that is to say, of rules – through a three-tier construction on top of the propositional calculus (which concerns elementary relations between propositions taken as wholes). Each tier adds logical operators to help specify those forms of propositions that, among the possible substitutions available to the propositional calculus, the logic of norms is especially concerned to identify. The propositional calculus itself is so general as to accept propositions of any forms as substitutions for the propositional variables, p, q, r, and so on; it considers those relations of such propositions to one another that are established by proposition-combining operators standing (approximately) for 'if ... then,' 'and,' 'or,' and 'if and only if.' $((p \lor q \to r \mathbin{\&} s) \mathbin{\&} \sim r) \to \sim(p \lor q)$, for example, is a symbolic sentence belonging to the propositional calculus; it may be read, 'If, if p or q, then r and s yet not r, then not either p or q.'

Consider a proposition p, which describes some state of affairs ('N holds office'); if the state of affairs does not obtain, then, of course, $\sim p$. Let there be an operator, T, to be placed between propositional variables (or combinations of these) and to be read 'changes into.' Four basic forms of propositions in a logic of change can then be envisaged: $pT{\sim}p$ – a world in which p changes into a world in which not-p; $\sim pTp$ – a world in which not-p changes into a world in which p; but also pTp and $\sim pT{\sim}p$, in which, significantly, no change in the ordinary sense occurs, but to which the T operator and the logic of change are conveniently extended by deliberate convention.

The logic of change constitutes the first tier above the propositional calculus. The logic of action, in von Wright's scheme, comes in the tier next above and relates change-propositions to human intervention by introducing d and f operators that indicate, respectively, acts and forbearances. These operators may be applied to any formula of the logic of change. While $d(pT{\sim}p)$, for example, might symbolize in an obvious way someone's acting to remove N from office – an example taken, like the following ones, from my discussion of Henry Parris's account of the introduction in Britain of the permanent civil service to replace the earlier system of patronage[5] – $f(pT{\sim}p)$ would symbolize forbearing to do so. But $d(pTp)$ and $f(pTp)$ are also intelligible formulas; they symbolize, on the one hand, acting so as to maintain a state of affairs that would otherwise change, and, on the other hand, forbearing to do so, letting it change though it could be maintained. Thus d(pTp) might stand for keeping N in office (when otherwise he would be ejected); f(pTp), for letting him be ejected (though he could be kept).

Finally, in the topmost tier of the construction, von Wright reveals his logic of norms, and with it two further operators: an O-operator (best thought of as standing for 'must') and a P-operator (for permission). The O-operator, applied to d-expressions of the logic of action, produces prescriptions: Od($pT{\sim}p$) 'N must be removed from office.' Applied to f-expressions, the O-operator produces prohibitions: Of($pT{\sim}p$), 'N must not be removed from office.' The P-operator produces permissions, either to do something – bring about some change – or to forbear. To these permissions, as well as to the prescriptions or prohibitions formulated with the O-operator, various conditions may attach, and von Wright provides for expressing them by associating further formulas of the logic of change with the formula representing the change to be brought about or forborne. Pd($pT{\sim}p/qTq$ & $rT{\sim}r$), for example, is the formula of a permissive norm with two conditions: It might be taken to symbolize the rule, 'It is permitted to eject N from office if (first condition, qTq) he owes his office to a patron and (second condition, $r/{\sim}r$) the patron himself has left office.'

However complex an O- or a P-expression may be, it can always be substituted for a propositional variable, p or q or r, in the propositional calculus.[6] Thus, all the connections, oppositions, and inferences made available by that branch of ordinary logic are available also for formulas in the logic of norms. There are, besides, some connections and oppositions peculiar to the logic of norms. Od(pTp), for example, is incompatible with Of(pTp) – they are contraries; though neither may hold, they cannot both hold together: it cannot at the same time be the case that one must keep p in being and forbear from doing so. Od(pTp) contradicts Pf(pTp): if one must do something, then one is not permitted to forbear doing it; and vice versa. Od(pTp), in fact, entails not Pf(pTp); and Pf(pTp) entails not Od(pTp).[7]

The application of von Wright's logic can be illustrated[8] by taking up a contention of Engels's in *Socialism: Utopian & Scientific*. Engels maintains that so long as artisans owned their own tools, it made no difference whether the foundation of their claims to their products was the work (w) that they put into making them or (then a secondary consideration) the fact that they owned the tools (t) (the capital equipment) used in making them. But once it ceased to be the case that the people who did the work were the same people as the people who owned the tools, a conflict in rules appeared between

$$Od(\sim rTr/\sim wTw),$$

under which people were enjoined to respect a right of ownership (by some specific person to some specific product) on the condition that the work of making it had been put in by the person in question, and

$$Od(\sim rTr/\sim tTt),$$

under which the right to the same product was accorded to someone on the condition that tools belonging to her had gone from not being used to being used in making the product. For suppose – as Engels supposes became generally the case – the person who did the work was not the same person as the person who supplied the tools. Which of the two claims was to be respected by other people? So long as those other people felt the force of both rules they were in a quandary that obstructed them from acting so as to respect fully either claim.[9]

The Logic of Rules Emerging from the Dalhousie Project

The multi-tier picture of rules given by von Wright in *Norm and Action* remains the fullest logical characterization of rules available in the literature (von Wright's remarks on aspects of rules that he does not include in the 'norm-kernels' expressed in his formulas are also rich in instruction). The philosophers in the project at Dalhousie University that culminated in the book *Logic on the Track of Social Change*[10] have kept the multi-tier picture in mind and intend in their own work to preserve its availability as much as the balance of considerations allows.

For example, as we have seen, von Wright asserts that in general we must expect to have added to basic rule-formulas a statement of the conditions under which the prescription or prohibition that may be in question comes to bear upon the people to whom it is addressed. This point is carried forward in our logic. (We leave permissions aside. They can be treated, following von Wright, either as absences of prohibitions in the case of some actions and forbearances [weak permissions] or as prohibitions against anyone interfering with given actions [strong permissions].)

The Dalhousie philosophers distinguish three features in our formulas for rules: **volk**, the demographic scope; **wenn**, the conditions under which the rule comes to bear upon conduct; **nono**, the routines (sequences of actions) that the rule targets in forbidding. For example, an example drawn from *Track*: under the feudal social order in France the king and nobility enjoyed the benefit of a rule under which, having appropriated the social surplus, they did what they pleased with it:

> **volk** = FRENCH
> **wenn** = $\exists(a)\exists(x)[\text{SURPLUS}(x) \text{ \& OWNS}(a, x)] \text{ \& } \textit{aft}\ (r)$
> $[\text{DISPOSES}(a, x)]$
> **nono** = BLOCKS (r', r).

The **wenn** component here says that x is a part of the social surplus and somebody a owns it and disposes of it by doing r. (r stands for any routine, i.e., any action or sequence of actions.) Given this condition, which notably leaves the way in which a has disposed of x completely unspecified, the **nono** component forbids any action or sequence of actions r' that BLOCKS r, the disposal of x by a.

Another example from *Track* is a norm consolidating advances in mechanization:

> **volk** = WORKERS
> **wenn** = $(\exists r)(\exists t)(\exists u)[(\text{TASK}(t) \text{ \& WORKSHOP}(u) \text{ \& } \sim\text{MECH}(t, u)$
> $\text{ \& } \textit{aft}(r)[\text{MECH}(t, u)]$
> **nono** = $\textit{aft}(r')\ (\exists a)[\text{HASRUN}(r, u) \text{ \& PERFORMS}(a, t, u)$
> $\text{\&}\sim\text{MECH}(t, u)]$.

$\textit{aft}(r)$ signifies that, after a routine r has been run, the proposition that follows is true. The rule in this case forbids workers to perform in a given workshop u an unmechanized task that has been mechanized there (by previously running an available routine for mechanizing it). It is a rule that prudent employers would adopt and enforce; if they did not, Marx, for one, would hold that they would be outdistanced by competitors who were more exacting about productivity.

Thus, the Dalhousie logic makes of von Wright's conditions for a rule coming to bear one (the **wenn** component) of the three characteristic features that it ascribes to rules. We make the doing or forbearing component (the **nono** component, in our case) more general, refraining from specifying that it applies only to actions with the form proposed for actions by von Wright. It embraces routines that may include series of actions.

Furthermore, we do not insist on describing actions in truth-functional propositions; we allow for three values where von Wright has one, truth (or its opposite). An action for us is just starting or not; is running now or not running now; has already run or not. The routines to which our formulas apply may involve many different actions and alternative routes to the same end. They may also belong to very different overall sequences; if we are forbidden to block some nobleman's disposal of his share of the social surplus, we are forbidden to do it in any way, and forbidden to do it in the course of bringing in the harvest as much as in plundering the granary afterwards.

Donald Davidson complained that von Wright's formulas for action do not take into account the variety of ways in which somebody might get from the state of affairs in which she begins to the state of affairs in which she ends (from p to $\sim p$ in d(pT$\sim p$).[11] We are better prepared than von Wright to satisfy Davidson's complaints about the ambiguity of von Wright's action-propositions, though we think von Wright could do a good deal to meet those complaints by simply having the actions in question specified in greater detail – as, for example, not just going from San Francisco to New York, but going by plane – or specified by analysing them more finely into sequences of actions. We are better prepared because our semantics brings in intermediate stages (INT) of a protracted action as well as the terminating stage (TERM). Thus, where for von Wright actions starting at A are differentiated solely in terms of what sentences they make true when they terminate, so that all actions starting at A and ending in B (with a certain sentence becoming true) are (without further analysis) identical, the Dalhousie logic treats every action starting at a as characterized by two sets. One set, TERM(r, s), is a set of ordered pairs associating every routine r turn by turn with the various states in which it would be said to terminate successfully; the other set, INT(r, s), is a set of ordered pairs associating every r turn by turn with the sequences of intermediate states that occur on various routes on the way to termination. The actions do not always terminate; there may be no sentence B such that TERM(r, s) = B.

Yet changing to our semantics does not mean a break with von Wright's – von Wright's is a special case of ours, in which the sets INT(r, s) are unspecified. We can accommodate in our routines all the forms of change that the actions and forbearances in von Wright's formulas involve; and all the actions and forbearances (which we treat as so many routines, simple or complex).

Our semantics also accommodates another complaint that Davidson makes about von Wright's logic. The set TERM(r, s') in which r terminates in Mary's being kicked viciously clearly relates to the set

TERM(r, s) in which r terminates in Mary's being kicked. The first set is, in fact, a subset of the second; hence, from Mary's being kicked viciously one may infer that she was kicked.

We do tighten up the logic in a way that von Wright did not anticipate: we follow a fruitful lead by the Australian philosopher C. Hamblin[12] and treat conflicts of rules as quandaries, in which all actions are ruled out. To express such situations as clearly as possible in accordance with common sense understandings of them, we furthermore reduce all rules to prohibitions (hence, the doing or forbearing component comes under the heading **nono**), where von Wright gives prescriptions an equal footing. We make of his prescriptions prohibitions of failing to provide for timely action on the routine prescribed in the routines that are done.

Our motivation in focusing on quandaries is to avoid the 'explosions' to which von Wright's, and other 'standard' deontic logics, are subject. Once a contradiction appears in any system of rules described within a standard deontic logic, the system explodes: one can infer that every action is permitted, indeed prescribed, which is tantamount to the system's being rendered useless for more guarded inferences. Is the lesson to be that one should refuse to recognize any contradictions? But conflicts between rules are common, especially when rules change, and to refuse to bring them within the ambit of a logic is to withdraw logic from full use in tracing changes in rules through stages in which conflicts between them exist. It means, among other things, sacrificing the possibility, long mistakenly beclouded, of making good sense of the notion of a dialectic operating in various historical sequences.

Another point of difference from von Wright – in this case, not so much a difference as a supplementation – is that whereas he treats goals as internal to the logic of change (thus, if one brings about the change pT$\sim p$ deliberately, for von Wright this is done with the goal of realizing $\sim p$), we (reserving the right to treat as goals also what von Wright treats as goals) treat goals as typically external to rules. Rules themselves, we insist, typically come into being in order to serve external goals – peace, order, and good government, for example – and among these goals may be the institution of other rules. (Thus, in Hobbes, there are rules specifying the form of contract that sets up a government able to enforce the basic laws of nature and other rules.[13])

The Dalhousie philosophers join von Wright in treating provisions for punishment as external considerations. In this sense, our formulas for rules are, like von Wright's, formulas for 'norm-kernels' and may serve as formulas for conventions and quasi-conventions as well. Under David Lewis's leading example of a convention (one that he says used to prevail in his hometown of Oberlin, Ohio) about resuming interrupted telephone calls, it is prescribed that the person who initiated the call make the connection again, while the other person waits.[14] This combines a prohibition imposed on the first party against doing any action or sequence of actions that precludes making the connection again in a timely way with a prohibition imposed on the second party of making the connection from her side.

With the reduction to prohibitions, the effect of escaping contradictions of the standard sort and the associated paradoxes of material implication is to substitute quandaries for contradictions. In quandaries, the rules accepted by the people affected combine to prohibit every action open to them. An example can be drawn from the debate in Parliament about abolishing the British slave trade, treated at length in *Track*, in which the action of abolishing slavery ran counter to the action (forbearance) of respecting private property, including property in slaves (which were held to be the only means of making plantations profitable).

Another example can be found in the prohibition, in force in England in the sixteenth century, against interfering with lords driving peasants off the land, conjoined with the prohibition laid down by Parliament in the act against vagabondage:
On the one hand, there was a rule f_t

volk(f_t) = ENGLISH
wenn(f_t) = [LAND(x) & HASDOM(a, x) & USEOWNS(b, x)
  & ~HASDOM(b, x) & *aft*(r) [DRIVEOFF(a, b, x)]]
nono(f_t) = BLOCKS(r', r),

which forbade anyone to do anything that blocked some a who, with dominion over a piece of land x, drove off someone b who, as a peasant, merely had useownership of the land.
On the other hand, there was a rule f_v

volk(f_v) = ENGLISH
wenn(f_v) = LANDLESS(b)
nono(f_v) = ~[WORKING(b)].

which forbade b, once b had been driven from the land and become landless, from doing anything that included a routine or sequence of actions that left him wandering about the country without working. But very likely there was no work for *b* off the land; he and thousands like him were in a quandary, forbidden to resist being driven off the land where they had been working and forbidden at the same time to be idle.

A quandary is certainly an uncomfortable situation, crying out for some change in the rules, but it is one that is, logically, perfectly in order. The going set of rules continues (by paraconsistent implication) to sustain nothing but reasonable inferences, even inferences from the rules directly in conflict. Partitioning the going set into subsets each of which by itself makes at least one action available that can be done without violating the rules in the subset has the effect here that in the propositional case comes from partitioning an inconsistent set of propositions into subsets each of which by itself is consistent.[15]

The Definition of Rules

Rules could be defined simply as whatever is expressed by the formulas of a logic of rules, like the formulas that we have inspected, either von Wright's formulas or those of the Dalhousie logic. This would at least be in one respect an advance over the most common definitions, which are circular – as 'normative constraints'[16] – or seem to leave the root-idea unexpressed – as 'systems of imperatives' (which prescribe or prohibit, too).[17]

However, it is quite unsatisfactory to treat rules as linguistic entities. The forms of words in which they are expressed can hardly, by themselves, be supposed to compel obedience, or indeed to influence conduct in any way. We can read in Empedocles 'Keep your hands off beans!'[18] and understand the words as conveying a rule (he is not using the same form of words to express a one-occasion imperative). Yet we may not be moved in the least to heed the words. If we move back from the expressions of rules to what in analogy with propositions they express, we have done no more to capture the action-compelling or action-guiding aspects of rules. We understand that one and the same rule can be expressed in English by 'Keep your hands off beans!' in French by *'Ne pas laisser les mains toucher de fèves'*; in Greek by *'kuamown apo cheiras'* – and not be moved by contemplating the shared meaning of these locutions.

What we need for a satisfactory definition is a definition that exhibits the place of rules in ordinary life and practice. Work on the Dalhousie project has led to just such a definition. We have found, in the course of formulating rules in one illustrative connection after another, that the notion of blocking was steadily playing an indispensable part in the ideas that we were working out of what the rules amounted to. This notion, in turn, has led us to an especially satisfactory definition of rules.

Rules, we say, are in origin physical blocking operations that prevent people from acting in ways prohibited; or, better, systems of such blocking operations, since unlike the imperatives issued for a moment, rules apply over and over again to many instances. Consider a child who is being blocked (by a successful blocking operation) from going into the street and, from this blocking, learning the rule against going there. When she comes to understand that she may expect to be blocked every time she tries, she understands the rule that she faces. In time, it will suffice for her mother to say 'Don't go into the street!' as she sidles in that direction; and this form of words serves as a verbal substitute for a physical blocking operation, just as the mother's speaking those words substitutes for her using a physical means in the blocking operation. She performs a blocking operation, whether successful or not, in either case. Thus, in general, we can define rules as systems, open-ended in time, of blocking operations physical or verbal. We can, furthermore, license under this definition speaking of physical imperatives as well as verbal ones. Different rules – different systems – are identified by different formulas from the logic of rules, a point that could be included in the definition or attached by way of explanation.

The blocking operations here, even the physical ones, are not instances of punishment; and both sorts, physical and verbal, may actually occur very rarely, and only at the beginning of any person's rule-learning history. Their rarity, and perhaps even more, their transience have no doubt contributed strongly to overlooking their importance for the definition of rules. They are rare because people internalize rules, so that rules learned from blockings physical or verbal are maintained usually without any need to repeat the blockings. With internalization, blocking operations are anticipated and forestalled. They are rare also, and their use transient, because, beginning early in childhood, people learn most rules simply by hearing them set forth; or even simply by observing examples of their application (as when a parent says 'stju' rather than 'stu' when stew appears on the table).

Yet the force of rules depends on the blocking operations that impend (or could be brought to bear). Rules are not linguistic entities, important as their linguistic expressions are for identifying them and understanding exactly what they involve. They are binding practices that involve people in structures of motivation for themselves and others and in structures of social control. Nor (as I myself long thought) are rules distinguished from conventions and the like by having measures of punishment attached to them. The physical actions that figure, in elementary cases, as blocking operations may sometimes be actions of the same sort that are imposed as punishments. However, they are not punishments when they serve as blockings – they are corrections, and as such belong alongside physical interventions of gentler, even caressing kinds, as well as verbal utterances that range from explicit imperatives to gentle hints. The mother may kiss and cuddle the child as she picks her up and takes her away from the street.

Conventions may originate as mutually advantageous solutions to coordination problems: in David Lewis's example, as a solution to the problem of who – the original caller or the original recipient – will start up a telephone call again after the connection has been broken. As such, they need not be taught by blockings or maintained either by blockings or by punishments. People may go on abiding by them, just as they started them up, simply from being aware of the mutual advantages. Yet conventions, once established, can in some cases be taught by corrective blockings, and as with rules there may be no occasion to go on to back them with sanctions. These observations reduce the distinction between rules and conventions to the vanishing point, even if one makes their being game-theoretical solutions a defining feature of conventions. Or rather, they reduce the distinction to accepting conventions as falling into a subclass of rules all of which are solutions to coordination problems, though some may not have originated because they were identified as such. (They may have been laid down by authorities with other things in mind.) Outside this subclass, there will be rules that do not constitute solutions to coordination problems and do not minimize costs.

Rules in Social Science and History

The definition of rules given makes it plain that there is more to rules in their workings upon people than there is to mere forms of words. Rules are robust, persisting social practices. Thus, the definition helps forestall any inclination to believe that rules must be (as mere words would be) superficial phenomena. There are important questions about society and history still to be asked when rules have been identified. Some of those questions are questions about rules. Where did they come from?

Who supports them, and why? Who benefits from general adherence to them? Rules may show up again, sometimes, in the answers to some of these questions; for example, some rules are inferred from others and get their support because people support those other rules.

Rules are not the whole story: power and interest (including class-interest) have to be considered. Some social scientists, and some historians, may be so much more interested in questions about power and interest that they hesitate to give the study of rules its due. I expect social scientists, however, will be easier to persuade than historians both that rules have some interest and importance and that a logic of rules is an aid to studying them. Historians have baulked at taking up any of the special techniques developed in the social sciences[19] (though they are taken up), while social scientists are used to having new techniques start up and used to trying them. We may expect there to be resistance among historians to the use of logic, too, especially since in this case its use – the use of a logic of rules – has not been established in the social sciences either. Indeed, our expectations are easily confirmed.[20]

We would ask, given the variety and ubiquity of rules, which we may expect historians not to deny, whether historians are already clear enough about them to have nothing substantial to learn from a logic of rules? They may nevertheless say they fail to see that translating the rules cited by historians makes any advance in clarification upon what Marx (in the examples given above) or other historians have done in expressing them in a natural language, German or English. Not only historians react in this way; as we have carried on the Dalhousie project from stage to stage, we have at each stage encountered philosophers who (perhaps not distinguishing sufficiently between the importance of having a logic and the importance of having a convenient notation for the logic) react on first sight by claiming that everything that needs to be done in treating rules can be done in English without any explicit recourse to a logic. Yet these reactions misinterpret the care that we have taken – notably, in the initial applications of the logic set forth in *Track* – to demonstrate that the rules for which we have developed the logic are rules of sorts that historians are concerned with. To comment that we seem to be only saying the same things but expressing the rules in different terms or a different notation is not an objection but a measure of our success in the demonstration that we intend.

It is true that – once we have got historians to acknowledge that we are talking about rules as they themselves already understand them – we have further claims to make for the logic. The first reactions fail to appreciate in this regard that those claims begin by citing only very modest possible advances on what historians are already doing, which we acknowledge that they could do, certainly without our notation and perhaps without any explicit attention to our logic or any other. They also fail (we think) to give due weight to the point that advances may be modest but nonetheless worth making.

Moreover, as a hypothesis in the psychology of scholarship, is it not probable that historians will actually make those advances in precision only if they make use of a logic of rules, even of a notation that continually reminds them of the components to look for? The use of a logic of rules is likely to alert investigators to logical issues that might otherwise go unnoticed and likely also to sharpen their appreciation of the variety of logical distinctions that issues call for once identified. Some examples bearing out the modest hypothesis can be found in the discussion in *Track* of the abolition of the British slave trade and in the discussion (also in *Track*) of the rise of clinical medicine. Dale H. Porter, one of the historians on whose account of the abolition of the slave trade we rely, omits to ask what happened to the rule of respecting the private property of the West Indian planters, which stood in the way of abolishing the trade in the 1790s (because cutting off their supply of fresh slaves would so far reduce the labour at their disposal as to make their plantations unprofitable).[21] Was the rule still in force when the slave trade was abolished in 1807? If it was not, how was it that the more general rule about respecting private property had ceased to give it force? It does not seem likely that the possibility of applying the general rule in this connection had simply been forgotten. Foucault, in his account of the rise of clinical medicine, identifies a rule forbidding giving diagnoses that did not relate external symptoms to internal pathologies correlated with them. However, he omits to consider that this rule, characteristic as it may be of clinical medicine once this has fully developed, could not be followed at the beginning of the development before the correlations in question had been identified. He has thus failed to see precisely part of what has to be brought into view (perhaps some rule under which the development could begin, which would also guide the development from stage to stage) to explain how clinical medicine came about.[22]

Here, we are already advancing – modestly – beyond the modest claims of the hypothesis set forth above. Attention to rules, with the logic of rules, has brought to light an aspect of the history of clinical medicine that even its most brilliant investigator, emphatic as he was here as elsewhere about the importance of identifying social rules, had not come upon. We claim in *Track* to make further advances. We identify quandaries and track social changes through the resolutions of the quandaries. We have found our illustrations in cases in which the resolutions came about by deliberations that cannot be made intelligible without identifying the rules at issue and their implications, including the implications that set some of the rules at odds with each other.

It may give an exaggerated impression of the extent to which a rule holds in a given society to formulate it exactly and then suppose that it holds exactly for every subgroup and every member. But this impression can be softened by consciously treating the rule as a sort of idealization familiar from accounts of language. (It is not everywhere in English the rule that the informal third-person singular negative form used for the verb 'do' is 'doesn't.') For some purposes, for example, constructing a perspicuous, simplified model of the rules in a given society (say, the rules of their kinship system), such an idealization is useful. It is useful, among other ways, as a benchmark for charting the variations on the rule found in different subgroups and with different persons.

One need not suppose that rules can be detached from the behaviour that is evidence for them – the behaviour of human beings doing things or avoiding things that we would expect them to do or avoid if they had invented and held to the rules in question. (I am using 'invent' here to cover processes of arriving at rules that are not deliberative and may issue in rules that the people who abide by them are not aware of.)

Our hypothesis does not exclude – nor should it exclude – the possibility that some rules may persist while the people who invent them disappear, so long as in disappearing they give way to other people who in their own time accept the rules. All along – consistently with the existence of the rules, so long as deviation is subject to blocking or punishment in some cases – some people, people in the inventing generation (supposing this can be identified), or maybe descendants or newcomers, may choose to defy those same rules. If defiance rather than conformity becomes paramount, the rules (not the formulas, or the possibilities of formulation, but the rules as practices) will disappear. Nothing in our conception of the logic of rules gainsays these points, or implies more in metaphysics than is needed to make them (e.g., that there are people, who act in various ways, and communicate about these actions).

Does ascribing causal efficacy to rules fail to take into account their dependence on the invention and support of the people who have adopted them as rules? One might be led to imagine the rules, though arising from human invention, operating regardless of human efforts to shake loose from them. But causal efficacy does not imply anything so bizarre. The most that it implies is that it may not be easy for some people, some of the time, to abandon a rule. Certainly, in many cases it is not easy for individual persons living under the rule; for them, taken singly, the rule as a system of blockings impacts them as an irreducible fact while it has general support from other people. It may not be easy to abandon the rule even when everybody wishes to abandon it. There may be no decision procedure for doing so in the society in question. Moreover, whether there is a decision procedure or not, other rules may go with the rule at issue, even rules not implied by it, but depending for continued support on powers and expectations that do depend upon the rule that invites abandonment. Think of the ramifications of abandoning the rule ascribing the power to dispose of the means of production to those who privately own the means (in accordance with the right to private property, of which I am about to give an illustrative formulation). It is not implied that the manufacturers of machine tools should have salesmen who heed a rule about approaching plant managers in other firms for business; it is not even implied that the manufacturers of machine tools should employ salesmen.

Changes in settled social rules is not a subject that embraces the whole of history; it nevertheless takes in a lot of historical phenomena, some very grand indeed. Changes of rules figure centrally in the conceptions, invoked in *Logic on the Track of Social Change*, of how the practices of feudalism came about and how they gave way to the practices of capitalism (which might, in turn, give way to another culture or social system defined by other rules). The rules for distributing the social surplus, for example, were very different under feudalism from what they have been under capitalism; under socialism, in principle, they would be very different again. At its most ambitious, the subject of change of rules rises to the heights of what Hegel or (in another version) Engels and maybe Marx discerned as the dialectic of history. Many people, not without reason, distrust such grand themes; changes of rules is an important subject for them as well. A great deal of the intimate tissue of social life under any culture comes from the social rules distinctive of the culture (e.g., rules about the choice of spouses, which may or may not give children at least a veto over the choices made for them by their parents); and changes in this tissue must be traced through changes in the rules.

To represent these changes, historians and social scientists must express the rules at stake in them, which the people affected heed, sometimes with full consciousness, sometimes not. The importance of having some logic of rules rests upon the importance of specifying the rules that change (the ex ante and ex post rules), along with the rules that define the context of change, some of them perhaps in ways that prescribe the path which change takes (recall the discussion, above, of Foucault on the treatment of diagnosis during the rise of clinical medicine). We must at least have a working idea of what sorts of content with what components to look for. Furthermore, if we agree that it is desirable to have a working idea that defines for prominent use clear views of harmony, connection, and conflict between rules, we have, in effect, agreed to welcome having a logic, because to define harmony, connection, and conflict between rules, expressible in formulas that represent them, is to define a logic.

The Logic of Rules Applied to the Right of Private Property

Before leaving the logic of rules behind, it is worth seeing how the logic applies to rights. Thus we return to rights, and I show what the formulas that identify them look like in the formalism of a logic of rules. The right of private property will serve as my illustration.

As a first approximation to formulating the right to private property, I offer a general formula for a right in which I leave some universal quantifiers to be understood. I let the letter 'a' be a variable implicitly universally quantified (in this connection it could also be read as a proper name). For a to have the right to do a certain sequence of actions or routines amounts in part to his being under no rule that forbids his doing it and also to its being forbidden by rule for anyone to block him from doing it should he wish to. Thus:

$$\text{RIGHT } (a, r_1) \Leftrightarrow \{(\text{Component}[1]) \sim \exists F \text{ \textbf{nono} } (a, r_1)\}$$
$$\& \{(\text{Component}[2]) \forall r_2 \, [(b \neq a) \, \& \, (\text{BLOCKS}[b, r_2, a, r_1]\}$$
$$\rightarrow \text{\textbf{nono} } (b, r_2)\}.$$

The formula can be treated as telling us among other things what we need to make sure of if we express the rule in English. Let us walk through the formula in English. a has a right r_1 if and only if the combination of conditions 'Component [1]' and 'Component [2]' holds. Component [1] is that there does not exist any rule F that forbids (**nonos**) a's doing r_2. Component [2] brings into the picture all routines (actions) r_2 under which everyone b who is not a might, by doing r_2, BLOCK[S] a from doing r_1. ('BLOCKS,' more vividly than anything else in the formula, ties the formula to the practice in which the rule identified by the formula operates.) Given these conditions, the rule for the present right forbids (**nonos**) everyone b who is not a doing the blocking action or routine r_2. (If it happens to be a routine that some rule requires b to do, b will be in a quandary.)

The view that I shall take here of the right to (some specific item of) private property seems to fit in an illuminating way the context of the dispute in Parliament about abolishing the slave trade and many other contexts as well. Even so, it does not capture all the features of the relevant right. People are held liable for damages to other people's property; for trespassing upon it; for putting it in danger of being damaged. They are held liable for BLOCKing a when she tries to carry out a routine that falls within the range of legitimate enjoyments of her property, whether or not the BLOCKing comes about by their intention; they must compensate the owner notwithstanding; so certain sorts of excuses are not available. I leave the right indeterminate to just this extent by not bringing these things into the formula. However, even matters that figure in the formula are no doubt indeterminate in the sense that in some circumstances they would be ambiguous in application, pending a resolution that might be only ad hoc.

People are also enjoined, we may suppose, from mounting certain operations that a reasonable person might think had a substantial chance of actually having the effect, whether intended or not, of BLOCKing r_2. Yet they need not refrain from all such operations. If they open up a shop nearby dealing in the same sorts of goods and attract a's customers, that is perfectly allowable. This is only one example, and the right as formulated so far – indeed as it might be formulated as fully as practical – leaves indeterminate what other sorts of examples might be allowable, too.

The complications and the indeterminacies continue with the enforcement of rights; for it is common for some people to be held responsible for the enforcement, and it will not suffice for them to say that they tried to BLOCK interference with the right though they failed. They might cynically have made a show of BLOCKing by mounting an operation that they knew would fail. I conjecture that the pattern of BLOCKings and BLOCKing operations prohibited, required, or permitted varies from one right or one class of rights to another, something that is to be taken into account in the close study of any right.

These various indeterminacies do not stand in the way of gaining valuable precision in other ways. If indeterminacies remain after the logic has been applied, that reflects, both in the idea that there might be alternative formulations and in the idea that there might be more, much more, to say, the general fact that all empirical concepts, among them the concepts of settled social rules, are to some degree vague, though typically not so vague as to be incapable of precise operation in many circumstances. We gain precision in some respects by formulating some features of the right to private property in applying the logic. Ironically, the formulation brings to light various indeterminacies. However, we learn from this exposure. The formulation, studied with care, allows us to say that the right (as so far formulated) may be indeterminate in just these ways. To say that is to assert an advance, humble though it may be, in our knowledge of rights.

The logic easily accommodates improvements in precision that go beyond the approximation given in the formula set forth above. However, I shall not try to include in the formula all the matters so far discussed; I shall proceed selectively and illustratively. First, it is an improvement to express the point that having the right is, in the first place, a matter of having a certain status to which the right is attached, with further rules determining how to acquire the status, for example, the status of owning some landed property, acquired by homesteading, purchase, gift, inheritance. For example:

$$\forall x\{[\text{LANDEDPROPERTY}[x] \ \& \ \text{PURCHASED}(a, x)]$$
$$\rightarrow [\text{STATUS}(a) = \text{OWNS}(a, x)]\}.$$

In English: 'In all cases, if there is a piece of landed property x and a has purchased x, then the status of a is such that he owns x.' Typically, alongside the licence that the right gives a to do a routine r, or r_1, there are rules that forbid other people from doing it, for example, planting a crop in land that a has cleared and ploughed. What matters is that a does not fall within the demographic scope of such rules. So we add a specification of a's STATUS with regard to r_1 to the right-hand side of our equivalence and revise Component (1) to incorporate a specification of the STATUS (r_1), which implies that, if there is a rule F that forbids r_1, a is not among the people to whom it applies, that is to say, a is not in **volk** (F).

The formula now runs:

$RIGHT(a, r_1) \Leftrightarrow$ (1) $[OWNS(a, x) \rightarrow ALLOWABLE(r_1, x)]$
(2) $OWNS(a, x) \& \sim (\exists F)$ **nono** $(F)(a, r_1, x)$
(3) $(\forall r_2)\{\sim RENOUNCE(a, r_1) \&$
$\sim COMPENSATED(a, x)$
(4) $BLOCKS[b, r_2, a, r_1, x] \& (b \neq a)$
$\rightarrow$ **nono** $(b, r_2)\}.$

The apparent need to have a new clause (1) came up when I thought for a moment that clause (2) would not suffice to circumscribe the right if it were not related to allowable actions only. On further reflection, it appears that (1) does no harm; but it is redundant. Clause (2) suffices after all: if a owns x, he can do with it what he pleases so long as it is not forbidden by some other rule. This answers (in part) the question about just what are allowable actions or routines – they are actions not forbidden by some other rule; and that is something that can be explicated in detail only by citing the main things that are allowable, selling x, giving x away, ploughing x, seeding x, gathering a crop from x, and so on.

In English, the improved larger (somewhat redundant) formula says that a has a right to do action or routine r_1 if and only if he owns it and it is allowable for an owner to do r_1 with x; there is no rule under which a is forbidden notwithstanding to do r_1 with x; a has not renounced the right to do r_1, nor has he been compensated for any interference with the right (clause (3) is added to spell out further what a's status amounts to). When all these things hold, then everyone b, other than a, is forbidden (**nono**'d) to block a from doing r_1 with x by himself doing r_2. We thereby leave it permissible for someone else to do so if a has renounced her right to do the routine with x or if she has been compensated. If some rights are such that no compensation for overriding them can ever suffice, they are covered by having $\sim COMPENSATED(a, x)$ always true.

It is to be noticed that though the use of the symbolization prompts these observations, once the observations are made, it may seem quite feasible to dispense with the symbolization. Feasible maybe, but not quite feasible. The benefits of the logic cannot be fully appreciated by anyone who has not done the work of filling in the formulas. This requires decisions, sometimes unexpected ones, at each point about just how to do so; and with each decision, the researcher learns something.

If a has the status of OWNING a piece of property x, then all the routines that constitute enjoyments of that property are routines that a has a RIGHT to do, though to say this we must understand 'enjoyment' as already controlled by various limitations protecting other people's interests. It does not count among the protected enjoyments of a town house that the owner should, at least without consulting the authorities, set it afire. In other words, as I have been assuming all along, though rules are ordinarily stated, as I state them, without enumerating limitations and exceptions, these are always to be reckoned with.[23] They increase the indeterminacies, which will remain in spite of the accumulation of precedents in the courts, hence of experience in invoking and applying the right. Yet the indeterminacies do not prevent numerous successful applications of the right of private property in resolving – or forestalling – controversies between persons.

On this approach, the assertion of a right – or, more specifically, the ascription of a right to some agent a – turns out, in accordance with the analysis earlier, not to be the assertion of one rule only, but an assertion about several interconnected rules. The character and identification of these rules will be in accordance with the definition of a rule as an observable system of blocking operations, which can be identified by a formula from the logic of rules (a formula that specifies the **volk**, the **wenn**, and under the **nono** the target of the blocking operations). Moreover, they will be in accordance with the main points of the earlier analysis in specifying rules implied by the *status* of having the right, rules for *acquiring that status*, and rules for *exercising* the right.[24]

To sum up the discussion of the right to private property, I lay out in **volk/wenn/nono** formulas a generalized selection of the rules that fall under the several heads of the combination of rules that make up the right to private landed property as treated here. (That the rules are a selection of the rules which the right embraces implies, in yet another dimension, that the right is not expressed by the formula with full determinacy.)

Thus:

For *acquiring* the relevant *status*, there is a rule Fp_q:

> **volk:** PEOPLE GENERALLY INSIDE AND OUTSIDE CANADA
> **wenn:** $\exists x$ (LANDEDPROPERTY[x]) & INCANADA[x] &
> PURCHASED [a, x]
> **nono:** $\forall(r) \ aft(r)$ ~[STATUS(a) = OWNS (a, x)].

For *status*, there is a rule Fp_s:

> **volk:** PEOPLE GENERALLY INSIDE AND OUTSIDE CANADA
> **wenn:** $\exists x$ [LANDEDPROPERTY(x) & OWNS (a, x) & ~RENOUNCE
> (a, x) & ~COMPENSATED FOR LOSING (a, x)
> **nono:** $\forall(r)\{$[ENCROACHES (r, a, OWNS[x])].

For *exercise*, there is a rule Fp_e:

volk: PEOPLE GENERALLY INSIDE AND OUTSIDE CANADA
wenn: $(\exists x)$[LANDEDPROPERTY(x) & OWNS(a, x) &
$\qquad \forall r$(LEGITENJOYMENT (a, r, x)
nono: BLOCKS$[b, r_1, a, r, x]$ & $(b \neq a)$.

'ENCROACHES' in the rule about status is to be taken as standing for all the variety of ways in which other people might interfere with or impair a's status as owner of x. The **nono** in the rule could usefully be made much more elaborate, specifying, for example, that every routine that takes part of x away from a or obstructs a's access to x or transfers x to someone else b without a's permission is forbidden.

I shall not walk the reader through this long multiple-part formula, but shall trust that the earlier walk-throughs show how this is to be done.

I leave out the associated rules for enforcing the right of private property, though they are of great importance and involve major social institutions. Should I add a rule that justifies the right by showing that it originates with an appropriate authority? This is another important feature of rules, which sometimes engenders great controversy. It is a feature that can notwithstanding be given a non-controversial specification in a fourth clause, say,

auth: CUSTOM(Fp) v COMMONLAWPRECEDENT(Fp)
$\qquad\qquad$ v STATUTE(Fp) v CONSTITUTION(Fp).

This formula gives a disjunctive list of the various non-exclusive sources of authority for the rule. I say the specification is, 'non-controversial,' not meaning to rule out some indeterminacy about which there is a current possibility of controversy; I suppose that the controversy would arise about one or more of the matters specified in my suggestion about how **auth** could be filled out. I say 'non-controversial'; I do not say 'uncomplicated.' But I think that it is not controversial that the complications arise like others under the heads such as those present in the formula. The right of private property originates so far in the distant past that we may suppose it precedes organized courts, where legal precedents could be set; and setting the right forth in statutes – which may sometimes precede, sometimes follow making it a provision of a constitution – is a later development still. Custom and the common law precede codification. The authority is multiple, and even if one ingredient of it or another has now become redundant, each ingredient has played a part in the historical development of the right.

PART TWO

AGGREGATING THE
FREE-STANDING STUDIES

Prefatory Note to Part Two

The idea of putting together the present book originated in the lecture on which the one chapter, chapter 6, in this part is based. The chapter was to serve as the keystone of the book; and anticipating its placement in the book, it has done so, in the historical sense of governing the plan of the book and the choice of contents. Is it still the keystone, in the plan now realized, with those contents? It is; and the fact that it will contain some repetitions of the contents of part one of the book does not stand in the way of its being the keystone. It is, as it were, the keystone both of an inner arch (parts one, two, three) and of a larger arch (parts one, two, three, and four) superimposed on the inner one. (Would such a construction be possible physically? Sure: imagine the two arches, with some bricks in the upper one duplicating some bricks in the lower one while others do not; the keystone, made up of the duplicating bricks, stretches through the top arch and then the bottom one.)

Chapter 6 balances and completes the contents of part one by bearing witness again to the rich variety of results obtained in analytical political philosophy, even on its humbler side, where in any given project it may be concerned to do no more than clarify a matter of conceptual detail on one or another disaggregated topic. It balances and completes the contents of part one, furthermore, by showing how those contents add up to a grand program for social policy and political organization.

It might well, therefore, figure in part one as its culmination, and the culmination of the main argument of the book. I give chapter 6 a part to itself, however, because it is not only the case that in it part one culminates. It also aligns with part four: I give in part four examples of grand programs (offered by Rawls, Nozick, and Gauthier) emerging from analytical political philosophy in a broad sense; and this chapter itself culminates in a program grand at least in the sense of being comparable in comprehensiveness with those other ones in spite of its humble origins in the free-standing studies.

In part three, to follow this one, which serves as a further test of the main argument of the book, I take up the challenge that recent political evils may pose for analytical political philosophy. People have reason to think that evil as a named, explicit topic has not been a preoccupation of analytical political philosophy, even in ethical theory, but that does not mean that analytical political philosophy has nothing to say about it, and in very recent years the picture has begun to change (see chap. 7, n.1).

Finally, in part five, I wind up the series of books to which the present one belongs by discussing, in the one chapter there, what might also have figured in part four, the relation of utilitarianism to natural law theory. In the course of doing so I add two further grand programs to the three taken as illustrations in part four and the fourth outlined in the present chapter, part two. Those two added grand programs, of course, gave a reason, which as I explain, I did not act upon, for including the chapter in part four.

In the present chapter (6) I shall repeat, in my discussions of needs, rights, and rules, some of the points made in the preceding chapters, though I hope only so far as is necessary for the chapter to do its work as a keystone. I shall take up the topics in a different order from the one used in presenting them, in part one; and I shall make some new points along with the repetitions. I shall come to the topic of needs last and come to it by way of a new topic of detail – how to deal effectively in choices of social policy with consequences or, more precisely, with uncertainty about consequences, a topic that the analysis of received moral discourse (and of the practices in which the discourse is immersed) illuminates. The chapter will end by adding up the results on these so far disaggregated topics of the free-standing studies in a grand program of their own.

6

(The Keystone Chapter) Aggregating in a Distinctive Grand Program the Free-Standing Studies and an Account of the Serial Evaluation of Consequences

Analytical Political Philosophy Sometimes Broad and Grand, Sometimes Narrow and Petite

In the broad sense, analytical political philosophy embraces works like those of Rawls, Nozick, and Gauthier that deploy social contract theory, principles of justice, and rights in grand programs for social policy and political organization.[1] Rawls, Nozick, and Gauthier will be treated in part four. Ronald Dworkin's recent work, *The Sovereign Virtue*,[2] which sets forth a grand program for equality, may justly rank with them in sweeping ambition. Also in analytical political philosophy can be found works (like those of Russell Hardin[3]) relating to the theory of what economists define technically as 'public goods'; works that reflect acquaintance with social choice theory in the style of Kenneth Arrow;[4] works that make use of the theory of games (Hardin's work[5] can also be cited here as among the most penetrating). All these works are analytical in spirit, because they unfold the arguments in them with a care that reflects some sophistication in formal logic for showing how the details fit in and stand in a relation of mutual support to one another; and because they reflect acquaintance with formalizing methods that are shared with economics.

Even results here may be dismissed as at most constructive only in intention, and useless because they are subject along with every alternative to endless controversy. This is a gross mistake, not only because of the spurious implication that other, non-analytical approaches are less controversial (though they may be controversial in less rigorous and hence less instructive ways). Rawls's elaborately constructed theory of justice has supplied a framework that, as it stands, invites political application at least pro tempore (see, in part, the comment that I have appended to chapter 8 in part four on Rawls's work). It has also supplied the basis for focused discussions of distributive justice, more precise than previous ones, within which many able philosophers have chosen to do their own work, and which others who do not choose to do this continually have in mind. I have too little sympathy with Nozick's work to find much use for it. It is fair to say, however, that it obtains attention for, among other things, the importance of received expectations in determining the justice of distributions, and this is a point neglected by Rawls and Gauthier. Gauthier's theory of justice, more elaborate and precise than Rawls's in its use of social contract theory, shows just what is at issue in the theory, something important in application to current politics and something that people attempting to do scholarship on Hobbes or Locke or Rousseau ignore at their peril. A full understanding of just what is at issue in Hobbes's doctrine of the social contract and the necessity for a Sovereign requires attention shaped by the theory of games (as in the late Jean Hampton's masterly work[6]). The mysteries that have surrounded Rousseau's concept of the General Will dissipate when, in a use inspired by Hardin and others, the theory of public goods is brought to bear on it. Simultaneously, an effective notion of the Common Good emerges as a counterpart, with useful applications to domestic and international politics.[7]

To become acquainted with these works, at least with the more famous among them, is to become acquainted with the main show in analytical political philosophy – the big tent, if you like, in the three-ring (n-ring) circus.

If the results that I have reached in part one of this book belong to political philosophy at all, however, they are results that in the first instance belong to 'analytical political philosophy,' not in the broad sense that I just referred to, with the grand programs sometimes produced there, but in a narrow sense, the sense in which what is continually of immediate concern is the analysis of disaggregated, relatively narrow topics about familiar concepts in the received discourse of politics. They are topics that demand close consideration of the words that figure in that discourse.

Linguistic analysis in the service of such close consideration awakens in many people a great deal of scepticism, and not merely scepticism. How can the discussion of mere words make any headway with matters of importance in politics? Such discussion awakens in many people distaste, perhaps invincible distaste, for what seems controversy that is not only endless but inevitably trivial. Some of those people may not like controversy anyway, and I am afraid that you cannot have political philosophy, grande or petite, without controversy. But perhaps the main reason for scepticism descending to distaste is that people fail to see that the focus on words is a means of identifying concepts, many of them of crucial importance to our conduct of political discourse and politics; and that concepts are not only matters of words, but matters of words deployed in specific social practices, like resolving an issue about policy and choosing a policy as a result. It is a trivial matter that we use the word 'rights' in the practice of politics; we might use any other vocable instead: 'pushpins' or 'pushkins,' for example; it is not a trivial matter that the word we use, 'rights,' repeatedly is used to achieve certain specifiable purposes in systematic practices where blocking operations and sanctions have a place.

The results that figure again in the parts of this chapter that first follow come from free-standing studies in the linguistic analysis of rules; of rights; of effective attention to consequences; and by way of the attention to consequences, attention to the concept of needs. The results on all these points are significant in themselves and assist in understanding what is going on in the big tent. The concept of needs, for example, plays a part in Rawls's theory of justice that deserves more attention than he gives it. His Difference Principle, for example, as I point out in the chapter (8) on Rawls, becomes much less compelling when what is at issue for the least advantaged is no longer meeting their basic needs. The results on needs and the other topics of detail also lead in many different ways to important questions about justice; I shall go on to discuss some of these questions. Then, after digressing to show that the results I have presented are useful to empirical political science, I shall show how, taken together, they make a far-reaching contribution to political philosophy – not simply tent-pegs, but a program comparable to the grand programs that I have mentioned, and thus an act in the big tent.

Rules

The results that I have reached practising analytical political philosophy on the concept of needs, the concept of rights, and the concept of rules have already been presented, in chapters 1 to 5, part one of this book. To make good the keystone claim for this chapter, I shall review the results here. However, I shall take them up in reverse order – rules first, rights second, needs third – giving an account of each that, though abbreviated, will still make some new points if only, now and then, by way of more visible emphasis. Moreover, I shall get back to needs by way of a discussion of the problem of dealing with consequences, another disaggregated topic, not yet examined, for analytical political philosophy.

One reason for beginning with rules is that I want to use the analysis of rules in the analysis of rights, a more glamorous subject, which in this review will come up next. Rules themselves, however, invite philo- sophical and political attention. They are everywhere in politics and in the outcomes of political processes, ranging from minor everyday rules like 'Don't litter' ('Don't Mess with Texas') to rules of much grander political significance. Consider the rule that votes for candidates be honestly counted and the candidate with the greatest number of votes be declared and accepted as a winner. Or, more poignantly, the rule that no one of military age and sound physique should avoid military service in time of war. These examples suffice to show that there are both rules that govern political procedures and rules (not a separate class) that, for better or worse, are the upshot of politics.

What do rules of any kind amount to?

Rules, to make again a point worth emphatic repeating, are generally given a definition with an essential element that is circular, and unhelp- ful insofar as it is circular. An example is the definition, frequently cited from St Thomas, applying to laws but also, through the theory of natural law, to moral rules: 'A law is ... an ordinance of reason for the common good made by the authority who has care of the community and promulgated.'[8] This is by no means uninformative; but it is circular, because of the presence of the term 'ordinance.'

How to do better? I stumbled upon how to do better in the course of a project that I carried on with others (issuing in the book *Logic on the Track of Social Change*[9]) to work out a logic of rules and apply the logic to social change, which is often in large part a change in rules. In the course of that project, a non-circular definition came to light from, first, setting permissions for the moment aside, and, second, reducing to prohibitions prescriptions in the narrow sense that opposes them to prohibitions. Hobbes, something we became mindful of after our work was done, treats rules as prohibitions, though the significance of his doing this is not likely to be appreciated without an excursion like the present one into the logic of rules.

Suppose we say an action is prescribed in certain circumstances if doing anything else is prohibited. This seems to work, though it will lead to certain awkwardnesses of formulation that can be addressed later.

Prohibitions command people not to do certain specified things. But there are many commands or imperatives that are prohibitions but not rules: 'Don't vote for George the Wrecker next Tuesday!' 'Don't throw that gum wrapper on the grass!' What is the difference? The major difference is that the prohibitions that are rules are more generalized, applying not just in this instance, but in many others where the action described is an option. Thus the rule 'Don't ever vote for a candidate who has led the country into war for spurious reasons'; or the rule 'Don't ever litter.'

The way is now open to defining rules ('Don't ever do that!') as systems of imperatives ('Don't do that here and now!'). This makes some headway toward a suitable non-circular definition. But does it make enough headway? Imperatives may well seem so close conceptually to rules as to create something like a circle themselves. Can we find a non-circular definition of imperatives?

If we look at instances of teaching rules that occur early in life, we can; and arrive simultaneously at a definition of imperatives that extends usefully beyond locutionary acts. Little Elizabeth, clamouring for attention at the dinner table, ignores the disruption that she is causing a conversation going on in the rest of the family. Papa puts his finger upon his lips and directs her attention to her bowl of mixed fresh fruit. He says, 'Quiet now, sweetie; the rest of us are talking.' Papa is mounting a complex blocking operation. It can be at once firm, successful, and affectionate.

It takes a little sophistication – that is to say, experience with physical blocking and experience connecting the blocking with Papa's saying 'No' – for Elizabeth to understand the physical sounds emitted in verbal actions as blocking operations. Nevertheless, she soon acquires this sophistication, as do numberless other children. The sophistication grows as life goes on. Later, Papa or Mama can block simply by saying, 'I would not do that if I were you,' or by frowning, or by setting an example (Mama turns her head and fixes an attentive gaze upon another member of the family, who is speaking). Language is very largely learned by having examples set and following them. As a high school student, Elizabeth writes 'Albeit'; Papa (with his teacher, Doctor Leavis, in mind) intervenes to say, pointedly, 'Though.' Or to use an example that is perhaps less of a lost cause (since the occasions for using either are so much fewer): Elizabeth, at university, says 'Mitigate,' and her professor says, pointedly, 'Here you mean "militate."'

The frequent absence of more explicit blocking operations has led many people to wonder whether the rules of language are properly rules. So has the absence of sanctions – specific penalties – in most instances. Sanctions are not blocking operations (though the threat of them may be); they are imposed when blocking operations cannot be relied on. But the sanctions are absent, to the degree that they are, because they are unnecessary in practice; for the most part people are eager to learn what is correct speech, at least up to the point where mutual communication with others that they encounter is possible. That is why the blocking operations, too, can be subtle and unobtrusive.

Nevertheless, somewhere in the practice of typical rules there will be provision for explicit blocking operations, even physical ones. If we define, as I now will, rules as systems of blocking operations, it is to be understood that the blocking operations vary greatly in character and are often, taking one sort with another, persistently latent. People learn how to learn rules in learning the first ones that they learn. There physical blocking operations are manifest; so are penalties. Later in life people will learn rules and in most cases conform to them just by being told what the rule is. When this does not suffice, as in the case of rules about violence and theft, for example, where there are strong temptations not to conform, both physical blocking operations and penalties may be kept up even with adults thoroughly acquainted with what the rules are.[10]

In the perspective of treating rules as prohibitions, all these points work out quite plausibly. But even in that perspective, not enough is made of the fact that there are rewards for heeding the prohibitions. Elizabeth gains Papa's approval and some gratifying cuddling if she desists from clamouring. Often, in learning rules, encouragement seems more in place than blocking; but blocking operations themselves may be encouragements, or be accompanied by them.

We can enlarge the perspective to include among rules prescriptions in the narrow sense as well as prohibitions by interdefining prescriptions and prohibitions. We would then have an operator '**must**' in the formulas for rules as well as an operator equivalent to '**forbidden**' (or '**nono**'). What we must do under any rule is something that we are forbidden not to do. The upshot is convergence with St Thomas in another passage, where he says of laws that through them 'a person is led to do something or held back.' This is the beginning of a non-circular definition, though St Thomas does not try to give one even in this passage.[11]

I referred to 'formulas' for rules, for instance, 'Don't ever litter.' These formulas themselves invite analysis, which in my case and the case of my co-authors of *Track* has as its outcome a standard formula in which there are places for the **nono** – describing the action prohibited; the **volk** – the people subject to the rule; and the **wenn** – the conditions under which the rule applies; perhaps also a place for the **auth**ority that has laid down the rule.

What is the relation of the formulas for rules to rules? One might say, quite in keeping with ordinary language, that they are rules themselves. Isn't the formula 'Don't ever litter' a rule? But to take the formulas as rules by themselves, without association with the underlying system of imperatives or blocking operations, is something like taking the names of the people on a list as the people. Formulas for rules are like names or descriptions, but they are not what rules are at bottom, which is shown by the possibility of having a rule – a persistent system of blocking operations – without having a formula for it. Many rules of language are like this. There is a rule in English about changing the sound of the 's' when one shifts from using 'house' as a noun to using 'house' as a verb; and this rule exists whether or not anyone has ever noticed it, much less produced a formula for it.

The most important thing that the formulas for rules do in connection with rules is express the distinction between one system of blocking operations and another. Thus, they identify rules. They tell us what system of blocking operations we are dealing with, imposed on what people (**volk**) under what conditions (**wenn**) and directed at what target (the **nono**). The formula 'Don't ever litter,' opened up to fit into its full expression in the logic of rules, makes littering the target of the **nono** and, by leaving open the **volk**, suggests that the **nono** applies to everybody, under any conditions (**wenn**) in which littering is possible, for example, conditions under which people have trash in hand. The formula 'Vote in the election for Parliament only if you are a citizen of Canada' opens up to apply to a **volk** that includes only people present or possibly present in Canada at the time of the Parliamentary election, under the condition (**wenn**) that a Parliamentary election is being held, and prohibiting people who are not citizens of Canada from voting.

Rights as Systems of Rules

Rights involve blocking operations. If we consider a typical case of a right, for example, someone's right to property in a house that she has bought, we immediately come across a scene for possible blocking operations. If a stranger enters the house and proposes to stay regardless of the wishes of the owner, the owner's right will be upheld sooner or later, if things go normally, by blocking operations. Indeed, even physical blocking operations may occur: the owner and her brother take the stranger by the collar, throw him out of the house, and chase him off the property. Blocking operations are prominently available for other rights, too. I wish to speak out against waging war in Iraq. If the Constitution and the rule of law prevail, blocking operations will prevent other people from interfering.

Does the occurrence of some blocking operations and the associated latency of others make rights rules? Rights are indeed rules, each right a bundle of rules, but the relation to blocking operations is less direct than it was with the rules I was previously discussing. They fall, in any given case, on other people. To say 'N has a right to do an action A' is to say that there are rules that block other people from preventing N from doing A.

In the case of any given right, there are a number of rules involved: rules about acquiring the right, whether by purchase or by going through some other qualifying procedure or simply by birth or more simply still just by being present in a given jurisdiction; rules protecting the status of the rightholder from attempts to take the status away from him; rules about how the rule is to be enforced, which may or may not involve penalties; rules about the exercise of the right; rules about how it is possible in some cases, if not in all, to alienate the right or to have it extinguished; rules about the authority behind the rules; rules about which rules are to take precedence when rules conflict. There is a good deal of complexity here. In practice, I doubt whether it often causes an insuperable amount of trouble, but in theory, it is no doubt desirable to have, if one can have it without prejudice to the complexity, a simpler idea of what a right is.

A simpler idea can be arrived at by selecting again and again a few sorts of rules that are present with all rights and invite special attention. This is what I did in chapter 3. We select for every right (1) a rule about status and (2) a rule about exercise. The rule about exercise will say what the rightholder can do under the protection of the right. A complete list is not to be expected, since not all the demands arising in future situations can be foreseen; but some leading examples will generally give enough to go on. A person's right of ownership in a certain house protects, subject to limitations designed to protect other people from harm, her exercise of the right in choosing which people will be admitted to her house and which will not; in choosing the equipment to be installed in the house; in choosing how to decorate the house; in choosing to shut it up when she goes away or to rent it to others. The rule about exercise blocks other people from blocking her in doing any of these things. Thus the exercise of the right is protected.

The status of the owner calls for protection of the same kind. The rule about status blocks other people from impairing the status, for example, by according to themselves the status at least in part, so that they, falsely claiming part ownership, demand to be consulted whenever the owner exercises the right. The rule about status also blocks other people from taking the status away by falsifying documentation in their favour or by expropriation without compensation. Where the right has to do with being given equal consideration for admission to a university, the rule about status will block imposing a quota on people of a certain colour or religion.

Given the simple picture of a right that includes with the rule about status and the rule about exercise the two most prominent rules associated with it, a number of interesting points about rights come up if to the rules about status and exercise we add, in the case of a given right, rules about how the status is acquired or given up. Some rights, I said a moment ago, are acquired by purchase (e.g., acquiring the property right in a house); some, by going through another special procedure (e.g., in acquiring the right to vote by becoming naturalized as a citizen); some, by simply arranging to be born in a given jurisdiction (e.g., the right to vote for native-born citizens); some, by simply being present in the jurisdiction (e.g., the right to a fair trial, or to security against theft or violence). How are rights given up? The rule for some rights says that the objects with which they are concerned – a house, a bundle of cash, a grand piano – can be sold or given away; other rights can be renounced, like the right to vote by someone who becomes, by renouncing her citizenship in one country, a citizen of another.

Can all rights be alienated? It seems very doubtful that anyone can give up his right to a fair trial. He can omit to invoke his right to a fair trial, but can he give it up to the extent of abrogating it, in a jurisdiction with a legal system in which no one legally competent to decide questions about rights would go along with his attempt to have it nullified? If he cannot give up his right to a fair trial, this is a very different sort of right from his right to a piece of property, which it is perfectly possible for him to sell or give away.

But may not people change their minds and cease to uphold the right to a fair trial whether or not the people actually to be tried want to give it up? With this question, the issue about whether a right can be given up, that is to say, about whether it is inalienable, changes into the issue about whether there are certain rights that cannot be extinguished. The right to a fair trial is again a prime candidate. The courts, as things now stand, would undo any attempt, by a prosecutor or an individual judge, or even by the legislature, to extinguish this right, in the case of any given person, or generally. But that, one might say in the United States, is because the right to a fair trial is embedded in the Constitution. Could not the Constitution be changed? One needs to pause to appreciate the importance of placing some rights in the Constitution, out of the reach of the legislature. Placing them there helps save them from hasty or petulant legislative acts.

Suppose the importance of this is dwelt upon and duly appreciated. Then, though it has been usefully postponed, the possibility of changing the Constitution comes up again. At this point one may shift to saying that, like a limited number of other rights, the right to a fair trial is a natural right. People with hard heads or hard hearts may deem this a very weak assertion, impossible to establish by rational argument. But I think a rational argument is available: show that the right to a fair trial belongs to a body of rules – rules that, along with St Thomas and David Hume, I am perfectly ready to call 'natural laws'[12] – that indispensably must have both legal and moral status in any society that is to thrive along with every person who belongs to it having a reasonable chance to thrive individually.[13] Then, in calling a right 'natural' we connect it with the natural conditions of human thriving. They are social, of course, as well as natural, like the rules combined in them, but many things about societies are natural, including the conditions of their thriving. Those conditions may on occasion be ignored by judges, legislators, and voters; but that does not do away with them.

This explanation of how rights can be natural falls in easily with the guiding idea in the approach that I have taken to rights: they are combinations of social rules and, as such, are inventions and institutions that originate in social practices and are kept up in social practices while they are effective. A firm grasp of this fact should discourage people from thinking that intuitions about rights without reference to their origin and reproduction in social practices are trustworthy. It might generate some resistance, though it would not be insuperable resistance, to Fichte's contention that rights come up in the very foundations of our knowledge of ourselves and others in a world external to each of us, taken one by one. Unless there is mutual recognition of each other's right to have some scope for freedom of action, we cannot understand how we are related to each other or to the world. This certainly makes more of rights than social devices, yet I think it is no more than a complication for the view that they are. Rights at this foundational level are not for Fichte already concrete moral or legal rights; they will have to be institutionalized, by way of a social contract and other arrangements, which will bring in systems of blocking operations, before they become concrete as social devices. The view that rights are social devices may be taken to be the view that they are social devices capitalizing on the presence of prototypes in the foundations of self-consciousness and knowledge.

To Needs by Way of the Problem of Consequences

Whether given rules or rights – given combinations of rules – are morally compelling enough to support and conform to depends on the consequences of having the rules or rights in question. The problem of consequences invites discussion under three heads. One may ask, 'How far should one go (both in the sense of how many and how far into the future) in considering consequences?' One may also ask, 'Just what, in the consequences that are considered, is to be given prime attention?' And one may ask, 'What form of evidence about what is attended to is to be taken as decisive?'

How Far Should One Go in Considering Consequences?

Even natural rights, on the view that I have taken of them, stand or fall with consequences. Were human beings or their circumstances radically different from what they are, there might be no serious consequences to follow from ignoring natural rights and natural laws, or at any rate no consequences that human beings would treat seriously.

Other, less sacred rights, no less fateful sometimes even if they are not always so ineluctable, also call for justification by consequences.

The key to dealing with the problem of how far one should go in considering consequences lies in limiting the search for topics and evidence that precedes the present choice of rules or rights while keeping open the possibility of considering further evidence afterwards and changing the policy accordingly. H.A. Simon advocated limiting the present search in his notion of satisficing.[14] C.E. Lindblom agreed and added, among other things, the point that, whenever possible, the present choice should be the choice of an alternative only incrementally different from the status quo.[15]

Lindblom did not arrive at incrementalism by linguistic analysis; nor did Simon arrive by linguistic analysis at satisficing. Yet they could have; linguistic analysis is another route to their results. It is a commonplace in the relevant linguistic practices that, of the options open to us, we should always choose the best one. If Simon and Lindblom had asked – in effect, at least, they did ask – how is the injunction to choose the best policy carried out in practice, they would have come to the position that normally it is carried out tentatively, with the assumption that revisions in further rounds of discussion will be considered. This is the position that Simon affirms and Lindblom agrees with. Given the limits of information that people choosing policies always have to cope with, it could not be otherwise.

'Best,' thus, in the practice of choosing actions and policies has a property that 'true' has in claims of knowledge. Compare 'This is of the options considered the one that we can reasonably defend as best to choose now, understanding that we may see our way to doing better in the future' with 'This is what we can reasonably and firmly say that we know to be true now, understanding that we may have to revise our position in the future.' The qualifying 'understanding' phrases are commonly left out, which heightens the paradox of the property involved. 'Best' and 'true' are notions both categorical (they do not admit of degrees) and tentative (they are subject to revision in later moments). Or, put another way, this two-faced property neatly fits neither under 'categorical' nor under 'tentative.' That helps explain why philosophers have often made such a mess of 'best' and of 'true.'

In the ordinary practice of choosing actions and policies, it would not be safe, furthermore, as Lindblom would say, to do anything but choose incremental departures. Only incremental departures will leave institutions in place that can undo policies that go wrong or remedy their unfortunate consequences, entirely or perhaps only partially unforeseen. Put another way, it is convenient and illuminating, as a move in linguistic analysis, to define 'incremental' so that it turns out to have this implication.

The results that I have just sketched supply an answer to the misgivings that, in a curious alliance, Joseph Butler, philosopher and sometime Bishop of Durham, Immanuel Kant, the champion of abstract rigour, and that philosophical guerrilla, Friedrich Wilhelm Nietzsche, have all expressed about consequentialist ethics, namely, that it could never tell us what is the right thing to do because we can never know all the consequences of our actions. We cannot know; but we do not need to know. We can attend effectively to consequences without ever attending to them all, much less to all that at any given moment are possible.[16]

What Is to Be Attended to in Attending to Consequences?

Limited though the number of consequences considered may be in any one instance of choice, a great variety of consequences come up for discussion in choices of actions and policies. This is so, at any rate, when the choices are not straightforwardly settled by unchallenged habits established by previous experience.

Are there any features of consequences that, if they do not always determine choices, at least must never tell against the ones that are made? Gratuitous reductions of personal happiness would be one such feature; but failing to meet needs, or to obstruct meeting them, claims even higher priority. It is commonly thought to be unjust that some people should have much more than is required to meet their needs, while other people fall short of having even enough; it is even more tellingly unjust to support social and economic arrangements that systematically deny some people the chance to obtain enough.

Happiness, which is what utilitarians originally aimed at in the Greatest Happiness Principle, has a claim to be a consideration that cannot in the end be set aside. But happiness is perhaps too elusive a concept to do the heavy lifting required. Utilitarians have championed utility as something more concrete. The greatest utility is to be pursued in every choice and in every revision of choices. Unfortunately, after two and a half centuries' hard work by some very acute thinkers, we still do not have a satisfactory concept of utility. A satisfactory concept would allow us to arrive at measures, not only of the utilities obtained by any one given person, but also, by comparing the utilities of different persons, of the total of utilities achieved by everybody affected by a given policy. Even this would not be enough to be satisfactory: the measures should not be measures difficult to understand and applied only in abstruse computations. Why should people be asked to accept policies whose consequences for them they cannot understand?

We do better to ask, on a first approach to considering the consequences of one option in social policy compared to another, 'How far do the options before us succeed or fail in meeting the needs of the people who will bear the consequences?'

The concept of needs has been so much abused, however, that many sophisticated thinkers place no confidence in it. Most important and most common among the abuses[17] is that too many people too much of the time claim to need things that they are only justified in saying that they want or desire. There is universally felt to be more force in asking for something that one needs than in asking for something that one would merely like to have. Beginning in infancy, people abuse the concept of needs by claiming that they need things just because they would like to have them.

This abuse, however, can be cured; and the superior force of needs restored. One way of doing this, in keeping with received linguistic practices, is to work out a construction in which the term 'needs' is given a firmly selective use. For example, draw up a convincing, brief list of what will generally be agreed to be basic – inescapable – Matters of Need: not needs that come and go with particular projects, but needs that people must meet to carry on their lives, whatever particular projects they take up. The list will include such things as food, water, clothing, shelter, companionship, and education. Second, identify for each of these Matters of Need Minimum Standards of Provision. These standards will vary from person to person, for example, in the case of food, since people vary both in appetite and in caloric requirements.

Now we say: let us make sure, whatever else we do, of meeting people's needs.

Is this all, however, that we want from politics? It is far from being so. We want good lives, what Hobbes would have called commodious lives. Here happiness returns. We want not just to have our needs met, but to be happy. We are not likely to be happy if our needs are not met, but they can be met – the needs on any trenchant short list at any rate can be met - without our being happy.

The difficulties about happiness being elusive do not demand so much weight after the agenda of needs has been taken care of; and so far as the difficulties demand consideration, happiness can be subsumed in Amartya Sen's 'capabilities.'[18] We would seek to give people the capabilities that they need to function with the skills and in the ways that make them happy.

What Form of Evidence Is to Be Decisive in Considering Consequences?

The form in which evidence about consequences is to be marshalled is not the calculus, since we do not have an accepted concept of the utility that is to be measured by the calculus, and the calculus does not apply (at any rate directly) to the concept of needs. The form of evidence is a comparative census, which applies easily to needs and even to happiness and applies better than any calculus, because, among other reasons, it does not lend itself to an opposition between making some people very happy versus making a greater number of people happy, though to a lesser degree .

The notion of a comparative census comes out of reflecting carefully (as Bentham and most of his followers, even Sidgwick, did not) on what we ordinarily mean by making people in a group happier. We do not mean maximizing a quantity of something measured and added up for the whole group, which might lead to painful sacrifices for people who are not suited to get high scores. We mean, starting with the distribution of happiness or provisions for needs that we have, moving to make more people happy or provided for while we make no one worse off in these respects.

I shall not repeat here the tables illustrating the census-notion given in chapter 1 or the points made there and elsewhere about safeguards in its use.[19] Suffice it to say here that it involves observing people with respect to their needs or their happiness being provided for and concluding that a policy that provides for the needs or happiness of more people and simultaneously reduces or at least does not increase the number of people not provided for is to be preferred, on the evidence, to a policy that provides for the needs of fewer or increases the number of people not provided for.

Shifting to the census-notion from the calculus is a repair to received utilitarian doctrine, but it is a repair authorized by the traditional slogan 'The greatest happiness of the greatest number.' The slogan has been felt to be an embarrassment by those utilitarians aware that it gives contradictory advice on occasions when the Greatest Happiness, taken as a sum over the whole group of people affected, lies in one direction, and the happiness of the greater number in another. Many more people may become a bit happier if they get fruit or ice cream for dessert every day; alternatively, a smaller number may be substantially happier if they get to go on a Caribbean cruise twice a year. The calculus, which is commonly and carelessly presupposed by writers on utilitarianism to be effective in principle, might well, if it were effective, encourage people to resolve the ambiguity of the slogan in favour of the aggregative score for the Caribbean cruises and let go of the Greatest Number, with the distributive consideration that it signifies. The census-notion makes good sense of both parts of the slogan. It accords with the Greatest Happiness in favouring movement from lower categories to higher ones; it accords with the Greatest Number in favouring having more people in the top categories. Furthermore, sensibly interpreted to resolve a certain ambiguity about whether advances for some worsen the conditions of others, the census-notion resists sacrificing some people's happiness to other people's happiness by refusing to support unqualified endorsement of such changes. Instead, it poses a problem for the Revisionary Process ubiquitously present in real-world politics about inventing another policy that does not require such sacrifices.

Questions about Justice

Justice did not figure among the advertised relatively narrow topics, the disaggregated topics, treated in the free-standing studies of part one; and I do not aim to treat justice at any length in this book, beyond what I shall be led to do in part four in the discussion of Rawls, Nozick, and Gauthier. However, there are significant connections between justice and the topics of detail that I have treated. Furthermore, these connections will lend strength to the program, about to emerge, that results from adding up my results on the topics of detail. So I should not let pass the opportunity to mention the connections.

Rules raise questions about justice. Do the rules under which the government raises taxes favour some people at the expense of others? Are any people excluded from having the status associated with certain rights or hindered in their exercise of those rights? Consider the right to vote, in the Southern states as they used to be; or, as shenanigans in 2000 proved, as they still were in Florida then.

Some of the worst injustices that governments and their supporters have perpetrated consist in violations of the rights of people they have chosen to victimize; others (sometimes in combination with violations of rights), in deliberate disregard of the needs of the victims. The denial by the Nazis of the Jews' rights to legal protection illustrates the first. The starvation of the kulaks under Stalin illustrates the second. The miseries to which the Gulag subjected its prisoners illustrate both, as do the miseries inflicted by the Nazis on people in the concentration camps.

On the other hand, rights, when they are respected, can serve as effective instruments of justice; and so do arrangements, whether they rely on rights or not, for meeting needs.

The use of the census-notion to deal with provisions for needs reflects a number of points of justice. Everyone in the population at issue is to be counted – put in one census-category or another; and everyone is to count for as much as anyone else – lending just as much weight by being placed in one census-category or another to choosing between policies as any other person placed there (or elsewhere). The connections do not stop there. Justice governs not only the evidence to be assembled in censuses, but what is to be made of the evidence once assembled. Consider again:

(i) On some one occasion, some people lose, even though there is in appearance a net advance.
Comparing a census ex post respecting a certain policy B with a census ex ante respecting another policy A, though there are fewer people not provided for under B than under A, everyone sees that some of the people who were provided for under A are now not provided for.
If there is no special reason for this misfortune, justice, brought to bear by the Gains-Preservation Principle,[20] requires turning to the Revisionary Process and revising Policy B to keep the advances that it makes without imposing the sacrifices now unmasked.

(ii) On one occasion after another, people in some identifiable subgroup never move up from a lower category to another. This is the sort of injustice (discrimination) that Black people in the United States have historically suffered.
Again, resort is to be made to the Revisionary Process, this time to give special attention to moving people in the subgroup up from a lower category to a higher one (without, other things being equal, pushing other people down or blocking their improvement).[21]

Benefits for Empirical Social Science from Analytical Examination of the Topics of Detail

To treat, as I shall briefly do, the benefits for empirical social science that emerge from the analytical examination of the relatively narrow, disaggregated topics that I have taken up is to digress from the main argument of this chapter, indeed (since the chapter is the keystone of the book), from the main argument of the book, which leads to a comprehensive normative program in political theory. Nevertheless, the benefits are worth looking at, since they are substantial and credit analytical political philosophy with accomplishments not so much to be expected on other approaches, in particular, an approach that concentrates on the history of political theory. The benefits, as it happens, are also available to pursuing the history of political theory; they increase the range and precision of questions, some of them relevant to current politics, raised about that history. Moreover, in general, analytical political philosophy is more favourable to empirical social science than other approaches are. Some analytical philosophers have objected to quantitative social science; but these objections (by P. Winch and A. MacIntyre[22]) express a one-sided view of social science, exposed as such by fuller analytical efforts.[23] Some analytical philosophers (among them, those just mentioned) have inclined to favour interpretative social science, which is closer in methods and outlook to their own activity, but this need not be one-sided favour; and on this point the reader should not be misled by my presenting here benefits to be realized, in the first instance, on the interpretative side.

Many of the benefits have to do with understanding better, with a more precise notion of rules, how rules govern social intercourse.

This is in part more a matter of future than of present illustration. A more precise notion of rules enables researchers to raise a variety of questions neglected hitherto, for example, 'Why are some rules on similar subjects more effective than other rules?' We can pursue this question by identifying in turn the appropriate formulations in the rule of the **volk**, the **wenn**, and the **nono**, and then considering their joint operation. Again, 'Why can many rules dispense with sanctions, while others may not be able to?' This is a question that arises after we distinguish, as I did in the treatment of rules in part one, between blocking operations and sanctions. Some rules are precise up to the point of leaving out exceptions, while others give only very general guidance, leaving details to be determined by discussion and negotiation. What approach works more effectively in what situations? The analysis in chapter 5 gives us models for precision that can be applied in answer to this question. If precision in one respect or another cannot be achieved, the formulas help make that fact awaken attention.

What makes some rules, and some rights, more effective than others, one may hypothesize, will have to do with how they affect meeting one or another need of the people who are to live with the rules or rights. What is at stake here and how groups of people are affected with respect to needs are matters on which the analysis of needs, the justification of treating some as more basic than others, and the census-notion figure, not perhaps as innovations in social science (though they are something like innovations in normative political philosophy), but at least as reminders of what to be firm about in studying related issues.

I say that these questions are matters more of future illustrations than of present ones. Some present illustrations of how such questions work out, as it happens, illustrations from history, are available, in addition to the illustration from the debate, mentioned in chapter 5, in the British Parliament on the abolition of the slave trade:

1. There is the issue, long a matter of debate among theorists of the Constitution, about whether and how the U.S. Constitution obstructs government by competitive parties. A rules-analysis leads to treating this as a combination of issues: Does the Constitution rule out parties? Does the Constitution put obstacles to the formation of parties nearly impossible in practice to surmount? Applying a precise notion of rules gives a negative answer to the first question. Applying the same notion makes some headway on a negative answer to the second when one possible obstruction after another is inspected. The most important part of the answer comes from history, though the rules-analysis explains how it was possible for history to work out this way. National parties with coherent policy platforms were formed under the Constitution during the first decade of its operation.[24]
2. As a second present illustration, consider again the account given by Foucault in *The Birth of Clinical Medicine* of the coming in, characteristic of clinical medicine, of the rule that diagnosticians are to include in their diagnoses (of mortal diseases) only external features of diseases that are correlated with distinctive internal features observed by pathologists in autopsies. There is a problem about how this rule could have been brought in before the correlations were discovered. Another rule to cover the development of the basis for the rule just cited must be postulated, and the rules-analysis indicates both the necessity of postulating it and what its content must be – essentially, that each stage of the development should rely on the closest approximation available to having internal features correlated with the external ones.[25]

The more precise notion of rules given in chapter 5 comes to bear not only with new questions on which research has yet to begin, but also with familiar questions that are staples of current research. Anthropologists and sociologists, including political sociologists, are always looking for the social rules that govern the behaviour of the peoples that they are studying. The more precise notion of rules tells them something useful about what to look for in rules that govern social intercourse. What is the **volk** in the postulated rule? What is the **wenn**? What is the **nono**? ('Don't just guess!' should be the motto for research; 'Formulate these aspects of the rule as precisely as possible.') For some researchers (e.g., J. March and E. Ostrom[26]), social institutions amount to systematic combinations of rules. The rules themselves and the logical features of the relations between the rules can be understood better with more precise formulations (as Ostrom, in particular, has fully realized, responding as she does in some writings to the challenge of using a formal logic of rules[27]).

Questions about social institutions often touch on the rights – bundles of rules – that the people who have to do with institutions claim from them. To flout these rights almost inevitably arouses resistance, resentment, failures in management, among other things (consider G. Homans on how important the feeling of justice is to morale in the workplace[28]). Precision about rules leads to precision about rights and what justice requires in respecting them.

More precise notions about rules, rights, and needs (as well as about how consequences are to be dealt with in evaluating policy proposals) improve the understanding of the policy-making process, including the policy-making process when it is concerned with modifying the rules that establish the character of institutions.

A useful definition of 'policy' can be given by defining a policy as a social rule. Then an issue (one important sort of issue, indeed, the basic sort) can be defined as a choice between rules, for example, between various possible rules for taxing personal incomes. One can then inquire into the consistency with which deliberations focus on a given issue of this sort; and into the reasons for departures from consistency.

It is clear from the analysis given of rules that rules impose burdens – they are upheld by people taking on the burden of associated blocking operations (and in some cases, sanctions). In crucial cases, the burden is taken up by courts and other agencies for the enforcement of laws. All this is true, as advocates of new rights need to bear in mind, of rules for rights. Every right is a bundle of rules, each of which must depend on self-restraint on the part of people conforming to them and on other people being ready to engage in blocking operations when conformity is not immediately forthcoming. In some cases, they must be ready to support (or themselves actually carry out) the imposition of penalties. Thus, of every right, one may ask: are people ready to take on the associated burdens?

The answer to this question will depend on how many rights are already recognized. And questions arise about what content and scope a system of rights will best have in any given circumstances. What will be the division, the content, and the overall scope of such a system? We must be mindful too, that effective use of the notion of a 'best' system will inevitably be tentative, something to improve on in later policy choices. Indeed, our focus most often will best be on whether adding a newly proposed right will fit in without trouble with existing rules or rights or will unsettle them, without any net overall improvement.

The Contribution to Political Philosophy: A Grand Program Brought into Being by Adding Up the Results from Analysing the Disaggregated Topics

The disaggregated topics that I examined in part one can hardly be dismissed as unimportant in politics, though by contrast to the grand programs to be treated in part four they are, indeed, relatively narrow. Even if we do not go on to define policies as rules, for example, it is clear that rules come into politics in many ways, sometimes as the object of political choices, sometimes as governing features of the process of arriving at social choices. Similarly, though we cannot take up rights without taking up the rules that combine to make each right, if we concentrate on rights, ignoring rules of other sorts, we still have a subject that has incited and continues to incite a good deal of agitation and controversy. Needs, often without explicit attention to rules or rights, continually call for political attention in all jurisdictions from the smallest to the largest: people lose their jobs or their homes; they suffer from assaults and life-threatening accidents. Statistics on these matters, when they show widespread lapses in provisions for the needs in question, become matters of concern at the highest level, even in governments that lag behind the best in promoting the general welfare.

So the several topics have a strong claim to political attention even taken individually. But how do the results on the several topics add up?

One way in which they add up is by being connected, each with every other. The results, moreover, are mutually helpful. You might believe, even at the beginning of reflecting on the topics, that rules are found everywhere in social life and institutions; and, in particular, that rules and rights have something to do with each other. Without reflection and analysis, however, you would not know just what rules were or, in particular, what distinguishes rules for rights from other rules. You might understand from the beginning that rules have something to do with consequences. But without reflection and analysis you would not know just what about the consequences of having any given rule, including rules for rights, would support having such a rule, or such a right; and what would not. You would understand, after reflection and analysis, what a heavy burden of justification you would be taking on if you held that some rules and some rights hold regardless of consequences. Some of the consequences might be very upsetting.

There is another way of adding up: what sort of figure do the results that I have described, operating together, cut in political theory? Combined, they take on the figure of another comprehensive program, a program according to which

Political institutions are to be looked for that
uphold reasonable rules (and a reasonable number of rules),
conform to and uphold rights,
    where the rules combined in rights and other rules can be
        justified by due consideration of their consequences
    in a policy-making process of which a Revisionary Process is a
        central feature,
    comparative censuses are carried out,
    and these take into account, with limits on inequality in
        distribution, provisions for needs as centrally important
    in consequences favourable or unfavourable.
It is further implied that whatever measures are needed to establish
    and preserve political institutions of this kind should be brought
    in and kept up.

This is just an outline, parts of which still cry out for filling in, especially with details about the needs to be considered, the rights to be recognized, and the limits on unequal distribution. On distribution, the grand programs of part four have much to suggest, but so, in rather more down-to-earth terms, does the discussion of the census-notion in chapter 1 and in the present chapter. Chapter 1 goes much, if not all, of the way toward specifying the needs to be considered. As regards rights, the received right to private property and an innovative right to a livelihood came in for substantial enough discussion in chapters 3, 4, and 5 to make a visible advance in the project of filling in the rights to be recognized; and other rights that the project may embrace have been briefly discussed or mentioned (the right to a fair trial, the right to free speech, the right to free association). Since rights are bundles of rules (systems of systems of imperatives), important instances of rules come up for discussion and specification in the project about rights; they and other rules inviting consideration are to be understood as falling in with the analysis of rules given in chapter 5.

Thus, an appreciable amount of filling in has been done in this very book. The effort here falls far short, however, of what sooner or later requires to be done. In some respects, it falls short of what is being done – has been done – all along in other quarters. Particular rights, for example, are continually being discussed in the courts, in the legislatures, and in treatises on law. At the moment of writing all those scenes of discussion in the United States have been concerned with the rights of people held by the United States government as 'enemy combatants'; there is a lot of discussion about curtailing the rights of consumers to sue corporations for damages. In this respect, the combination program offered in this chapter – I shall call it 'the needs-focused combination program' – has vigorous roots in a current agenda for people practising politics in accordance with the program; the program is not merely a subject for debate among theorists. Many people with relevant roles are already busily at work carrying out the program, and here it has distinctive strength.

Even where the combination program is not already heavily involved in a current practical agenda, the theory has practical advice to offer. In respect to rights, for example, before they are assented to there is a need to know whether the burden or the added burden of having them will be accepted by the people who will have to uphold them. That is one reason for my interpolating the reference to 'a reasonable number of rules.'[29] Anarchists should not stand alone against having too many rules and the vexations that come with them. We need to inquire, for normative purposes as well as scientific ones, whether we are moving away, just in adding rules, from net improvements in the current system of rules or rights or moving forward.

Added up, the results that I have surveyed thus pose an elaborate, programmatic, global challenge for political theory, a challenge that the theory of democracy may be required to face up to. From Plato on, there have been philosophers who have argued that politics is best conducted by an elite; and there have been theorists who have argued that, for good or ill, politics is inevitably so conducted. If this is so, it is still vital to distinguish elites that pursue humane, responsive, and progressive policies from elites that do not.

Will democracy do better on these points than alternative political forms? A democratic theorist is bound to argue that, if we have to have elites they will be more reliably humane, responsive, and progressive if the elites are under democratic control. What forms of control will serve best? What conditions must they meet? Among them may be that democracy is to play a part on each topic: in choosing rules; in choosing rights; in deliberating about consequences; in demanding that needs be met; in insisting upon justice.

Late in my reflections on these matters, indeed, only after sending off to the publishers a full draft of the present book, it became clear to me that my labours on needs, rights, rules, and dealing with consequences can be justified, even if the labours were not more than intermittently consciously driven by any such aim, by the aim of restoring credit to familiar ideas that inexpert citizens can use to reach sensible judgments on ultimate issues of politics. I say 'inexpert' citizens: to speak of 'ordinary' citizens or 'average' citizens, as is commonly done, is patronizing and unjustifiable. We are all inexpert citizens in regard to most policies. Yet we must believe that concepts and procedures within the power of all of us are adequate for deciding ultimate issues. Where would democracy be if this were not so? Yet experts of one sort or another have cast elaborate doubts on the concepts of needs and rights; failed to make clear the relation of these concepts to rules; and time and again such notable lights as Kenneth Arrow and Thomas Scanlon[30] have missed the salient feature of dealing with consequences, namely, that they are dealt with serially, making one revision after another. Inexpert citizens themselves have had misgivings about the concept of needs and the concept of rights, since doubtful applications of those concepts are as common as well-founded ones.

Inexpert citizens may have given no thought to the problem of dealing with consequences; or to the ways in which rules come up in providing for needs as well as in establishing and maintaining rights. In practice, however, they are used to doing by and large what I say they should do about these things. They know what it means to heed rules, old and new, are used to heeding rules themselves, and are used to expecting others to heed them, too. They are used to having rules repealed, or fall into disuse . They are used to having new rules adopted. They are used to having rules, once adopted, revised stage by stage. They are familiar with the connection of some rules to needs (e.g., the rule of compulsory attendance to the need for education); they are familiar with the rules that come with rights (e.g., the rule that one must be a citizen to vote in a general election). It is a merit of what I say about rules, I would claim, that it is fully intelligible to inexpert citizens and will even seem familiar to them once they are reminded.

The same is true of what I say about needs and rights. Inexpert citizens recognize when claims of needs have become far-fetched; they will recognize that firm grounds for claims of needs can be found in what everyone must have to carry out basic social roles and lead a reasonably full life. The construction that I give for the concept of needs does no more than take simple steps, all of them easy to understand, toward making this recognition systematic.

People may not be spontaneously mindful of the structures of multiple rules that come into operation when rights are invoked or proposed; but I am confident that they will recognize the pertinence of the structures once they are pointed out. They do not have to inquire into abstract theories of social contract or subscribe to theories that cannot be given current application about the histories of supposed rights. Everything that comes up in my grand program is familiar or immediately recognizable; everything is within the powers of application of inexpert citizens.

That is not to say that no philosophical work was required to make these concepts fully intelligible and vindicate (careful) use of them by inexpert citizens. On the subject of needs, for example, my account arises after I have cleared away confusions created by experts disdainful of the concept; and after I have set at rest misgivings that inexpert citizens themselves have, aware of how often and readily the term 'needs' is abused to make claims that careful use of the term does not support.[31]

The needs-focused combination program set forth here solves one problem about how the citizens of a democracy can know what to do about issues that they face. It tells them what to do in the decisions that they have to make, ultimately, about their aims in politics for themselves and for the societies in which they live. If their needs are not met, and their rights are disregarded, how can what is happening in politics be acceptable to them?

The combination program does not solve another problem about how the citizens of a democracy can know what to do: They can tell when their needs and other people's are being met, but they will often have to turn to experts (fallible as these experts will be) for advice about the social arrangements that will best meet the needs. How are they to deal with experts? My program does not save them for having to take some advice from experts on trust, at least for the time being. However, the combination program does show what they should expect the experts to attend to in the ultimate aims of policies. No mystifications about utility, please, or about the aggregation of preferences! The program also reminds inexpert citizens that they can tell when the trust that they have temporarily given the experts has turned out to have been misplaced. Then people – the inexpert citizens themselves, or people whose condition they are able to observe – are by and large worse off rather than better off after one policy or another has been adopted on the advice of experts.

The program does not solve a third problem, which is how to get inexpert citizens to attend to what is happening in respect to needs and rights; and to act upon the shortcomings that they observe. The citizens may not take the trouble to distinguish between the average benefits of a cut in taxes and the benefits that most people will get. They allow themselves to be misled on this and other simple points. Worse, they will simply ignore the evidence that on one point after another a politician in office has introduced policies that do not, on even the most obvious points, support or advance the common good. Ignoring growing pollution, understaffed and underequipped schools, and declines in occupational health and safety, to say nothing of costly and unnecessary military adventures, they will vote for a plausible ignoramus who looks as if he would be good company at a barbecue rather than a thoughtful man who would do substantially more to meet their needs.

Here, the results that I have surveyed and the program of problems that emerges from their combination arrive in the neighbourhood of James Fishkin's concerns with deliberation in democracy.[32] Analytical political philosophy may have something to say about the design of democracy – Fishkin certainly has something to say – in these connections, but for a lot of the action from this point on the ball is in the court of empirical political science.

Would democracy, in meeting the demands of the program, demand anything more of citizens than that they be

peaceful in disposition,
law-abiding
and alert in supporting what the program would deem improve-
    ments in social conditions?

It might require argument – strenuous, if not far-fetched – and a good
deal of evidence to show that more has to be added, such as

religious belief
or abstinence from various sexual practices.[33]

About some sexual practices we shall never have enough information
to judge whether or not there is an adverse connection with civic character. With others, we have the information and the irrelevance seems
clear. Was Voltaire's lead in public-spiritedness on certain subjects to be
repudiated because of his contempt for the Christian church, or because
he had an incestuous relation with one of his nieces? Or Wilkes's leadership on behalf of political liberty in eighteenth-century England, because he was a member of the Hellfire Club and merrily involved in
orgies at High Wycombe? Wilkes is not, I think, remembered as a very
devout churchman. He could have been – he was – a very useful friend
of liberty notwithstanding. Sade's life and work should check us from
thinking that every champion of sexual liberty is also a consistent
champion of liberty in that connection or others. But we can hypothesize that there is no obstacle in the combination program to its being
supported by people with a great variety of religious beliefs or with no
religious beliefs at all, and supported as well by people engaged in a
great range of disreputable sexual practices, some of them very disreputable in socially conservative eyes.

This is a strength of the program if it is to be carried out in a pluralis-
tic society. The program, even when the details of institutions and civic
training necessary to carrying out the program have been filled in, lays
down minimal requirements regarding moral character and moral or
religious beliefs. It thus gives a favourable reception to concerns like
those of Joseph H. Carens, Benjamin Gregg, and J. Donald Moon[34]
about how to establish an effective democracy with enough community
to win support for enlightened social policies, and enough institutionalized patience to bear with a great deal of diversity in people's cherished
beliefs and practices.

My grand program does not invoke Providence or the history of the class struggle. It does not depend on unmasking deceptive practices associated with current oppressions (though, if they come up as obstacles to carrying out the program, they will require unmasking). The census-notion, to which it gives such prominence, is hardly as dramatic an idea as the social contract, the original position, a mythical history of private property, an elite's claims to know what is good for people better than they know themselves. To return to a theme broached in the introduction: does it answer to the longing that Mark Lilla expresses 'to render political life more coherent, more just, [nobler]?' Does it give 'a compelling, synthetic account of our present situation and how to address the new challenges of our time?'

I think it does all of these things, in spite of its mundane and undramatic appearance. At first, the program may seem a combination of commonplaces; but they are refined commonplaces mutually reinforcing in a complex combination, and the combination poses not only a searching test of more dramatic doctrines, but also an arresting challenge that governments have rarely if ever lived up to. At its best, the government of the United States might have been awarded a B-minus for meeting the challenge. As I write, before and after the presidential election of 2004, government in the United States is moving rapidly in the direction of D or even F, with schools starved of funds, children dropped from health insurance rolls, and, by a spectacular lapse in attention to the census-notion, some millions of the poorest citizens losing rather than gaining from the latest Federal measure on prescription drugs. It will take energy and ingenuity and an engrossing struggle to get the United States just back to B-minus. It will take even more of these things to make comparable advances in the poorest parts of the world, to say nothing of the problems of keeping the peace in order to make way for the advances.

Suppose, somehow, B-minus returns and is even surpassed. When the United States or Canada reaches A or even A-minus, will not politics become boring? Suppose it did. Why would that discredit the needs-focused combination program of refined commonplaces as a political philosophy? People could still be active and excited in public spectacles: Rousseau's festivals; concerts and operas; sports. Everyone could give more time to the excitements, the anguish, and the joy of their private lives. People would go on playing music and composing it. They would go on painting, and writing novels about the tensions of family life. Some people have thought that you cannot have interesting art in the absence of agonizing social problems.[35] But I do not think that

Mozart's or Mendelssohn's piano trios presupposed any concern with agonizing social problems. Nor did the watercolours of Francis Towne or John Sell Cotman.

Moreover, issues for public disputation will not disappear. People will disagree about the character of the festivals, the concerts, the operas, the arrangements for sports and sports competitions. Many public projects, not so exciting as killing people by the thousands perhaps, but exciting as peacetime pursuits notwithstanding, will remain: an enormous proportion of the public spaces of Canada and the United States, to say nothing of private houses and commercial developments, call for being ennobled or at least re-imagined. The Acropolis can be outdone.

Moreover, if we do arrive at a point at which everybody's needs are adequately met under arrangements that assure them of being met indefinitely, we would still have bafflingly intricate social problems to deal with, for example, how to give everybody a steady variety of meaningful work – real work, not make-work in connections where machines could do better – and still enjoy a comfortable level of prosperity. Lots of work for political philosophy and political science will remain to be done on this topic.

Have I allowed sufficiently for competitiveness, aggression, and violence, to which human beings have been all too prone, even in prosperous circumstances? (Cf. Blues fighting Greens in ancient Constantinople; South Sea Islanders, with all their needs easily met in a lovely climate, making war on each other; English football hooligans, drawn in considerable numbers from people with respectable jobs.) One could say that my programmatic challenge lays out a desirable alternative to violence. It carries out a traditional task of political philosophy by offering a picture of the good society that sets up a usefully sharp opposition to social breakdown and violence. It sketches, ready to be filled in, the picture of a thriving society in which as much as possible the people belonging to it thrive, too, given due encouragement, including a moral education of the sort that human beings are naturally suited to benefit from.[36]

Is this enough? Will encouragement and education eliminate the inclination to violence? In normal circumstances, the inhibitions against violence installed by suitable moral education should prevail with most people most of the time. Will there not perhaps be some restiveness under the inhibition-controlled surface? Should not the Good Society have some way, other than repression, of accommodating the inclination to violence that in some people survives moral education; or remains latent beneath a moral order fragile as every moral order may be? This problem shows up in conflicts between religious groups and ethnic ones; and (with special concern for the violence tending to arise from conflicts about religion) it was the chief preoccupation of Thomas Hobbes, who also thought, entirely realistically, that any conflict whatever, even conflicts on trivial points of honour and the like, could lead to violence, and needed to be stopped, if necessary forcibly, by an alert and reliable authority, an absolute Sovereign. (He allowed for the possibility of this Sovereign's taking the form of a representative democracy, but he did not foresee that this form would turn out to be more reliable and stable than autocracy.) Nor did Hobbes consider, as William James did in suggesting that we need to find a moral equivalent to war, whether some forms of accommodating the inclination to violence might allow for its safe expression. I think such forms (violent, even extreme, sports, for example) might be found, though I think that analytical political philosophy has not done what it could to search for them. It might become more dramatic in the course of the search; but there is drama enough to preoccupy most people's tendencies to conflict in the so far unending struggle to find the policies that best meet people's needs and enable them to live commodious lives. Nor should we want dramatic ideas to divert us from this struggle.

PART THREE

ANALYTICAL POLITICAL PHILOSOPHY DEALS WITH EVIL

Prefatory Note to Part Three

The discussions and illustrations of the preceding parts of the present book have established that analytical political philosophy can generate grand visions of political society, one of them at least a vision set forth in a program that adds up the useful results of analysing particular concepts like needs, rights, and rules, and combines them with an analysis of the practice of evaluating consequences. The program is applicable to many choices of social policy and to evaluating the results of the choices afterwards. Thus, the preceding parts have fulfilled the undertaking made in the introduction.

Two of the questions broached in the introduction have not had full-dress treatment: first, the capacity of analytical political philosophy to deal with unsettled social conditions and (as a special case of these) far-reaching social change; second, its adequacy in coping with evil.

My answer to the first question, about social change, is, to be found as one theme in the chapter (5), which gives an analysis and definition of rules. There I illustrate how a logic of rules, coming out of analytical philosophy, can give precise accounts of such social changes as the inception of the permanent civil service in Britain; the onset of a division between tool-owners (capitalists) and tool-users (workers); revolutionary shifts in the appropriation of the social surplus; advances in mechanization; and the clearances of peasants from the land.

In the keystone chapter (6) just preceding this one, moreover, the discussion of how choices of social policy are to deal responsibly with the consequences of policy, never fully foreseen, bears upon social changes, in particular, the changes brought about by deliberate choices of social policy. So I say enough in this book, and give enough in the way of potent examples, to rebut any charge that analytical political philosophy does not and cannot deal with social changes.

However, as I said in the introduction, the answer to the charge – an answer that in my case is quite substantial – is mainly to be found in other works of mine – in the collaborative work *Logic on the Track of Social Change*[1] and in my work on 'issue-processing.'[2] In this book, I shall take up for full-dress treatment only the second question, about evil, and that is the subject of chapter 7, the one chapter in Part Three. However, I shall return briefly to social change in chapter 11, where at the end of a discussion comparing the grand program of this book with other grand programs offered in analytical political philosophy, mainly Rawls's program, I shall briefly consider the challenges presented to Rawls's program and mine in times of upheaval and turbulence.

7

Through the Free-Standing Studies and Their Aggregation in a Grand Program, Analytical Political Philosophy Can Deal with Evil

Leaving concentrated treatment of the connections that analytical political philosophy can make with social change to other passages in this book and elsewhere, I concentrate in this chapter on the question, 'How can analytical political philosophy deal with evil?'[1] If analytical political philosophy could not do this, it would fail an important test, which thinkers of another bent would justly hold against it. Appropriately enough for an entry in the present book, to establish a perspective for dealing with evil I shall use the list of things to be accomplished in politics that I have given in my discussion of particular, disaggregated topics in part one and then aggregated in the program with which part two concluded. The list, aggregated or disaggregated, is easily converted into a convincing basic list of evils, though each item on the list has to have a certain magnitude to be fully reckoned as an evil. How do these evils arise? I shall expand my account of evil to consider evil deeds, evil intentions, and evil characters. These all have a place in the general picture of evil, and sometimes attract as much attention as the basic evils that they impose, or more. However, even when human agency has the predominant role in generating evils, there may be vanishing little in the way of evil characters, or even of evil intentions, to invoke in the explanation of evil deeds; and the evil of evil deeds may not be commensurate with the basic evils that they generate.

In the last part of the chapter, I shall argue that this account of evil is rich enough, even if it is not fully comprehensive, to refute the suggestion, entertained by Susan Neiman[2] and others, that evils on the scale and with the character of Auschwitz outrun our concepts (in one sense in which this challenge might arise) – both the concepts on hand and even perhaps any that we could invent.

Lists of Needs, Rights, Rules Transform into Lists of Evils

Evil is not the subject of this chapter alone. The treatment in preceding chapters of needs, rights, and rules has identified by implication at least a number of important instances of evil.

Consider, first, a list of basic needs, such as the one that I give in *Meeting Needs*[3] and invoke in chapter 1 of the present book, which includes a first part, with needs for a favourable physical environment, food and water, excretion, exercise, periodic rest, bodily security (the need to keep the body intact); and a second part, with needs for companionship, education, social acceptance, sexual activity, being spared harassment, recreation. There is evil, often poignant evil, to be found in unmet needs; indeed, reversed in each case, the list of needs converts immediately into a list of evils. Recall from the introduction the little boy in a western American state who prays every night that he will be able to learn to read, but whose brain was damaged by the toxic dust surrounding his home. The dust was left over from mining operations profitable, one imagines, but insufficiently regulated. The absence of regulations restraining pollution or the disregard of such regulations, when they exist, may not always be as vivid and poignant in effects as this, but there are plenty of examples that are poignant enough, often affecting millions of people.

Rights on a list of rights violated or disregarded offer comparably many examples of evil, some of them, like being subjected to torture, equally poignant or more so. There are men and women – tens, indeed hundreds of thousands of them, some of them victims of American policy under a president who is much advertised as a Christian believer – living in unlucky parts of the world today whose lives have been shattered by military action or by torture and public humiliation violating their right to security of life and limb. There are as many, or many more, whose lives have been ruined by wrongful imprisonment. There are thousands of children – and not only children – forced into slave labour or prostitution whose right to freedom has been entirely disregarded. There have been hundreds of thousands, even millions, of people massacred in recent years in the Sudan, in Rwanda and the Congo, in Bosnia, in Cambodia, and elsewhere.

Vivid and poignant or not, but consequential even so, are the evils on a third sublist arising from flouting and undermining wisely chosen social rules (besides the rules combined to make rights), among them rules designed to check pollution or injury and loss of life in house fires. In the train of political corruption, for example, come failures to make sure of elementary provisions for public health and safety – classically, for example, the sort of graft repudiated by the Tammany Hall politician George Washington Plunkett, which consists in taking money to overlook violations of provisions in the building code about fire safety, an evil raised exponentially in shoddily built apartment houses in earthquake zones.[4]

Failures under each of the three subheads in the three-part list are patent evils, by which I mean that we do not need a definition of evil to know them as such; on the contrary, their inclusion is a basic test of any definition. It is an evil for people to starve; to die of thirst; to be exposed to the elements without shelter or clothing. It is an evil for them to be denied rest and recreation and in consequence to suffer physically and mentally from stress. Many, perhaps almost all, of the most serious evils that afflict human beings come down sooner or later to disregard of meeting needs or active obstruction to meeting them. The rules for rights and other rules that it is most important not to violate are rules that have to do with meeting needs directly; or indirectly, as in protecting opportunities to protest not having needs met. The right to free speech derives a good deal of its power from its service to protests against all sorts of evils.

Let us concentrate for the moment on the evils of unmet needs. Sometimes, I say, the evil lies in disregard and neglect; sometimes in active obstruction. (There are borderline cases, like the starvation of the kulaks: they were left to starve, but they starved because their crops were taken away from them.)[5]

Evils, even patent evils, vary in degree: neglecting to feed a child for a couple of days is on its way to being a patent evil, but it might not be thought significant enough to warrant the heavyweight epithet 'evil.' Neglecting to feed a child for a couple of weeks is surely significant enough. Is the difference between something that would not invite the term – though it is, as it were, on the way to inviting it – and something of the same sort that invites, indeed, compels the term, the difference between not being (yet) life-threatening and being life-threatening for sure? In many cases it is.

People may be, and should be, reluctant to accept it that magnitude is the only consideration and that the picture is complete without bringing in human deeds, human intentions, human characters. Basic evils –

for example, the evils of not meeting, even thwarting the meeting of, needs – are already recognizable as such, however, before the picture surrounding them is complete.[6]

The term 'evil' often gives way to a more specific term, for instance, 'starvation' or 'exhaustion' or 'fright,' the use of which makes the use of 'evil' redundant; this reduces the frequency with which 'evil' is used over the whole general range of particular cases. That makes the use of the term to designate a basic evil – one or another – on the three-part list somewhat less familiar.[7] The term comes into its own, however, when it is desired to speak of 'the evils neglected by the present government' or 'the evils of a depressed economy.'

The criterion of being life-threatening will capture many sorts of above-threshold evils when they become serious, but not all sorts. Denying girls schooling for a week or so is objectionable; preventing them from going to school entirely, as the Taliban did in Afghanistan and would do everywhere if they could, is an unqualified evil, on the received use of the term. But it is not life-threatening. Uneducated, the girls may still live to old age; because they are uneducated, they may live to old age under the arbitrary domination of men, fathers, brothers, husbands, and live miserably. The criterion to capture this sort of evil must be something like being life-confining or life-blightening.[8] Too many of the enjoyments of life, including (to invest the enjoyments with maximum ambition) the exercise of personal autonomy, are denied women who have been denied education.[9]

Adam Morton gives prominent place in evil consequences to 'suffering'and 'humiliation.'[10] 'Suffering' embraces all the unmet needs on the basic list (less readily, perhaps, 'the need for education' and 'the need for recreation,' but still, even these). 'Humiliation' can be taken to run counter to 'the need for companionship,' 'the need for social acceptance and recogntion,' or 'the need to be free from harassment,' but it is an important thing to keep in mind and deserves specific mention. It is an interesting example of a need that fits both 'the life-blightening' criterion and 'the life-threatening' one. 'Humiliation' may lead adolescent boys, bullied at school, to take their lives. Japan has had many sad cases of this kind in recent years.

Bringing humiliation into the picture illustrates how simply converting the list of basic needs (together with rights and heeding well-considered rules) does not quite suffice to give an adequate list of basic evils. Some adjustments are needed, bringing some concepts only implied to the fore, retiring others to being implied. Rape and incest call strongly for places in the list of evils, but they are not fully accommodated under the need to keep the body intact. One does better to adjust the concept defining this need and speak of the need to keep the body unviolated.

Another important case of adjustment is giving an explicit place to pain. Indeed, anyone mindful of the horrors of politics, war, and revolution in the past 100 years might well be inclined to give it top place, or even a department with a priority for remedying all its own. Politics aside, the priority might arise in medical connections, where sometimes the measures to relieve pain themselves cause pain (which can be reduced or eliminated by adopting better techniques). Pain accompanies many cases of violating the body; and some sort of pain occurs when the environment becomes too hot or too cold or too dusty, and also when other needs are disregarded, like the need for exercise or the need for periodic rest. Pain, however, even debilitating pain, can occur without any of these things. So pain must be added for its own sake; at the same time the lesson should be taken to add to the list of basic needs the need to be free of pain, which may be tolerable below the threshold of significance, but becomes an evil above the threshold.

The list of evils requires amending in another way, not by adding another category of evil corresponding to another specific need, but by setting aside a presupposition with which the list of basic needs may be used. The list of basic needs is a list for providing living people with the means of living, so the list invites being used with the presupposition that even if people are on the verge of losing their lives, there are still ways of preventing them from doing so – often provisions for needs. When we convert the list of basic needs into a list of basic evils, that presupposition falls away. When the evils are life-threatening, the continuance of life is at stake; and the worst of all evils to be associated with the list is having the threat fully realized, for one or more of the basic evils. I want to treat loss of life as the worst of the evils associated directly with the basic list, and in that connection the worst to figure in the consequences of evil acts.

Neither 'life-threatening' nor 'life-blightening' suffice as criteria to capture all the sorts of evil that arise on the disaggregated topics of the present book. Evils having to do in the first instance with contravening rights, bundles of rules, or with other rules, when the rights and the other rules both are well founded, are in many cases neither life-threatening nor life-blightening. It is an evil to deny someone free speech; and though to do so does confine his life within limits that he may feel –

indeed ought to feel – uncomfortable, he can still make music and listen to it, write poems and stories and read them, and lead a full, civilized life in many other respects. The threshold of significance criterion needed here (call it the 'institution-impairing' criterion) will bring in considerations of what social institutions must be like if they are to be useful to having people thrive in a thriving society and hence should be valued by the people who benefit from them. That criterion will capture the evil of disregarding judicious social rules generally. Not only are well-founded rights (special combinations of rules) not to be flouted. Other useful social rules are not to be flouted either, for example, the rule of taking turns at four-way stop signs or the rule (designed to reduce public drunkenness) that alcoholic beverages are not to be served outside the home except when they accompany a substantial meal.

The three criteria for rising above the threshold of significance must be matched against the three parts of the list of basic evils laid out just previously. This will produce a definition, which can be exhibited in the following 3 × 3 table:

Nine-Categories Table

	Against Needs	Against Rights	Against Rules
Life-threatening	x	y	z
Life-blightening	t	u	v
Institution-impairing	w	q	r

Every basic evil will fall into at least one cell; and that will suffice to bring it under the definition. One might speak of 'the 3 × 3 definition of evil,' but I shall call it the 'nine-categories definition' instead: a condition or an event that befalls a person is an evil if it imposes on the person in question a deprivation on the three-part list that is, according to one or another of the three criteria, an above-threshold deprivation. The deprivation may relate to provisions for a basic need or to life itself; or to respect for a right; or to the benefits of a well-considered rule.

References to evil deeds, evil intentions, and evil characters have still to be added; I shall treat them all as figuring in the generation of one or another of the basic evils falling under the nine-categories definition. Even then, the definition may fall short of including all evils. Claudia Card puts forward a category of 'diabolical evil,' which has to do most strikingly with corrupting another person's character.[11] Even if this is brought into relation to the list of evils falling directly under the nine-categories definition, it will be an evil of a second order – the person with the corrupted character is more inclined to generate one of the evils on the list than before; and changing a person's character for the worst is not in all cases easily related to the list, even indirectly. It is an evil (often practised upon women) to undermine a person's ambition and self-confidence, so that she settles for a more modest role in life than she could perform; but this is consistent with her leading an unblighted life in such a role, and with having rights, though she may be softly discouraged from exercising them.

The definition can be put to immediate use in dealing with some observations on evil by John Kekes.[12] Kekes holds that an evil is 'an undeserved harm.' This is not an accurate representation of ordinary English, since we speak of 'evils' that 'people bring upon themselves,' implying that they 'have only themselves to blame.' But it does bring up a little tangle of complications. Being confined or suffering capital punishment may be evils that people bring upon themselves, but even so we may be hesitant to call them 'evils' if they are justified punishments. Why the hesitation? It appears that if an event befalling N is an evil, then if someone M (or some agency) imposed the evil or let it happen, M is somehow to blame. We do not want to say this if M (as judge or prosecutor) was only doing his duty in enforcing the law. (A similar point may be made about doctors taking measures that are painful but unavoidable.)

So, if we are going to speak of the event as an evil and the question arises whether it was imposed on N as punishment, we have to take the precaution of saying it is an evil 'for N.' This qualification is, in effect, anticipated by the basic definition of 'evil' just given, since it makes every such evil an evil for some person; and this provision is founded on other considerations, for example, that an evil for an enemy is not necessarily an evil for us. The provision does not, of course, mean that it is an evil only from N's point of view. What an enemy suffers is real suffering.[13]

The nine-categories definition does not, unless supplemented on this point, take into account the variation in numerosity to which the evils in the categories are subject. An evil of a given intensity will be greater the more people that it affects. To have one child starve is an evil; to have a hundred, or ten thousand, do so is certainly a greater one.[14]

Above-threshold evils are evil regardless of their relation to evil deeds, evil intentions, or evil characters, though all these things must be brought into the definition, and the above-threshold evils often originate with one or another of them. I shall say that, with exceptions noted above, what makes all these things evil is that they tend to generate above-threshold evils meeting one or another of the three criteria for significant impact on needs and other matters on the three-part basic list. An evil deed has the expected consequence of thwarting the meeting of basic needs or drastically limiting people's rights and benefits from well-chosen rules. An evil intention aims at just such thwarting. It may, of course, not succeed in doing this; but then a deed may be evil without having the expected consequences: it is an evil deed to spray poison gas in the direction of a subway station; but a wind may come up and blow the gas harmlessly away. An evil personal character is one steadily disposed to have evil intentions. A person with such a character defies normal expectations; it may even reverse them, taking pleasure in inflicting pain on other people.

However, the above-threshold evils need not originate in any of these ways. Above-threshold evils that meet the criteria of significance are evil regardless of provenance. Here is this girl of thirteen from a village in Sierra Leone; she has lost both her arms. What has happened to her is an evil; it remains so if we learn that it came not from a cruel deed of a rebel soldier, but from having a tree fall on her, with gangrene developing afterwards; or from surgery to check the spread of necrotic fasciitis.

Provenance

The provenance of evils is a topic of which the following schematic representation exhibits the range:

Basic above-threshold evils may come from nature
   without the agency of God
   or by the agency of God
   or by human agency.
They may have been invited by lapses on the part of the people
   suffering the evils
   or not invited
      hence coming about by human negligence
      or coming about because intended by someone for whom the
      suffering is
         a matter of regret
         a matter of indifference
         a duty to impose as in a just punishment
         a pleasure to behold.

The nine-categories definition leaves room for basic above-threshold evils that originate through negligence or omission, without any evil deed, maybe without any evil intention or evil character either. An omission may have evil consequences even if it is itself to some extent excusable as the effect of distraction or thoughtlessness. It may in other cases be a grave dereliction for which the agent or agents in question are to be severely blamed or punished. Moreover, the story of omission may include details about evil intentions, and the evil intentions may be persistent features of an evil personal character. It is true, real-world cases in which omission alone is in question might be hard to find. Almost always, one may conjecture, culpable actions accompany culpable omissions. Clinton and Albright (along with a number of other people on the scene at the United Nations) did not just omit to arrange to strengthen the military forces at the disposal of General Dallaire in Rwanda; they actively obstructed proposals at the UN to make such arrangements.[15]

Allowing for cases in which basic evils originate in omissions, and accepting their presence, I shall not discuss omissions further. I shall also set aside the agency of God. This subject has preoccupied a good deal of the traditional discussion of evil. How can there be the evils in the world not attributable to human agency, like earthquakes, floods, tornadoes, and hurricanes, if God is a creator both omnipotent and benevolent? How can there be the evils that are attributable to human agency, supposing that human beings might not have had the faults that led to evil-doing? I accept the demonstration in Susan Neiman's book that a full understanding of the history of philosophy, even in modern times, must allow for the preoccupation of the major philosophers before the twentieth century with these questions. I shall not, however, pursue them here; I think they remain unsettled – indeed, I think quite unprofitable. So I set aside God's part, if any, in the provenance of evils.

If one should wish to consider only those evils that are consequences of human acts and intentions, this self-restriction would not, perhaps, much reduce the quantity of evils brought into view. Even in the eighteenth century, the quantity of evils imposed by natural disasters could be significantly reduced by effective action on the part of alert governments (consider the Portuguese statesman Pombal's prompt and effective leadership after the Lisbon earthquake in the mid-eighteenth century). Since that time, the measures available to human beings to prevent natural disasters (dams to curtail flooding, vaccines to ward off diseases) or reduce their impact (forecasts of hurricanes, evacuations, quarantines) have significantly increased, so much so that, in upshot, natural disasters of the kinds just mentioned nowadays always, or almost always, have consequences attributable in large part to human intentions or failures of intention. Such is the case with global warming, by scientific testimony an impending disaster of unprecedented magnitude.

At the same time, as Susan Neiman remarks in *Evil in Modern Thought*, human beings have acquired the power to initiate disasters as great as any initiated in nature. Hiroshima and Dresden matched the devastation of the Tokyo earthquake of the 1920s. Had the United States and the Soviet Union ever engaged in an all-out exchange of nuclear missiles, the world as a whole would have been made uninhabitable, or nearly so, in a 'nuclear winter.' It seems highly unlikely that the world will escape nuclear warfare entirely during the next several decades or the next 100 years, and if it does not, the evils generated may region by region exceed those generated by any hurricane, earthquake, or volcanic eruption.

The schema given above, therefore, has to be applied to a quantity of evils not much diminished by concentrating on those that come from human agency rather than from nature. There are diseases (bone cancer suddenly seizing the life of a happy teenage boy) that we do not know how to prevent or cure, so we cannot quite say that disasters that come from nature alone are falling into a vanishing residual category. They do, however, fall into a category that human efforts are steadily shrinking.

A great variety of evils figure with incomparable vividness in a work by an author with a very different perspective from mine – the *Inferno*, by Dante. Blasphemy, heresy, disrespect for God's will, and lack of faith I shall set aside; they invite condemnation and punishment only under the auspices of religious belief. Some of the other evils that Dante depicts being punished offer a challenge to my nine-categories table and definition that I should say something to meet. For it may appear that some of them escape my definition, and maybe escape any relation to the evils on my list.

How does the definition apply to gluttony, for example? And if it applies to betraying a friend, does it capture the hurt that the friend feels about being wronged from just this quarter? I think that I could shoehorn the hurt into my list of needs as contravening the need for companionship or maybe the need for social recognition and acceptance, but doing that does not make sure of covering the poignancy of the upset. On the other hand, this manoeuvre does show that treachery is not to be regarded entirely as a second-order evil having to do with intentions that lend themselves to creating first-order ones; it is at times a first-order evil also, obstructing provisions for a basic need. Gluttony is not a second-order evil at all, except insofar as it may lead (through some other vice) to misappropriating provisions that other people need. It is primarily a first-order evil that involves damage that someone does to her own body.

The *Inferno* does not merely list evils to be punished: it gives, very vividly, picture after picture of the punishments. These all consist of evils on my list, indeed of evils in the first subclass, of unmet needs. In some cases they exhibit great ingenuity (for which Dante does not omit to praise the Deity), for example, when the sinners are severally thrust upside down into specially provided earthen funnels. The sinners are burning with fire, hot beyond human bearing; or else icy cold, locked into a lake of ice as an alternative to being submerged in boiling pitch or immersed in their own shit. (Where does the shit come from? The dead do not eat. At one point Dante gives an explanation: the flatteries that the sinners uttered in life turn into shit in the afterlife, since the flatteries were worth no more than that.) The flesh of other sinners is bitten into or clawed away from them. Some are continually whipped, another way of invading bodily security. It cannot be said that Dante's view of evil entirely omits to give due consideration in cases of individual persons to the points on which I rely in mine.

Moreover, the overall picture that he gives of Hell is of an environment polluted as thoroughly as unrestrained capitalism (or unrestrained industrial socialism) at its worst has managed to do, or even more so: smoke; malignant, murky air; nauseous stinks; dirty rain; fire on every hand, some of it raining from above; mud; slime; filthy water. There is no sewer system to accommodate the need to excrete. But it is not only sewage sloshing about; at one level, the sinners are immersed in a river of boiling blood. That goes beyond anything that capitalism has done so far,[16] but it is still something that creates evils where needs could otherwise be provided for. I shall not pretend to compete with Dante's account of evil in its vividness, but vivid as it is, it is, except for the theological vices, in entire keeping with my account of evils.

Adam Morton[17] has worked out what he calls 'the barrier theory of evil' as a framework for explaining how people come to do evil deeds. The theory postulates that normal people – as distinct from 'sociopaths' – have built-in barriers or inhibitions against inflicting suffering on others. The inhibitions may be to some degree instinctual; or readily acquired in the course of being brought up. They stand in place sufficiently often for most people to lead a peaceful social life together. However, they stand at different places in different people's behavioural repertoires. They can be overcome on occasion, sometimes by violent rage, which is triggered more quickly and easily in some people than in others. Sometimes, even in people who are to begin with non-violent in disposition, they are overcome by military training, which may be useful in the defence of the community, but has some tendency to unfit people for peaceful social life. Analogously, and much more perniciously, the inhibitions may be overcome by ideological training, more or less explicit, which may lead to the subjects acquiring persistent dispositions to ignore the inhibitions when they deal with classes of other people deemed dangerous in some way or in some way unfit for association and sympathy. This is the route to racial and ethnic conflicts.

Morton concentrates on evil deeds, but his theory embraces consequences in suffering and humiliation (which can be specified in detail by filling in my amended list of basic evils; see above). The theory also embraces evil intentions in the picture of motivations, in those cases in which motivations that go beyond the normal inhibitions supplant motivations that do not. The theory can be extended to include evil people – what I have been referring to under 'evil personal characters.' These are people whose inhibitions against inflicting basic evils fall away more frequently, more quickly, with less provocation than they do in normal people. They vary, of course, in their capacity to lead normally peaceful lives some of the time. All too often, they pass as normal, so that other people do not keep on guard when they encounter them.

Once on some occasion they have overcome their inhibitions against inflicting evils upon others, what will be the mood in which they do their evil deeds? The schema offers four possibilities: regret; indifference; dutifulness; pleasure. They are not mutually exclusive possibilities. Reminded of a child of his own at home, a concentration camp guard may regret killing the Jewish child who has been thrust into his hands, his turn to kill having come; if the guard has any tendency to indifference, it is therefore a precarious indifference; but the guard may still feel dutiful and take some pleasure in helping to exterminate a race that he thinks has put true German identity in jeopardy. Other guards may be simply indifferent; still others, some helped by ideology, some not needing the help, may unambiguously relish the killing and the suffering that accompanies it. The pull of a disgusting pleasure may have helped to overcome the inhibitions. There are chilling precedents in theology and the history of the Christian church; St Augustine, St Thomas, and Protestant reformers like Calvin[18] agree in picturing the elect in Heaven rejoicing in the sight of the non-elect suffering in Hell. In some cases, perhaps, the elect helped put the non-elect there, by provoking their sins (infuriating them, for example); or, at least, by burning them at the stake or by other means hurried their descent.

Morton founds his model on the work of psychologists; and to psychologists we must leave the work of filling it in with behavioural explanations. I trespass upon their work, I hope, only insofar as is necessary to justify including one or other application in my nine-categories table and the associated definition, of the uses of the term or concept of 'evils.' Finding other people's suffering a pleasure to behold is itself evil, I think, a feature of an evil personal character if it is not an evil deed or an evil intention. Is it just an additional evil, which supplements the evil of suffering? I think not. It colours the evil of suffering by associating it with perpetration by morally perverse characters, whose psychology, at least in part, sometimes, runs directly contrary to the psychology of normal human beings and is therefore at least emotionally utterly foreign.

Does Auschwitz Outrun Our Concepts/Means for Moral Condemnation?

Susan Neiman says that Auschwitz (in contrast to Hiroshima or 9/11) embodied an evil to which we do not know how to respond because it outruns our concepts, in particular, our concepts of moral evil, intentions, responsibility, and blame.

There are at least two different ways in which this judgment can be understood. Auschwitz may outrun our concepts, because no one yet has assembled and organized the concepts required to make the evil in it fully intelligible, though these concepts are already available. I shall not try to refute this proposition; indeed, I shall show why it cannot ever safely be regarded as refuted. On a second understanding of the judgment, we do not have the concepts to make the evil in Auschwitz fully intelligible (and maybe cannot even see our way to inventing them). I can make some headway toward refuting the judgment so understood, but I do not think that I can bring the refutation to an end.

Neiman seems inclined to understand the judgment about outrunning in both of the two ways (which she does not distinguish). She is perhaps more inclined to the second, more radical one, though (as I shall show) her commitment to it is not a firm one.

Auschwitz represents for Neiman a breakdown of the position that we can understand evil adequately by refusing to think of metaphysical evil and natural evil, insisting instead that all the evil in the world is created by human beings. She resists any attempt to put Auschwitz on a scale for comparison with other evils, for among other reasons the fear that such attempts raise the possibility of reducing the enormity of Auschwitz to just a very much more far-reaching example of familiar sorts of cruelty. She resists making any comparisons of evils, saying that they are both pointless and impermissible (286)[19]: impermissible because they inevitably underrate the evil in some cases and do not do justice to the mystery of them; pointless because they do not advance our capacity to deal with the evil that we are confronting. Whatever is new about contemporary evils, she says, again forestalling comparisons, is neither relative quantity nor relative cruelty (256).

Neiman gives great weight to the idea that the evil of Auschwitz escapes the grasp of our present concepts. She cites Adorno as holding that poetry (and, I suppose, music, fiction, drama) cannot be written after (about?) Auschwitz,[20] beause instead of giving any real consolation, it seems to 'drown the cries of the victims in the attempt to overcome one's own dejection' (262). She cites Guenther Anders as holding that while Hiroshima betokens a threat to humanity as a species (a horrible threat, but perfectly intelligible), Auschwitz is a deeper, even more unsettling threat 'to the human soul' (251–2). For her own part, she says 'Auschwitz was conceptually devastating because it revealed a possibility in human nature that we hoped not to see' (254). It thwarts 'the possibility of intellectual response' (256), and on this point she converges with Adorno's holding that 'moral integrity' demands that we respond to Auschwitz with 'helpless silence' (262). In the same spirit, Neiman holds that after Auschwitz all the latest attempts at 'theodicy' must be reckoned to have failed, and we no longer know what we mean in speaking of moral evil (257–8). Again, Auschwitz raises doubts about the sense in which we apply moral categories at all (240).[21] The difficulties of coping with terrorism (e.g., the attack on the World Trade Towers of 11 September 2001) are not conceptual; terrorism is a recurrence of 'old-fashioned evil' (283). The difficulties of coping with Auschwitz are, precisely, conceptual difficulties. Until these are dealt with, we shall be 'proceeding as if questions' have been 'settled' that have simply been 'left hanging'; attempts hitherto to deal with the evil in theory have 'left residues that cloud our attempts to eradicate evils today' (250).[22]

Whatever the conceptual difficulties may be, however, Neiman holds that we must try to solve them, if not by assembling concepts already on hand, I presume by modifying our present concepts or by inventing new ones. She does hold, dauntingly and somewhat mysteriously, that to accept that nature has no meaning leads, in those who 'refuse to give up moral judgments,' to 'accepting a conflict in the heart of being that nothing will ever resolve' (268), but given the tenor of her remarks elsewhere, I do not think that she means to imply that we should consider returning to the pre-Lisbon view that natural events are intentionally evil, invited by human beings and laid down by God as penalties.

Moreover, Neiman, in spite of the discouraging things that she has to say about these conceptual difficulties, takes some heart from what she takes to be signs that progress in dealing with them is possible: 'The very multiplicity [of sources of evil has] suggested something new and fundamental that was common to all these forms' (253). This by itself does not seem entirely plausible (might not multiplicity make exactly the opposite suggestion?); and it runs contrary to Neiman's disinclination to define any 'evil.' Nevertheless, it compels us to acknowledge the multidimensionality of the evils of Auschwitz.

Neiman makes a good deal of Hannah Arendt's reflections on the evils of the Holocaust, but in this connection she does not make as much use of them as she could. Of all the authors that Neiman treats, Arendt has the most arresting things to say about evil, and one of them is to make the point that the complicity in great evils – the disconcerting evils of modern times – of the general public as well as of the people active in the final stages can arise, not from any one personal or collective choice, but from the spread and accumulation of a lot of petty choices, some of them on the limited view taken of them by the people involved not directly evil in intention, but simply careless or indifferent about the collective consequences, or even just ignorant of them to some extent. People joined Nazi-sponsored organizations to have employment for the first time in years; they took jobs in the agencies that drew up lists of neighbours and fellow-countrymen to be sent to the camps; not to speak of jobs as guards, I suppose they took jobs as clerks or typists in the concentration camps or related administrative offices outside the camps. The evil of Auschwitz was, according to Arendt, like a fungus (301), spread by myriad small actions, many of them taken within the ordinary limits of getting and keeping a job to support one's family, the ordinary limits of what might pass for perfectly respectable (271–7, 301–4).

Neiman says that intention, personal or collective, cannot bear the weight that contemporary forms of evil bring to bear on it (281), and she says, 'Auschwitz embodied evil that confuted two centuries of modern assumptions about intention' (271). Yet Arendt's approach implies that intention can bear the weight. Given at most some evil-precipitating intentions on the part of Hitler, Himmler, and a few other leaders, the only intentions needed as ingredients of explanation and moral assessment are the petty, circumscribed intentions of many people caught up at one place or another in a social structure that they had no thought of being able to control. The extermination could have been done in every detail (it largely was done) without overt violence.

Moreover, we do already have the concepts – concepts of circumscribed motives, concepts of complex rationalizations, and concepts of organization – to deal with various features of Auschwitz, and arrive at some intelligible approximation to adequacy. On the central subject of evil, we have the concepts, too, both for the aspects in which it represents familiar evils carried to stupendous lengths and for the distinctively new aspects that I agree with her must be ascribed to it. The nine-categories definition, amplified to take intentions and personal characters into account, will serve to give a substantial account of the evil done at Auschwitz and the other camps: basic evils – life-threatening, life-blighting, and institution-impairing – were the consequences of evil deeds done in sending people to the camps and dealing with them once there, of evil intentions, and of evil personal characters, though these things were allied with what in many cases were deeds, intentions, and characters not themselves remarkably evil.

Auschwitz was in large part a combination of familiar evils. The fact that in this case and a few others they were each separately and all in combination carried to stupendous lengths does not mean that they outrun the concepts under which the evils are familiar. They were not, one by one, distinctive. Consider, for example, that the prisoners in Auschwitz were denied sufficient food; in this aspect, their plight resembled (though it did not in fact go so far – most of them were killed by other means) the starvation to which the Stalinist regime subjected the kulaks. Or consider that, frail as their health was, the prisoners were grossly overworked (so long as they were allowed to live); in this aspect, their plight resembled that of prisoners in the Soviet Gulag.

Auschwitz and the system for drawing people into the camp denied the prisoners' rights to freedom and to humane treatment in and out of prison, along with their rights to a fair trial on actionable charges. Those evils were present and widespread in the Soviet Union, too.

In all these connections, rules that are the hallmark of any reasonably civilized society were flouted or fell into disuse. Consider the rules for helping neighbours and fellow-countrymen out of disasters that befall them. People who would have rushed to help free survivors from the rubble of a collapsed apartment house stood by when the police came to take neighbours into custody (and on to the concentration camps). In a civilized society would not there have been protests on the spot against the police action and complaints filed afterwards? I realize that the Nazi and Soviet regimes offered (though not with entirely systematic efficiency) terrifying deterrents to any such protests or complaints. That is a mitigation of the bystanders' conduct; but the evil done, both in the police taking people away and in the absence of protests by their neighbours (and, sometimes, surely, their friends) remains intelligible under familiar concepts.

Some distinctively new aspects of the evil of Auschwitz may be conceptually elusive to a degree just because they are new, but they are not impossibly elusive.

People were singled out arbitrarily for brutal treatment and others spared (at least for a time), equally arbitrarily; aid, even sympathy, was sharply discouraged; rights were not only denied, they were derided; people were sometimes encouraged, sometimes forced, to take part in their own abasement (274–5). The evils inside the camps were abetted by evils outside them, for example, enlisting the connivance of local populations. This can be treated as one aspect of the transformation of social structure that occurred with both of these evils – a transformation more radical and pervasive as it came to bear in the camps, but still significant in the surrounding society. The transformation involved, in the first place, lapses into disuse of the normal reinforcements to good conduct: praise for working hard and purposefully; praise for acts of kindness; blame for disregarding the rights of other people; blame for not respecting them as human beings. The transformation went beyond this: as Neiman recalls, what otherwise would have been normal reinforcements were given sometimes for good conduct, but as often for bad, and sometimes not at all (256–7, 259). In this way and others, the people taken into the camps after extraction from the structure of the surrounding societies found themselves hopelessly disoriented, in a situation drained of meaning, in which no substitute social structure giving the victims intelligible roles was present, or was present only in a gross deformation of anything that the prisoners had experienced in life outside. If the prisoners were made complicit in their own victimization, complicity in people outside (people not targeted for imprisonment in the camps) was induced in ways to some extent unprecedented. Here is an example, in which both inside and outside complicity seem involved, that has haunted me ever since I read it: about to be shipped off by train to the camps (but still outside), a mother, believing that unencumbered young women stood a better chance of surviving, tried to abandon her little girl, who was running beside her, shrieking with fear.

Some of these things were present in the slave system in the American South, but not as a sudden transformation victimizing people with hitherto full membership and citizenship in the society transformed, and all these things were present in a country only recently in the forefront of civilization. Thus, new and distinctive aspects of Auschwitz (and the Gulag), which I do not deny, can be captured by concepts already in hand: reinforcements under familiar rules of good conduct, here falling into disuse; the impairment of meaning fostered by these lapses and other lapses from the rules of the social structure outside the camps; social structures, regarded as systems of rules, in which some – many – of the familiar rules, become deformed (no longer serving to uphold civilized social practices) or vanish.

Have I refuted, or at least discounted Susan Neiman's misgivings about the adequacy to deal with Auschwitz of the concepts that we have in hand?[23] So many items in my account are perfectly commonplace that I may seem to have made much too easy work of the misgivings. I would say, in defence of analytical philosophy, that its job is often just to restore to credit commonplaces that have been disregarded, overshadowed, or thrown into confusion by high-flying thought. In this case the restoration takes on special importance because Neiman's misgivings are the misgivings of the most notable scholar of the history of evil in modern thought and an author specially concerned to bring her scholarship to bear upon the enormity of Auschwitz.

Moreover, I do not concede that my account is entirely commonplace. That some items in it are commonplace – the various kinds of basic evil; the criteria for being above threshold – means only that they are familiar; and that helps make the point that I contend for, that we have the concepts in hand to capture at least a substantial amount of the evil of Auschwitz. It is not so commonplace, however, to show that a pretty comprehensive list of basic evils can be generated corresponding point by point to lists of needs, rights, and well-considered social rules; to show that these evils fall under the three criteria of being life-threatening, life-blightening, and institution-impairing; to show that the further evils of evil deeds, evil intentions, and evil characters are held to be evil because they generate the basic evils. From these observations emerges an organized view – the nine-categories definition, amplified to bring in human agency – of the evils to be looked for at Auschwitz and elsewhere.

Finally, reflecting some points made in the discussion of provenance, but responding specifically to a story[24] about an Iranian mother who was glad (she said) to have lost five of her six sons in the war against Iraq and gladly ready to have the sixth die in the cause of Allah, I want to emphasize that my account of evil in all its parts, items, criteria, additions, and supplements, is resolutely secular. Not only have theists not yet produced a convincing theodicy to deal with the problem posed for them by the evils present in the world; they have lent a spurious cover to many evils by providing (as they have provided the Iranian mother) with a form of excuse and apology that enables people to accept evils that they should not accept; and the many evils that fall into commonplace categories do not become more acceptable because they are commonplace.

The Remaining Mystery of Auschwitz

Some mystery may be felt to remain after the nine-categories definition, amplified, has been used to sort out evils combined in Auschwitz. I can think of four ways to account for this remaining mystery, all of which invite sober reflection.

First, the evil of Auschwitz is, all told, so awesome – a word that needs to be recovered in its basic use for this application – that we expect to find evil in every feature of it and, behind it, monsters of depravity. There are some monsters to be found, but, disturbingly, they turn out not to have been indispensable. The evil could have been produced as a whole, as it was for the most part produced in fact, by a lot of very ordinary people whose motives were only somewhat different from normal ones. Even at the top of the Nazi regime, the people responsible, like Hitler and Himmler, were people somewhat more twisted in determined commitment to 'the final solution,' but otherwise very ordinary, certainly in cultivation and in their powers of thought. We resist the suggestion that we have in these people a sufficient account. Moreover, they are, unsettlingly, not so very different from ourselves; and we want to resist the suggestion that we could have done such things. We still look for monsters and are baffled when we do not find any, or at least any that are indispensable.

Second, even the most morally sensitive people among us cannot literally feel the evil of Auschwitz in proportion to its enormity. At any given moment, the revulsion that we feel for the brutal mistreatment of one person, or a handful of people, can use up our emotional capacity. So far as literal feeling goes, we do not, and cannot, feel any more revolted by the evils done to hundreds of thousands, to millions. Yet though we know that sympathy and horror are equally called for in a million other cases, we cannot feel a millionfold intensity. But if our emotions fall short, are we giving the evil due weight? We may feel, uncomfortably, that we are not; and we feel guilty about this. Due feeling eludes us; we may then, by projection, consider that a dimension of the evil, something in the phenomenon of Auschwitz, mysteriously eludes us, too, and will go on doing so.

Third, we may feel unsatisfied by the account generated on the basis of the nine-categories definition, amplified, not just because most of the items mentioned in the account are commonplace, but because we know that there is more to say, and that there will always be more to say. That account has been built up by analysis and addition. We add, for example, a reference to the guards' taking pleasure in the suffering that they cause; we add a reference to the gratuitousness of the whole project of extermination; we add the staggering defiance of human inhibitions, normal in the surrounding society and previously normal for the perpetrators, against causing suffering. The account grows in mass, but is there not always something more to add? The account is incomplete and does not ever completely match the phenomenon. We must admit, again and again, that there is more to the enormity of Auschwitz, and more evil, than we have discerned. I have not mentioned that Auschwitz figured in an effort at genocide, that is to say, at the extermination of a whole people; and this may be held to be an evil distinct from the evil of murdering a miscellaneous great number of human beings.[25] I have not mentioned, either, the evil created by irresponsible aesthetic visions,[26] but this can play a vicious part in diminishing sympathy for the victims of evil and readiness to help them.

I do not think we can ever assemble an entirely satisfactory account of the evil of Auschwitz from concepts available. Hence I do not pretend to resolve the first of the issues that Neiman broaches about

Auschwitz's outrunning our concepts. Nor do I resolve the second issue: analytical and additive treatment offers a substantial and (I think) illuminating account of the manifold evil that Auschwitz presents; but the present, third point about the remaining mystery shows that the issue about whether our available concepts suffice has not been laid to rest. Something may always come up that does not fit into an available concept or available combination of concepts; something may have come up already, and I not have realized it.

Fourth, and finally, the spirit of the approach taken in analysis and addition may arouse grave doubts and resistance in some quarters. A friend and colleague[27] suggests that analysis and addition belong with one of the two concepts of infinity discussed by Descartes in the third Meditation, a concept that does not capture the infinity of God, which, being absolute, cannot be conceived of as admitting any additions; nor can His infinite goodness, which likewise must be appreciated as already an indivisible whole. Just so, someone who insists (more firmly than Susan Neiman insists) that the evil of Auschwitz escapes conceptualization may really be insisting that it escapes analysis. The evil of Auschwitz may seem infinite, like the goodness and power of God. It has to be confronted as a whole and accepted as something that transcends any internal distinctions.

The Lessons to Be Drawn from Auschwitz

People like me with an incorrigibly analytical temperament can hardly fall in happily with the suggestion that Auschwitz has to be accepted as a global mystery. Moreover, even if the points made in the analytical and additive account fall short in the ways that I have discussed (I daresay in other ways, too), are they not significant so far as they go? There are practical lessons to learn from them about preventing evils in the future, which is not something that, I think, can be said about the global mystery.

The main lesson to be drawn from Auschwitz and the Gulag, and from other events of our time like the civil war in Bosnia and Kosovo, is the fragility of moral education and the dependence of moral conduct upon social structures themselves fragile.[28] People themselves, placed in the wrong social structures, are not reliable enough. Overnight, it seemed, people who had been living in Bosnia on reasonably friendly terms for generations turned into ruthless enemies; even the successfully mixed community in Sarajevo broke down as the country was swept by wild beatings, rapings, torturings, and killings of Bosniaks, for example, in camps like Omarska run by their Serbian neighbours.[29] The hold that humane dispositions have on many, perhaps most people, when the people are not bound by roles and expectations in normal social structures, is astonishingly feeble.

I do not mean to suggest that there are not some people in whom moral education sends down deep roots, so that even in extreme situations these people will, from the beginning, resist being made complicit with the evils pressing upon them. People who do not resist from the beginning may resist later on, as the evils intensify.[30] One trouble (mentioned by Arendt; see Neiman, 260) is that we cannot tell in advance (even of ourselves) who these people will prove to be. That being so, to forestall evils like Auschwitz, the Gulag, Srbrenica, Rwanda, the Congo we must construct and keep up social structures within which people are steadily encouraged to behave in civilized ways. Their manifold petty choices in taking jobs, in hiring and firing jobholders, in marrying or ceasing to be married, in advancing religious causes, in supporting political candidates must steadily fall in with the common good.

Is this a new lesson? It may seem a very old lesson. Hobbes, assuming people inclined to heed the natural laws, held that they could not practise them without belonging, along with the other people that they had to deal with, to an authoritative social structure. Locke, assuming people inclined to heed the natural laws and already practising them to some extent, held that they could not escape incessant conflict without belonging, again, to an authoritative social structure. Surely, Hobbes and Locke had a lesson to teach about the dependence of humane conduct on social structures.

The present lesson goes hand in hand with this old one, but it is not the same lesson. It does not concern people who have the basic motivation required for good moral conduct, but who cannot without great trouble act on it outside an appropriate social structure. The people in question are not people who are in danger of losing the social structure that restrains them from becoming wolves pouncing on one another in a war of all against all. The present lesson concerns people who belong to an appropriate structure, and continue to belong to it along with most of the others who have been their fellow-citizens. They have been up to now acting without reproach. But now, while the structure to which they have belonged continues to obtain their allegiance and foster upright, indeed humane, conduct toward people accepted as fellow-citizens, they are called upon to deal with people outside the structure: people already outside, like Jews in Eastern Europe and the

Gypsies; or, even more poignantly, people who have been thrust out-side, like the Jews (the mentally impaired, the physically disabled, the terminally ill, homosexuals) in Germany itself; or, like fellow Russian citizens, dehumanized, animalized as enemies of the people in Moscow trials during the 1930's.[31] In former centuries (let it not happen again!) insiders who deviated in religion were thrust outside the elect to much the same effect. A further parallel, which has had its dangers and its part in the generation of innumerable evils, lies in the hostile identifica-tions of social classes in the class struggle; or of some people classed with terrorists as terrorist suspects.

It is this division, first in opinion, then in organization, that requires special vigilance. Hobbes, for one, was well aware of this in his view of the relation of religion to politics, though his view, like Locke's, of the fragility of peace and order gives equal weight to disorder started by personal quarrels. The vigilance may be specially hard to maintain in modern societies, with huge, diverse populations served in their diver-sity by multiple mass media; and sometimes beset by disciplined orga-nizations whose purpose is to foment social division and mobilize 'negativistic, punishing' attitudes directed at scapegoat subgroups.[32] The existing structures may be shallower than they used to be in respect to individual people's habits and motives; and it may be easier, with modern communications in societies committed to freedom of speech and association, to create organizations with divisive purposes.

Indeed, the structures that foster humane conduct may be more precarious than anything that Hobbes and Locke imagined, just be-cause, as it turns out, it is so easy to redirect the motivations of the people who belong to them. How much redirection of motivations was required for most of the people who had a part in the evil of Auschwitz? All that was called for as deviation from normal conduct was some-thing so petty in itself as to be nearly invisible. Consider the *Reichsbahn* clerks[33] who scheduled transport to Auschwitz, assigned places to the passengers, and calculated the fares; everything they did fell into the rounds of their familiar duties, except for features that they could easily ignore or rationalize. Easy as redirection was in the first place, it was made even easier for them by the stock rationalizations available, pro-moted, as Stanley Cohen shows, from private delinquencies to the political plane: denial of knowledge ('We didn't know just what the purpose of the trip was'); denial of responsibility; denial of harm done; ascription of guilt to the victims; condemnation of critics as hypocrites and unfair; appeal to higher loyalties.[34]

These stock rationalizations, of course, were available when redirection had to surmount more resistance. It was harder, no doubt, to surmount the inhibitions against doing face-to-face violence to other people than to go along with the violence at one or more removes. Even here, however, redirection was easier than would have been expected. In experimental situations, Milgram and others[35] have shown how easy, even when ideological indoctrination was not present. The ad hoc authorization of the experimenter sufficed. Ideology can do even worse.

What can be done? One important and necessary thing to do may be to examine in detail the features of current social structures and revise them one by one so that wherever possible they henceforth carry with them precautions against moral failure. People's roles in the structure might be redefined to embrace the precautions. A beginning might be made with professional roles, like those of physicians and lawyers; in Nazi Germany physicians and lawyers evidently did nothing to set up in themselves Adam Morton's barriers against inflicting evils upon other people. Numbers of doctors and lawyers were found to have cooperated with torture and extermination; or at least to have averted their eyes when the evils befell other people, among them neighbours. We need not look to Nazi Germany, however, to find definitions of professional roles that have proved inadequate in this connection. The infamous advice given the Bush administration, about loosening the rules constraining torture, by John Yoo and Alberto Gonzales disgraced their profession.[36] The loosening was acomplished by legal artfulness, adopting a definition of torture so narrow as to leave many things ordinarily regarded as torture outside the definition and hence freed from constraints.[37] How could these people have learned their law at Harvard and Yale Law Schools without becoming acquainted with barriers (inhibitions) against practising or permitting torture broadly defined? They may not have had any course in ethics and not having one would not have helped. However, I suspect that more than a course in ethics is needed: taking part in skits where the moral limits of advice to a client are exposed; further devices to practise acting responsibly; pageantry, ceremonies, solemn oaths. Families should attend. Gonzales's wife and children attended the Senate hearings at which he gave testimony slickly disavowing any responsibility for encouraging the practice of torture. It would have been better for them had there been another ceremony to attend in which full weight was given in explicit commitment to moral constraints on the practice of law, among them a firm barrier against torture.

THREE FAMOUS GRAND PROGRAMS IN ANALYTICAL POLITICAL PHILOSOPHY, WITH COMPARISONS

Prefatory Note to Part Four

One thing that I aim at in Part Four of this book is to remind readers of three grand programs that have been generated in recent analytical political philosophy, the programs, respectively, of John Rawls, Robert Nozick, and David Gauthier.

One way of doing this would be to exhibit excerpts from those authors or set forth synopses of their works. That would be uncalled for, since the works in question are all readily available and excerpts from them or synopses can be found in dozens of textbooks and encyclopedia articles. Moreover, it would be misleading to present the positions of the three authors without making it plain that they have in each case been subject to major objections. I do better than this, giving some idea of the current state of discussion about these programs, by exhibiting as samples of the objections to which they have been subject previously published articles of my own. This part also includes, besides some notes interpolated in the article on Rawls and a new general comment appended to that article, a newly written chapter (11) comparing the needs-focused program of this book with these other programs. The comparison with Rawls's program is the most extensive.

The critical article on Rawls, in chapter 8, is a very early review of Rawls's *A Theory of Justice*.[1] Is it too early to be still current? I would hold that it is still current in every part, and evidence of this currency can be found in the treatment of some of the same topics in recent articles by G.A. Cohen and David Estlund, which I discuss here in a comment appended to the review. Rawls, in his later book *Political Liberalism* (1993), undertook to answer an objection, which he attributes to H.L.A. Hart, about the liberties in *A Theory of Justice* (1971) being insufficiently defined to sustain the absolute priority that Rawls would have the agents in the original position give them there and in ensuing discussion. He says some illuminating and judicious things about how the liberties can be further specified first in a constitution and then in legislation, but he does not seem to me to lay to rest, as applied to the original position, Hart's objection, much less the more exacting objections that I raised in the review about the composition of the list of liberties and the priority to be given to any and all of them over opportunities, income, and wealth.

The other articles that figure in this part of the present book were published recently enough, I think, to incite no worries about timeliness.

Representing the positions of the three authors by exhibiting the positions in the midst of current critical discussion has the added advantage of giving me occasion to lay to rest the common impression that because there is endless controversy about everything said in philosophy, including political philosophy, there are no useful lessons to draw from the fate of these authors' works or any others', except maybe lessons about failure.

Lessons about failure are themselves useful. Gauthier does not succeed in embracing the whole of what we want to cherish in ethics by taking a rigorous egoistic approach to a comprehensive ethical theory; but the care and precision with which he carries out the approach gives us reason to think he has shown once and for all the limits of egoism in ethics. Nozick does not succeed in showing how the right to private property can be an adequate basis for a comprehensive ethical theory of politics; nor does he succeed in showing how a historical approach to such a theory can be adequate. What we learn from him is the care with which we should treat historical considerations when we undertake evaluations of current actions and policies. We can learn, moreover, a good deal about the interconnectedness of ideas about the right to private property and the indispensable qualifications about the condition of the people affected, adequately protected by that right or not, that we must accept insofar as we do rely upon that right. (Nozick makes a beginning to spelling out the qualifications in his 'Lockean Proviso,' an idea that Gauthier takes over for his own purposes.)

Of the three positions, I think that it is Rawls's that turns out to be most current in application to contemporary politics. Rawls's position does not have the precision in logical imagination of Gauthier's or the enchanting historical mythicism of Nozick's. But, as I shall maintain, Rawls's principles, including the Difference Principle, indeterminate as they turn out to be in a number of respects, still offer a useful guide to social policy at least during the current epoch of economic growth. As a guide, to cut through at one or another of the right places, it does not need to cut finely.

It is sometimes thought, in some quarters, that analytical philosophy, analytical political philosophy included, neglects to consider seriously the history of philosophy. This is as good a point as any for a brief digression treating this misgiving.

It is true that the history of philosophy demands serious attention. An important task of philosophical work is to keep up a range of reasonably convincing views of the ideas of philosophers in earlier generations. Consider the objections that I raise (in *Natural Law Modernized*),[2] against Leo Strauss's confused account (in the *International Encyclopedia of Social Science*[3]) of a supposed difference between modern natural law and natural law as conceived earlier.

Analytical political philosophers do not, it may be conceded, have historical work as a central preoccupation. However, there are many instances of their working to preserve useful results of earlier philosophers. In this part of the book, chapter 9 brings up Sidgwick's results in work a century earlier for new attention, in a comparison of them with Nozick's position. In other books, I have upheld the continuing usefulness of results by St Thomas, Hobbes, Locke, Rousseau, Hume, Bentham (and other classical utilitarians). Gauthier has offered historical studies of Hobbes and Rousseau. Rawls has continually had Aristotle as well as Kant in mind; Nozick and Gauthier give the same devoted attention to Locke.

8

Utilitarianism with a Difference:
Rawls's Position in Ethics[1]

Rawls's book *A Theory of Justice* did not need to be completed to inspire dozens of seminars based on advance instalments; it must have inspired dozens more[2] since its completion, with hundreds yet to come. No wonder: the book has in certain respects created the subject of social and political philosophy anew. It has the substantial mass and systematic aspirations that most contemporary works in social and political philosophy have lacked; indeed, few contemporary works in any field of philosophy have been as substantial. A philosopher could spend a fruitful lifetime pondering the connections and implications of the topics that Rawls has assembled – many of them former topics regained for philosophy, reappearing after the vicissitudes and transformations of a long sojourn in economics and politics. By an effort longer sustained than anyone else in the history of philosophy has expended under the heading of 'justice' (distributive justice) Rawls has brought these topics into perhaps as much comprehensive order as they are susceptible of. Will in the nature of things any such order be tentative and transitory? The order that Rawls imparts to his topics may soon disintegrate. Other philosophers will nevertheless usefully begin their lifework with his book, taking it not as a point, but as a frontier of departure, and continue through their careers preoccupied with the topics arrayed there, which taken together will give social and political philosophy lasting new weight and a new claim to central philosophical attention.

What distinctive lessons will philosophers in the end draw from the book? I conjecture that once some confusion about the relation of Rawls's position to the historical tradition of utilitarianism – a confusion that Rawls himself does more than a little to aggravate – is disposed of, the chief novelty of the book will be seen to lie in its having established once and for all that to utilitarian criteria for the choice of social policies a constraint must be attached with a sense at least neighbouring the sense of what Rawls calls 'the Difference Principle': 'Social and economic inequalities are to be arranged so that they ... are ... to the greatest benefit of the least advantaged' (302; cf. 75ff.) Rawls's own version of the constraint is far from being entirely satisfactory, as I shall explain at length in the latter part of this chapter. Moreover, the importance of having a constraint in this neighbourhood has been appreciated before – for example, in the grounds on which such egalitarian champions of the poor as R.H. Tawney[3] and Barbara Wootton[4] have been willing to concede some inequality in incomes. Rawls, however, has, I think, been the first to succeed in making the constraint explicit and unavoidable as a central topic of ethics applied to social policies. It will not, one may hope, soon be lost from sight again or fail to obtain due appreciation.

In General Scheme of Attractions, One Utilitarian System among Others

My stress upon the Difference Principle may be surprising. Rawls himself might claim that his most important innovation was something broader in import, namely, to have found in the complex of ideas defining 'the original position,' where the Principles of Justice are imagined to be chosen, a systematic basis for a 'moral geometry' opposed to utilitarianism. For Rawls, if he is a utilitarian at all, is certainly a utilitarian in spite of himself. Yet what Rawls offers, in the principles that emerge from 'the original position' in a 'lexical' ordering calling for one to be perfectly fulfilled before the next is invoked, is essentially a number of constraints (the Difference Principle among them) upon the Principle of Utility. They are not all of them constraints that the classical utilitarians recognized; but all the classical utilitarians did at least presuppose some such constraints, so that insistence upon having some constraints along with some concern with happiness and with the means to happiness (which Rawls expresses in his concern with having people able to settle on satisfactory life-plans) does not separate Rawls's doctrine from the utilitarian family of ethical theories.

Rawls's list of constraints – the Equal Liberty Principle, the Fair Opportunity Principle, and the Difference Principle, in that order – is longer than some, and more explicit. Once those constraints have been satisfied, however, it becomes legitimate even in his view to ask whether people are as happy as they could be. Indeed (as he himself argues at great length), satisfying them already embraces providing people with the means or conditions of happiness – 'primary goods': chiefly, liberties, opportunities, income, self-respect, and (so far as they are subject to provision) health and intelligence. Everyone's demand for primary goods will have been so far attended to, in the course of satisfying the constraints, that the whole society will have been brought to a point on the efficiency frontier, that is, one point among the many at which it is no longer possible to give anyone a larger combination of goods, or a combination otherwise preferable in that person's eyes, without giving someone else a combination less attractive than he now finds that he has. Moreover, the point among the many which the constraints select is the one that most favours the least advantaged stratum; it is the point at which that stratum receives the greatest flow of primary goods, as measured by an index based on the preferences of a representative person in the stratum (92).

[Note 2005: *However much Rawls may have wanted to bring these preferences into consideration, he does so only indirectly, through an index of income, and of money income at that. It would be exceedingly inconvenient to do anything else: Real income, especially the real income of 'a representative person,' presents intractable measurement problems; if these are to be solved by measuring utility, which Rawls gives no indication of expecting, there are problems of interpersonal comparison still unsolved by the most sophisticated attempts at measurement. So I carry on the discussion of the Difference Principle in terms of comparisons of money income.*]

Given even a modestly prosperous frontier-output, everyone is to have a decent minimum of primary goods coming to him; if people are not happy in consequence, they have little excuse for not being. How happy they will in fact be depends on the soundness of their individual plans for living, according to which they aim to realize by use or exchange the benefits of the primary goods that they receive. Rawls does contend that they will succeed in being happy enough to give persistent, stable support to the Principles of Justice once established.

How different is this scheme of attractions – the claims of justice satisfied, and everyone's happiness promoted in due proportion – from the general scheme offered for moral assent by a utilitarian ethics? It is true that professed utilitarians have typically expected assent to be forthcoming because the attractions of their schemes would awaken feelings of humanity; they have explicitly appealed to such feelings in arguing for the attractions. Rawls, for his part, wishes to renounce in arriving at his principles any such appeal. It is true also that professed utilitarians have tended to treat the claims of justice as themselves founded on considerations of social utility; whereas Rawls would treat them as irreducible to such considerations. However, attractions like the attractions of utility are present in Rawls's scheme, too, and will appeal to humanity whether or not humanity is invoked. Moreover, his Principles of Justice, though they may not be reducible to any simple consideration of promoting happiness, are evidently designed to provide for the diffusion of some subclass of the means of happiness. They are more than constraints; they are also arguably aspects of the Principle of Utility.

Taken as constraints – constraints upon the promotion of everyone's happiness – the principles are not reducible to being mere means to social utility. However, in spite of a good deal of confusion about this point in the minds of professed utilitarians themselves, it is hard to imagine how a form of utilitarianism that placed no irreducible constraints on the Principle of Utility could even be fully stated; and impossible to make such a form intelligible. At the very least (as Rawls himself sees [182–3, 324], without, I think, drawing all the right inferences) every intelligible form of utilitarianism must have some settled way reflecting constraints of taking into account the utilities of the different people affected by an issue. Otherwise, not merely can no one say what alternative the Principle of Utility will favour once applied; no one will know enough about what evidence to collect to know what applying the principle amounts to.

The traditional assumption is that the interest of everyone affected by the issue will be taken into account.[5] Moreover, as Rawls notes, 'Everybody to count for one, nobody for more than one (182).'[6] Here are two constraints that correspond to some of the same elementary notions about justice that Rawls's principles reflect. Even if the classical utilitarians adopted them without any regard at all for their appeal to moral sentiments, which is hard to believe, the constraints serve justice as far as their force carries.

All the leading historical exponents of classical utilitarianism impose further constraints as well. Even Edgeworth, who comes nearer than any of the other writers that Rawls cites to offering a target identical with 'classical utilitarianism' as Rawls conceives it, would evidently not carry the maximization of social utility to the point of putting hopelessly morose people to death. It is true that he did not confront this question. He was diverted from confronting it and like questions, perhaps, by another, broader question of life and death, namely, whether 'the lower classes' might be pressed to the starving point in order to increase the means of happiness obtained by more sensitive people. He thought this question had a negative answer. Before that point was reached, the marginal privations of the least favoured would outweigh the marginal pleasures of the most favoured; moreover, too feeble or too unwilling, the least favoured would cease to work, thereby jeopardizing the income of the whole population; they might even become restive.[7]

That answer, however, does not apply to hopelessly morose people, who might be so few and so unproductive as to make little net difference to social output. Why not modify the population directly and eliminate such people? Edgeworth is perfectly ready to consider direct modifications. He advocates emigration by the least favoured classes, in their own interest, and in the interest of the community left behind, until the condition of even the least favoured class at home is 'positive happiness.'[8] Why not cull the hopelessly morose beforehand and simply put them to death? This sort of modification, significantly, does not occur to him. May we not reasonably ascribe to him, as a firm though implicit presupposition of his doctrine, a constraint operating against such modifications and prohibiting killing people gratuitously merely as a means to increase total utility? It may not be a sufficient constraint, but it is hardly an unimportant one.

If Edgeworth is not a 'classical utilitarian,' one might wonder, who is? Yet whatever gestures Edgeworth and other professed utilitarians may have made toward 'defining' 'the good' as 'the satisfaction of desire,' none of them, given the presence of the constraints just mentioned, has invited us to maximize anything the degree of which can be judged 'without referring to what is right.' In Rawls's view, however, to be a form at least of pure, 'classical' utilitarianism an ethical theory must be teleological in the sense of requiring that something of this sort be maximized (25; cf. 30). The historical utilitarians that he mentions do not. They invite us to maximize, for example, as Rawls concedes, 'the greatest sum of satisfaction of the rational desires' (25) of all the persons affected, which is something that cannot be determined except under constraints serving justice.

To this paradoxical consequence of Rawls's discussion, that no historical examples of utilitarianism can be found, one might fairly wish to oppose, as equally paradoxical, my own tendency to use 'utilitarian-

ism' so broadly that it is hard to see how among ethical theories historical examples can be found of anything else. If Rawls himself is a
utilitarian, as in my view he is, one might fairly ask, who is not? And
when I reveal that I am even ready to argue that (in spite of himself,
though not so much in spite of himself as Rawls) Kant, too, was a
utilitarian, one might be inclined to think, regardless of the points I
have just made, that my use of 'utilitarianism' is both bizarre and
empty. Not at all. It is no more bizarre than Mill's perfectly natural
endeavour in *Utilitarianism* to show that all the attractive and reasonable features of received ethical views can be incorporated by the theory
that he calls by that name.[9] It is not empty, since it excludes the ethical
views classified and rejected by Bentham under the two heads of
'asceticism' and 'the ethics of caprice,'[10] under which fall such purely
deontological varieties of ethics as the Ten Commandments and the
Book of Leviticus, rigidly interpreted without reference to the greatest
happiness.

The point at stake, however, is not whether we can find another
significant way of using the vocable 'utilitarianism.' The point at stake
is whether the fact that constraints are accepted on the Principle of
Utility is an issue between Rawls and his chosen historical opponents. It
is not. The issue between Rawls and his opponents is not whether
constraints must be present, but what they shall be and how far they
can be systematically connected.These are respects in which forms of
utilitarianism vary among themselves. They vary, of course, in other
respects, too: for example, in the honour that they are prepared to show
subjective preferences as against objective determinations of happiness;
or, given an ultimate commitment to objective determinations, in their
intention to rely on the unrealized project of measuring happiness by a
felicific calculus. They may choose, instead, to extend to happiness the
familiar practice of assessing social conditions by taking censuses, in
this case censuses designed to find out (say) how many people fall into
the category 'happy' (tolerably happy), how many into the category
'unhappy' (grossly unhappy). Forms of utilitarianism vary in the operating criteria that they use besides happiness, as practical signs of it.
Health, for example, is a utilitarian criterion – indeed, perhaps the
criterion through which philosophical advocacy of utilitarianism has so
far had most decisive effect upon social policy.[11] Among these variations, I think, Rawls's incidental complaints about the vagueness of
utilitarianism find firm answers. Rawls mentions (175) the possibility of
a form of utilitarianism that simply calls for increases in 'the relevant

indices' of primary goods; but he does not discuss it, considering it only remotely relevant to the issue about utilitarianism that preoccupies him. That issue concerns variations in constraints, among which the variation marked by the Difference Principle will turn out, I think, to repay discussion most; and variations in systematic connection, where Rawls hopes to minimize the number of separate intuitions from which constraints arise and which bring them to bear.

Hardly More a System Than Other Utilitarianisms

One may ask of any form of utilitarianism how far the irreducible constraints which it accepts have been given one unified rationale outside the Principle of Utility. Rawls offers as a rationale for the constraints that he advocates the thesis that they all would be chosen (along with their implications for the pursuit of happiness) and given a certain order of priority by agents who, in an 'original position' where none of them enjoys an unfair advantage, have to reach agreement with one another about the basic structural features of a society to which they will all belong. He elaborates this thesis with great ingenuity and brings to light a thousand philosophically interesting points in the course of doing so. I think, however, that he depends much more often on separate intuitions than he realizes; and that resort to the original position cannot give a convincing foundation, free of anomaly, to the rationale that he seeks.

Relies as Much as They Do on Miscellaneous Intuitions

Rawls does not argue against classical utilitarianism that it depends on too many intuitions, compared with his own doctrine. Although he might have made something of the possible need that classical utilitarianism would have for an intuition to fix upon a procedure for measuring well-being (324), even so, there would be perhaps just one intuition to add to the one that the Principle of Utility itself might require. It is as opposed, not to classical utilitarianism, but to various 'mixed' conceptions of justice (124, 315ff.), that Rawls claims his doctrine reduces demands for intuitions. In the 'mixed' conceptions, the Equal Liberty Principle is imposed as a constraint on the Principle of Utility, with perhaps further constraints added about the distribution of material goods. Rawls finds distasteful the fact that the constraints in question then just derive from so many miscellaneous intuitions – from judgments assenting to them that cannot be supported by constructive ethical arguments – rather than from a unified rationale (317–18; cf. 34ff.). He also objects that further intuitions, operating without the benefit of an 'articulate' conception of justice, will be required to give them effect in any circumstances where their dictates will have to be balanced against one another, or against the end of utility itself, in order to establish the priorities required for a definite decision on policy.

The constraints that Rawls himself invokes – his three principles[12] – seem, however, to depend as regards their content upon quite as many intuitions, that is to say, at least one for the content of each constraint. Other intuitions must follow to establish priority. It is doubtful whether priority among the principles can be established once and for all in advance. Even if it could, it could not be arrived at in the original position without additional intuitions; nor could it be applied outside the original position without further intuitions at the time of application.

In spite of the language in which he is often inclined to invoke it (shifting significantly between 'basic liberties' [61] and 'fundamental liberties' [199], on the one hand, to 'liberty' without qualification [195, 204, 210]), on the other, Rawls's Equal Liberty Principle does not defend liberty in general – or, as with such writers as H.L.A. Hart, liberty in every respect not justifiably qualified in the interests of other people.[13] The principle says, 'Each person is to have an equal right to the most extensive total system of equal basic liberties compatible with a similar system of liberty for all' (302). Conceivably, a system of liberties might be 'most extensive' by embracing more liberties than any other. Nowhere in the book, however, does Rawls argue for extensiveness so conceived; and he explains 'extensive,' where he does explain it, as having to do with the several basic liberties' being more or less extensive when adjustments are made for their mutual accommodation and protection (203–4; cf. 244). The basic liberties, which are to be given priority when the Equal Liberty Principle is given priority, are specific items on a finite list. As given in the present book (I shall allow in what follows that it may not be given completely), the list runs: 'Political liberty ... liberty of conscience ... freedom of the press along with the right to hold (personal) property ... freedom from arbitrary arrest and seizure' (61).

These are all fine things, which I expect most utilitarians (perhaps with some reservations about the right to hold property) would be chagrined to learn that the Principle of Utility might override. Does it not seem a very miscellaneous list, however? And an awkwardly incomplete one? It does not even mention, for example, freedom to marry. The list seems to invite, in a manner congenial to a 'mixed' conception of justice or a 'mixed' utilitarianism, a series of separate intuitions, one for each basic liberty, and one (now, or perhaps better after further development) for the completeness, or approximate completeness, of the list. If each liberty is to share in the absolutely comprehensive priority that Rawls ascribes to the principle when circumstances permit all of them to be fully exercised, perhaps the most direct and satisfactory way of reaching them is, in fact, by the operation of such intuitions. How otherwise is one to believe that abating any one of them even in the slightest to gain enlarged opportunities or more material goods is always wrong in the circumstances assumed?

It might be suggested, drawing upon the final chapters of Rawls's book, that one knows the liberties on the list are to be accorded absolutely comprehensive priority because with the agents in the original position one understands that they are needed to carry out rational plans for the pursuit of happiness. Rawls concedes that his principles are incomplete (303). Should one not treat the list that he gives of basic liberties as an incomplete sketch of a list that in the end would suffice to cover all the liberties needed? I sympathize with this move – but does it not jeopardize the irreducibility of the Equal Liberty Principle, taken as a constraint, by veering close to giving the basic liberties a unified utilitarian justification? Will they constitute an irreducible constraint if respect for them is called for on grounds of their service to (plans for the pursuit of) happiness? On the other hand, insofar as it is insisted that the chief business of the liberties is not to serve those plans but to constrain them, excluding some as unjustly interfering with the plans of others, the liberties move back toward dependence on separate, miscellaneous intuitions; then it will be only a fortunate coincidence that people can (as Rawls believes) be happier under the constraint of respecting the liberties than otherwise.

Does reference to agreement reached on the basic liberties by agents in the original position reduce the apparent dependence on intuitions? The agents must concede to each other the liberties on the list to make sure of the liberties for themselves. I do not question that the mutual advantages of this concession reveal an important aspect of the moral standing of the liberties. Until the list of basic liberties is complete, however, the agents must be supposed to be ascribing absolutely comprehensive priority even to items on the list as yet unknown. What grounds can they have for doing such a thing? They are not claiming as much liberty as possible to establish a future bargaining position. Without even knowing what all the liberties on the list are, they renounce once and for all the right, in circumstances where all the liberties can be fully exercised, to abate any of them in the slightest for gains in opportunities or material goods. How can they know, not merely that there are liberties yet to be identified as helpful to carrying out rational plans of life, but also that some, at least, of these unidentified liberties will be such that giving up any small part of them will wreck some plans? How can we know that the proper lesson to draw from the agents' reasoning on this point is that it would be wrong not to guarantee the full extent of the unidentified liberties before there is any opportunity to choose those plans? And wrong afterwards, even for a community none of whose members choose the plans to give any part of the liberties up in marginal exchanges for opportunities or material goods? It is not merely an intuition that seems required here; it is an act of faith.

Or an act of definition. Let the Equal Liberty Principle be so defined as to embrace only those liberties that claim absolutely comprehensive priority over opportunities and material income, once all of the liberties on the list can be exercised effectively. Must not one then ask if any such liberties have been identified so far? Consider, for example, the priority that is supposed to be accorded political liberty, one of the items that figures on the present list. Is this liberty (when it and the other basic liberties can be fully exercised) to be given absolutely comprehensive priority in future constitutions, legislation, and decisions over the fair opportunity principle? (The Fair Opportunity Principle says, 'Social and economic inequalities are to be arranged so that they are ... attached to offices and positions open to all under conditions of fair equality of opportunity' [302].)

The intuition in this case, if it is forthcoming at all, does not seem very reliable. Suppose majority rule (for Rawls an indispensable implication of political liberty [224]) turns out to interfere with fair opportunity, for example, because a majority of voters (perhaps including even a majority of women voters) will not support laws against certain subtle discriminations against their sex. Would it contravene the priorities of justice to abate majority rule a little by transferring such matters for decision to institutions (like courts with judges appointed for life) that are to a degree insulated from popular desires? To recognize, as Rawls does later (354ff.), that majorities may be mistaken does not do away with the problem. Can their mistakes always be remedied without setting aside priority? I am not saying that there is always a remedy –

judges may turn out to be more sexist than the run of voters – just that refusal on principle to look for a remedy seems to be implied by Rawls's theory of justice, once the lexical ordering called for by 'justice as fairness' is in force, and that this implication in respect to political liberty, as Rawls currently characterizes it, seems to depend on an intuition that not every enlightened person is likely to share. The other liberties on the present list seem equally open to question.

Let us suppose, however, that all the liberties to be embraced by the Equal Liberty Principle have been identified; by reliable intuitions or other means we are assured of those liberties' warranting absolutely comprehensive priority sometime or other. How are we to know when? The lexical ordering does not, in Rawls's view, come into force until people have sufficient primary goods of all sorts for everybody to exercise the basic liberties. It is no use, for example, insisting upon full political liberty for people none of whom are in sufficiently robust health to follow the news; or all of whom are too desperately concerned with surviving from day to day to care whether their protectors are democratically elected. Some exchanges of basic liberties for opportunities and material goods may go on until a minimum of primary goods sufficient for exercising the liberties is available, for most people at least; and a minimum of opportunity, too.

One cannot quite say, 'an acceptable minimum' and argue that this minimum would exclude at least the grosser forms of discrimination against women. To do so comes too close to granting certain forms of opportunity priority over the basic liberties. We must rely, as regards the priority (of the basic liberties), on the criterion of full, effective exercisability.

It seems unwise to leave the application of the criterion to the people affected. They might be too tempted to argue that there were still opportunities and material goods to be gained before the society would be prosperous enough for all the liberties to be exercised. To be sure, the temptation would disappear if economic development should ever reach a point at which the marginal significance of every one of the basic liberties will have shifted for everybody (perhaps because of their importance to self-respect [544]) permanently above the marginal significance of opportunities to hold office, which in turn will have shifted permanently above the marginal significance of income in material goods (cf. 542–3). At that point no intuition would be needed to bring in absolutely comprehensive priority. Unfortunately, the people affected may be so ignoble that they never reach this point; or at least so ignoble that they value material goods more than opportunities, and opportunities more than basic liberties, long after they have become quite rich.

The criterion of full exercisability must be kept in the hands of independent moral criticism and used to call for the lexical ordering just as soon as it is called for morally. However, we, too, acting as such critics, as sincerely and disinterestedly as anyone could wish, will have some difficulty in discerning just when there are no further gains to exercisability to be had from increased opportunities and increased material incomes. What is worse, we shall have to defend the criterion. We shall have to say why, at just this time, when full exercisability has been attained, all room has vanished for morally acceptable marginal exchanges between liberties and opportunities or between either of them and material income.

Nothing about the original position explains why this room should have vanished, or explains why full exercisability should be a sign of its vanishing, though the agents do, supposedly, foresee that they will each find it intolerable not to have the liberties unabated once the liberties are fully exercisable. Do they foresee that the best plan of life for each will require that each of them should have all the liberties to the fullest extent throughout their lives? The crucial point, however, is the wrongness of renouncing any portion of the basic liberties. To support the coincidence between the first moment of full exercisability and the first moment of absolutely comprehensive priority, another intuition will be required, to the effect that thenceforth it will simply be wrong not to accord the priority, whether or not it is intolerable.

Can these difficulties be escaped by qualifying the priority to be accorded the Equal Liberty Principle (and, in its turn, the Fair Opportunity Principle) so that the priority is not absolutely comprehensive? One might as well treat all counter-examples as arising in circumstances that the ideal theory of justice does not fit and admit that mankind will never leave such circumstances. What in either case would become of the prized priority supposedly established in the original position? Would it not become in perpetuity perfectly irrelevant? We will then understand that in some cases opportunities and material income should be considerations marginally subordinate to specified basic liberties; and in other cases considerations of liberty should at least marginally be subordinate to opportunities and material income. Rawls surely aims at establishing somewhat more stringent and comprehensive priority. Can he succeed in his aim, however, if reliable intuitions are not forthcoming at the points mentioned? In their present state, moreover, the content of the Equal Liberty Principle and the Fair Opportunity Principle is not precise enough to make fully intelligible what is being demanded in the name of priority.

Foundation (in 'Original Position') No Less Anomalous

There remains to be balanced, against the objections to these puzzling demands for separate intuitions, the very real virtues of the unified view that the hypothesis of the original position offers of aspects of social justice and connected matters, including most of the chief points of ethical theory. One sees, for example, taking this view, not only that there are mutual advantages to be obtained by mutual concessions in respect to liberty; but that since these advantages include opening up a variety of ways to pursue happiness, through the use of different combinations of primary goods, it risks frustrating many people's best plans, perhaps most people's, unless those concessions are made at least in part. Liberty has at least that much claim to priority. Rawls, developing the unified view offered by the original position, is led in the end to giving a richer and more exciting account of the value of personal liberty than exists anywhere else in philosophical literature.

There is no doubt that the idea of the original position contributes a high degree of system to Rawls's theory and that many of the insights that he arrives at depend heuristically on his systematic development of this idea. However, can a system founded on the hypothesis of the original position be in all important respects an entirely appropriate one for either justice or ethics? I think there are too many anomalies associated with resort to the original position for deliverances from that position to be accepted as morally authoritative. The doubtful intuitions, already surveyed, required at crucial points may be reckoned among these anomalies; but there are serious anomalies in other respects, too.

What can be supposed to motivate people to heed the principles forthcoming from the original position? The agents are prevented by the veil of ignorance from knowing anything about their personal advantages or personal tastes. Will people who do know their personal advantages in wealth (say) or power accept the same principles? The veil of ignorance is, of course, a picturesque device for answering the familiar demand that moral attitudes be disinterested. Real people, however, cannot be counted upon to meet the demand when it jeopardizes any advantages over other people that they may happen to possess. Rawls might fairly argue, however, that there is not much of an objection to the hypothesis of the original position in the fact that no one who does not already have a relatively profound attachment to justice would be much moved to resort to the hypothesis or to heed the principles that it favours; Rawls means to be explicating a conception that may appeal only to people who, through a decent upbringing (462 ff.), have already become convinced adherents of its main features. Yet this limitation jeopardizes the chances of his principles' making any straightforward appeal (in the manner of Hume's conventions of justice, at the stage of 'natural obligation')[14] to the self-interest even of selfish people in the real world; and the chances are not improved by Rawls's reliance upon hypothetical interests in the original position. There is, furthermore, a serious objection on other grounds to this imaginary assignment of motives.

The terms of the original position are fair to all in the sense that they prevent any agent from taking advantage of any other in the course of the deliberations or in respect to the Principles of Justice that are to be arrived at. The terms do not, however, preclude any agent from being primarily motivated to protect her own interests; indeed, Rawls assumes that each agent will be exclusively motivated by this consideration. As Rawls is concerned to insist, the assumption does not imply that the agents are egoists; they do not know enough about the particular characters and tastes that they might have on the other side of the veil of ignorance to know whether they are egoists or not. Nevertheless, in the original position each agent strives, unmoved by the least concern for the fate of any other agent, to make sure that the principles chosen will guarantee her as large a minimum quantity of primary goods as possible in the basic structure discovered when the veil of ignorance is withdrawn.

Once she has them, an agent may find that her character is so ascetic that she has no desire for any of them. Even then she may enjoy disposing of a substantial quantity of them as charitable contributions. Beforehand, with the veil of ignorance in position, she must safeguard herself also against the discovery that she is sufficiently sensual to make use of all of them in personal consumption. Each agent acts on behalf of the unknown character corresponding to her on the other side of the veil of ignorance as an ordinary economic agent – not necessarily egoistically, but certainly no more than '*non-tuistically*,' to use P.H. Wicksteed's phrase.[15] Moreover, she acts with this motivation in circumstances where its effects will not differ in the least from the effects of purely egoistic motivations.

Is it not highly anomalous, however, that the people expected to heed the deliverances of the original position, because they already possess a sense of justice, should be expected to give so much respect to (the operation of) this motivation in such circumstances (the circumstances of the original position)? Their moral consciousness, as is implied by their possessing a sense of justice, has in every case got beyond egoism and beyond *non-tuism*, too; they are ready, as egoists would not be, and *non-tuists* need not be, to sacrifice some of their personal advantages over other people in response to the demands of justice. Is it not an anomalous retrogression in moral consciousness for them to consider themselves bound and bound only by conclusions arrived at by *non-tuists* (who for all the difference it makes to those conclusions might, in the circumstances, be simply egoists)? There is no such retrogression in the alternative of being bound by conclusions that are supported by direct concern for the fate of other people, even strangers – that is to say, by feelings of humanity.

The anomaly is not removed by citing the formal conditions (generality, universality, publicity, ordering-capacity, finality) that Rawls imposes on all the candidate-principles to be offered for consideration in the original position (130–6). These conditions do, as he claims, eject merely egoistic principles from the field of candidates and in this and other ways bring considerations important to ethics to bear upon the choices that are made in the original position. All these formal conditions, however, might have been demanded by the agents themselves (rather than imposed on their field of choice during the construction of the original position). All the conditions assist in achieving what each of those agents is aiming at: the protection of his own interests (cf. Rousseau on the social contract). Their presence does not make any agent other regarding. The agents are not moved by the other agents' prospects of happiness. The happiness of other agents is an instrumental consideration for them, since evidence that their happiness is to be expected, given institutions that fulfil certain principles, is evidence that those principles will receive stable support. But the agents can hardly take the happiness of others (along with their own) as an end to be promoted by the Principles of Justice without becoming utilitarians themselves; and, though I hold that Rawls's doctrine is utilitarian in general effect, I do not think the agents in the original position are utilitarians.

Another drawback to the hypothesis of the original position, as serious as the anomaly of moral retrogression, is that it gives a new lease on life to the very feature, ascribed to 'classical utilitarianism,' to which Rawls most strongly and cogently objects.

[Note 2005: *As I remind the reader in the propositions immediately following, this is the feature of reducing the means of happiness going to some people so that they can be given to other people, maybe people already happy, who will gain more happiness as a result than those who are making the sacrifice will lose. My statement about giving this feature 'a new lease on life' is very misleading. I do not mean – I did not mean then – that this feature would become a free-standing principle, or become a living part of Rawls's own doctrine. (It does, as I shall make clear later, play a part – an unacknowledged part – in his treatment of the distribution of income within the least-advantaged stratum, but that is not my present point.) As can be inferred from the several pages of discussion following, the present point is that the reasoning ascribed by Rawls to the agents in the original position, which leads them to shun even the least chance of not having a minimum of primary goods in the society to which the principles chosen in the original position apply, seems in the end no more reasonable than reasoning to classical utilitarianism, given evidence that the probability of anyone's losing out in this way is very little.*]

Classical utilitarianism (in the teachings at least of Sidgwick and Edgeworth) appears not only to allow, but to require, in some possible circumstances, that the quantities of primary goods – the means of happiness – going to some people shall be reduced simply in order to make other people happier by increasing the quantities going to them; the circumstances are those in which the people so favoured increase more in happiness than those disfavoured decline. This perverse requirement is a feature of 'average utilitarianism,' which Rawls considers the chief rival in the original position of his own Principles of Justice lexically ordered. Average utilitarianism calls without qualification for maximizing the average measure of happiness. Why do agents in the original position reject average utilitarianism? On Rawls's account, it is chiefly because they apprehend the possibility of being compelled to give up primary goods to increase the happiness of other people for whose happiness they may have no direct concern, perhaps even being reduced for this purpose to poverty, below the minimum income of primary goods that will give them any chance of happiness themselves.

David Lyons has objected, however, that from the general knowledge of social phenomena which Rawls assumes the agents to have, they may be able to infer that opportunities to increase some people's happiness more than sufficiently to offset severe forced sacrifices of primary goods on the part of others will not occur empirically.[16] They may have some way of anticipating and comparing the effects on happiness, increased or decreased; and the comparisons may indicate that people are, as Edgeworth thought, too similar in the extent of their dependence for happiness on primary goods to open up such opportunities. Then the agents would run no great risk in adopting average utilitarianism.

Rawls may reply that neither the agents' general knowledge nor ours does, in fact, reach so far. There is no felicific calculus available for practical applications and no way of knowing what results to expect in the course of such applications. However, Lyons's objection can be pressed home by asking how Rawls can forestall knowledge from increasing so that these matters are covered and the uncertainty about average utilitarianism resolved in its favour. Unless this possibility can be forestalled, the agents that Rawls now speaks of cannot be said to be choosing principles in perpetuity (131). Moreover, so far as resort to the reasoning of agents in the original position implies any advantage, the advantage of the Principles of Justice over average utilitarianism with the perverse feature mentioned will consist in a contingent and possibly temporary fact about the limitations of empirical knowledge. It will not consist in a permanent point of moral superiority. Yet how can Rawls forestall this outcome, without stipulating a priori that the general knowledge ascribed to the agents will fall short of excluding circumstances in which the objectionable distributions would be called for? To make such a stipulation, however, would render the victory over average utilitarianism empty.

Would it worsen matters to forget about the original position in this connection and simply reject the perverse feature of average utilitarianism by a separate intuition? The hypothesis of the original position does not free us from dependence on intuitions, some of them more doubtful than this one.

The Difference Topic: A Lapse to be Rectified in Other Utilitarianisms Regarding Inequalities in Distribution

Perverse distributions are licensed, indeed required, in the forms of utilitarianism offered by Edgeworth and Sidgwick by the presence of what I shall call 'the Capacity Principle': 'The means of happiness shall be distributed to people in accordance with their capacity for happiness.'[17] Since this principle has such objectionable consequences, when it is allowed that people's capacities for happiness vary, it invites being replaced by a better one. Rawls offers as a replacement (which he intends to replace the Principle of Utility at the same time) the three principles – the Equal Liberty Principle, the Fair Opportunity Principle, and the Difference Principle. He is justified in thinking them, in respect to blocking objectionable distributions, superior to the Capacity Principle – indeed, so obviously superior that one cannot help asking how writers as intelligent as Edgeworth and Sidgwick could have given any credit to the latter. What can Edgeworth have meant by frankly and cheerfully adopting it? Or Sidgwick, by at least lapsing into language that may fairly be taken to endorse it?[18] And what did it mean to their contemporaries, not one of whom seems to have thought to object, at any rate in the pages of *Mind*, either to Edgeworth or to Sidgwick, on a point that seems (to say the least) so debatable to us?[19]

I think the clue to an answer lies in Sidgwick's saying, in the course of a general review of his own work in ethics, 'The principle that another's greater good is to be preferred to one's own lesser good is, in my view, the fundamental principle of morality.'[20] The Capacity Principle, first in its implied prescriptions of possible sacrifices by oneself, then in prescriptions regarding possible sacrifices by others, follows directly, given the identification of any person's good with his happiness, and given the identification of his happiness with a variable quantity of satisfactions. Sidgwick may indeed have thought of the Capacity Principle as hardly more than another way of expressing 'the fundamental principle of morality.' It emerged too close to the centre of his moral vision for him to focus upon it or its consequences.

Moreover, not all its consequences are perverse. There are plenty of circumstances in which the distribution of means called for by applying the Capacity Principle is not perverse at all, but morally compelling. Consider, for example, whether Sir Philip Sydney should have accepted that drink of water, instead of asking that it be given to the worse-wounded soldier lying beside him. Or consider whether the one piano available to the community should be broken up for firewood by the person who discovered it or given to someone who knows how to play it.

To be sure, these are questions of distributing once-and-for-all stocks rather than questions of distributing flows of goods. Rawls considers, justifiably, that the distribution of flows is a more important consideration for the justice of basic social structures than the distribution of stocks; and consequently, he sets questions about stocks aside (88). A complete conception of social justice should, however, have something to say about the distribution of stocks; and questions of flows pass into questions of stocks as the periods during which the flows are taken to occur shorten. Hence, one might expect a conception of justice to have to strike some sort of compromise with the Capacity Principle insofar as that principle correctly prescribes distributions of stocks. Moreover, the consequences of applying the Capacity Principle to flows, even long-term flows, are sometimes morally appealing. Like the British in war-time, people might invoke the principle to ration weekly supplies of eggs and vitamins so that persons who had most need of them – growing children – got increased flows, while the flows going to other persons diminished, with some cost to them in the primary good of health.

The examples just given suggest very strongly that the moral attractions of the Capacity Principle, which are genuine, even if in the end overshadowed, lie chiefly in its association with serving needs or (in the case of the piano) preventing waste. This association with needs is not present in the objectionable cases, where the principle is used to sanction diminishing the happiness, perhaps already marginal and uncertain, of some people solely – gratuitously – to increase the happiness of others, who may be tolerably happy already.

If he had inquired into the import for the principle of the concept of needs, would Sidgwick have qualified or replaced the Capacity Principle? I expect so; but then he might have been expected to realize much earlier, from the barest description of the objectionable cases, that something was wrong with the Capacity Principle. It was, however it came about, a calamitous lapse of insight on his part not to have anticipated such cases.

Was it more than a lapse? There is a difference between Sidgwick and Edgeworth on this point. Edgeworth champions the Capacity Principle with silly enthusiasm.[21] Sidgwick, when he formulates it, does so as a matter of incidental comment.[22] In both their cases, however, the Capacity Principle, so far as it is objectionable, represents an aberration from the utilitarian tradition. Rawls charges, 'The striking feature of the utilitarian view of justice is that it does not matter, except indirectly, how the sum of satisfactions is distributed among individuals' (26). Yet is not the Capacity Principle itself an expression of concern as direct as one could ask for (and so far as unobjectionable at least in harmony with the Principle of Utility)? It does not stand alone. Neither of Bentham's basic formulas – 'the greatest happiness of the greatest number' and 'the greatest happiness of all those whose interest is in question' – easily reduces to simply insisting that everybody be counted (important as this point itself is).[23] Mill declared that, according to the Greatest Happiness Principle, morality ought to consist of 'the rules

and precepts for human conduct, by the observance of which an existence ... exempt as far as possible from pain, and as rich as possible in
enjoyments ...' may be 'to the greatest extent possible, secured to all
mankind.'[24] Is this a sentiment indifferent to the question of distribution? A sentiment indifferent to the objections that tell against the Capacity Principle when the Capacity Principle miscarries?

Rawls may fairly object that Bentham and Mill failed to make anything definite of the sentiment; and fairly claim that he has done something substantial and memorable to repair the omission. Would not
most historical champions of utilitarianism have been entitled, however, to a degree of being taken aback, on first hearing of the rectifications that Rawls proposes, if they heard also that those rectifications
were opposed to their beliefs and intentions? They would have thought,
as Rawls acknowledges (159, 181), that such things as basic liberties and
fair opportunities, serving as they do to promote happiness, were already secured by the Principle of Utility. They might have argued that
so long as the chief consideration in promoting the greatest happiness is
meeting needs – vital, even desperately vital, needs – as it almost
always has been, and in most countries continues to be, their Capacity
Principle and Rawls's Difference Principle would have much the same
effect. 'Social and economic inequalities are to be arranged so that they
are ... to the greatest benefit of the least advantaged.' But the people
whose needs are most urgent – the least advantaged – will presumably
be just those people whose happiness will most increase with further
primary goods, and hence the people to whom the Capacity Principle
will assign the goods.

Sidgwick and the others might have regretted, furthermore, both the
disappearance of the appeal, present in the Capacity Principle, for self-
sacrifice in cases to which the Difference Principle does not apply; and
the disuse into which feelings of humanity – supporting such sacrifices
so far as such feelings have weight – fall if Rawls's method of constructing the foundations of ethics is followed. Suppose there are two people
with equal incomes in material goods. Is it not possible that a transfer
from one to the other would be justified if it enabled the one who
gained to train for a splendid singing career, while it made little difference to the simple rural life-style of the one who lost out? (Both, let us
assume, already have the same opportunities to try out for the same
careers.) Could not provisions for such transfers be made in the basic
social structure, as matters of family or tribal custom? Rawls would
perhaps assign them, along with altruistic motives, to 'moralities of

supererogation' (478–9); but all that the Capacity Principle asks for in such cases is an attitude that defers to other people's interests when, impartially weighed, those interests in a given issue are more substantial than one's own. This attitude is arguably not altruism, since it counts one's own interests along with the rest and on an equal basis. However, there is no use for it in Rawls's foundations. Sidgwick, I think, might have been inclined to consider that, in leaving it out, Rawls leaves out any support for 'the fundamental principle of morality' and for all distinctively ethical prescriptions, which, effectively or not, call men [people!] beyond *non-tuism*.

Defects in the Difference Principle, Considered as a Formula for Rectification

Nevertheless, I agree with Rawls that the Capacity Principle obviously demands rectification. Otherwise, it can be used, as Edgeworth is prepared to use it, not merely to justify some transfers of primary goods to people with more substantial interests in having them, but to justify such transfers to the extent of keeping whole social classes poor while their more refined contemporaries revel in luxurious pleasure.

In Rawls's scheme of rectification, the Equal Liberty Principle and the Fair Opportunity Principle have an important share in the work of protecting the interests of the poor, who especially need the protection of those principles. I shall now concentrate, however, upon that part of the rectification intended in the Difference Principle; and, given the guarantees of the other principles respecting other primary goods, I shall treat the Difference Principle as entirely concerned with money income.

The Difference Principle, as a device for doing (under the guarantees of the Equal Liberty Principle and the Fair Opportunities Principle) in part the same job as the Capacity Principle, certainly has important attractions. Not only does it block Edgeworth's defence of class privilege. It reverses the effect of the Capacity Principle as used by Edgeworth in this connection. Unfortunately, the Difference Principle, as it stands, has several serious drawbacks, even apart from its forfeiting, perhaps needlessly, the overshadowed moral attractions of the Capacity Principle.

One drawback belongs only to the principle in the simple form that I have quoted. Satisfying it does not, strictly speaking, ensure satisfying the principle of efficiency for social strata. It might conceivably be satisfied and yet improvements in economic condition remain which would not affect the least advantaged, but which would benefit some other stratum or strata. To avoid gratuitously forfeiting these improvements, Rawls would have what he calls 'the Lexical Difference Principle' used as the ultimately decisive form: 'In a basic structure within relevant [strata], first maximize the welfare of the worst-off representative man; second, for equal welfare of the worst-off representative, maximize the welfare of the second worst-off representative man, and so on until the last case which is, for equal welfare of the preceding (n – 1) representatives, maximize the welfare of the best-off representative man' (83).

Another drawback can be managed at some cost to Rawls's hopes for geometrical precision in the ideal theory of justice at least; and some cost also to his conviction that he has found a simple way out of the problem of interpersonal comparisons. The chief business of the Difference Principle is to make sure of maximum benefits for the least advantaged stratum; and it is simple enough, Rawls thinks, to measure this maximum by an index (92ff.) founded loosely, on the opportunities for expressing preferences given by money income, and on preferences representative of the least advantaged stratum, once this stratum has been fixed upon – for example, as including everyone with less than half the median (money) income (98).[25] Are we, however, to apply the Difference Principle in favour of the people who compose the stratum that fits such a description now and work our way to the efficiency frontier and the point on that frontier at which benefits are maximized for the stratum so composed? There are grounds for acutely distrusting such a policy. It is possible – indeed, likely, as the mix of factors and skills changes during successive reorganizations of the economy – that some people, say the set of people $x = Ax$, who were in the least advantaged stratum ex ante, will in time move above what is then half the median (money) income, while other people, say the set of people $x = Bx$, who were not in the least advantaged stratum ex ante, move below.

Suppose such a change has, in fact, occurred by the time the economy reaches a stage one move away from the efficiency frontier. The Difference Principle, invoked on behalf of the least advantaged stratum ex ante, will favour, other things being equal, moving to a point that increases the income of $x = Ax$ without doing anything to increase the income of $x = Bx$ over a point that does almost, though not quite, as well by $x = Ax$ and increases the income of $x = Bx$, too. What credit can be given the Difference Principle then? So applied, it will favour the relatively rich over the relatively poor.

Nevertheless, questions about the composition of the least advantaged stratum can be decently managed. We can even take some comfort in this connection from the fact that no one now knows where the efficiency frontier is on which the least advantaged stratum, however its composition is determined, will find maximum benefits. Suppose we begin, in practice, by making an incremental move to raise the benefits going to the least advantaged stratum ex ante; then we make another move to raise the benefits of the stratum least advantaged at that stage; and so on. Though the composition of the least advantaged stratum changes from stage to stage, the changes are so small as to be negligible on any one move; moreover, anyone who is reduced to the least advantaged stratum on one move can expect to recoup, in benefits at least, if not in relative position, on the next move or a later one, provided that he gets at least an average share in the benefits seized for the least advantaged stratum then current. The point finally reached on the efficiency frontier may not be the only one that justice would have accepted – it may not even be the only acceptable efficiency frontier; it will nevertheless be a point that justice, as Rawls conceives it, may insist upon, during the last stages of approach. One might, it is true, wonder whether the force of justice – or of any moral consideration – would carry so far, insisting that movement toward the frontier be kept up perhaps long after everyone had become comfortably affluent. On the other hand, the successive applications of the Difference Principle might meanwhile have had the laudable effect of rescuing everyone from actual need.

The other drawbacks of the Difference Principle belong to it in both forms in which Rawls gives it; and they cannot be managed without major modifications to either form. They are defects of omission – major omissions having to do (i) with distributing income inside the least advantaged stratum; (ii) with conceding relatively productive people the whole of their marginal value product as income[26]; (iii) with accepting less than full effort from people in any stratum; and (iv) with compelling a productive elite to serve the tastes of other people no longer in need.

(i) The Difference Principle, in both forms given, operates by strata (or by 'representative men' standing for the different strata); and what it would maximize is the mean of the incomes received in the least advantaged stratum, which contains possibly millions of people. Rawls adopts operation by strata out of laudable care, shown throughout the discussion of the original position, for keeping the information problems generated by his theory at a minimum. Unfortunately, operation by strata lays the Difference Principle open to the very objections that arise against utilitarianism in forms committed to the Capacity Principle.

Since it is a mean for the stratum, the income of the least advantaged representative man can obviously go up even when simultaneously the incomes of most people in the least advantaged stratum drop. To be sure, there is a (moving) upper limit to which the gains of a few can be pressed, and yet still be counted as income to the least advantaged stratum, namely, the limit beyond which the incomes of the few begin to equal incomes received by people in the next higher stratum ex post. Moreover, a minimum level of income is assured to everybody in the least advantaged stratum by way of protecting their capacity to exercise the basic liberties[27] and by way also of protecting their opportunities for employment. The skewing within the stratum may still be substantial enough to be felt by the people affected. Conceivably, many people in the least advantaged stratum ex post may have belonged to the least advantaged stratum ex ante and be worse off than they were before the journey to the frontier began. Moreover, in the course of the journey to the frontier, the Difference Principle would have ridden roughshod – just like the Capacity Principle, pressed without qualifications – over the social provisions (job contracts, seniority rules, veterans' rights, rights to compensation, etc.) that protect, though very imperfectly, ordinary people against individual victimization by departures in social policy. Disregarding these provisions would violently upset long-standing expectations respecting income. Would such disregard not seem to ordinary people the very height of injustice, the Capacity Principle, the Principle of Utility, or the Difference Principle notwithstanding? The Difference Principle would, in fact, leave even greater grounds for resentment in this connection than the Capacity Principle, since, unlike the Capacity Principle, it neither limits nor rationalizes any shift and skewing within the stratum; it simply ignores the fate of the people victimized.

Rawls may, of course, be ready to allow that even in societies (like Canada and the United States today) perhaps affluent enough already to invite the application of the Principles of Justice in lexical ordering, it might still take some time to bring about their fulfilment without undue disruption of present arrangements. Perhaps it would take a generation or two, while people's expectations about present arrangements for income-security gradually weakened, and the arrangements themselves folded up. Rawls and his principles might be ready to wait out the process. However, does their patience meet the objection? So far as the Difference Principle is concerned, the present arrangements are not necessarily going to be perfected; they are not even necessarily going to be replaced.

One might wonder why Rawls's *non-tuistic* agents do not call for more sensitive protection than the protection by stratum authorized by the Difference Principle in either given form. No doubt they should be hypothesized to be practical men, who are properly wary of insisting on principles too exacting in demands for information to administer. They would be mistaken, however, if they thought that adding provisions for individual protection to the Difference Principle would be impractical. Some provisions of the kind in question already enjoy a working existence, as present arrangements for income-security show.

The agents would not be mistaken in thinking that it would be impractical to provide for individual protection by formulating the Difference Principle in lexical form, but lexical by persons rather than by strata. Yet it is worth looking at this form for what it reveals about the attractions of the Difference Principle in the forms given. To satisfy the Difference Principle, in a form lexical by persons, all persons would have to be strongly ordered, when the efficiency frontier is reached, from least to most advantaged;[28] and the point selected on the efficiency frontier would have to be that for which the least advantaged person had as much or more in benefits as at any other, with the next least advantaged person getting the most benefits compatible with those benefits for the least advantaged, and so on. (A weak ordering [allowing for approximate ties between persons], which could be invoked to much the same effect, would be easier to carry out, but is harder to talk about.) However, the moral attractions of strictly adhering to the Difference Principle tend to vanish when the principle is put in this form. Consider a stage one move away from the efficiency frontier; and suppose that though the same people will rank (counting from the bottom) as 111th and 112th least advantaged in either case, there is a choice between moving to the frontier at a point that will give the 111th only a little more material income, but the 112th a substantial gain, and moving to the frontier at a point that will give the 111th somewhat more, but forfeit the chance of giving the 112th any significant increase at all. Strict adherence, lexical by persons, to the Difference Principle, requires movement to the second point, since the 111th person is relatively less advantaged; but where is the moral attraction, let alone the moral compulsion, of this requirement? The attraction and compulsion might be restored by assuming that there would in any case be a big gap between the income of the 111th person and the income of the 112th; but they vanish again if we assume that the gap, viewed as an incident of approximately continuous variation over the whole society, is rather small (though still significant to the two persons concerned).

Evidently, given continuous variation, the Difference Principle lexical by persons stands at one extreme of a process of moral dilution: the more finely a population is divided by strata, the less moral force there will be in the Difference Principle in this form, strictly applied. (The less reason also, I would think, for agents in the original position to care about its strict lexicality as a means of self-protection.) Can it be that the moral attractions of the Difference Principle in the forms given by Rawls reside almost wholly in the broad priority which those forms assign to the needs of the least advantaged stratum, taken together with the tacit assumption (all too commonly borne out in experience) that people in this stratum are otherwise unlikely to have enough income to live decently? (Assuming a big gap between the incomes of the 111th and 112th persons almost inevitably brings in its train the tacit assumption that the 111th can make a case based on needs; without this further tacit assumption it is questionable whether the gap makes any moral difference.) This suggestion, however, still leaves shifts and skewing within the least advantaged stratum to be guarded against. It also brings in the concept of needs, which Rawls's Difference Principle does not employ. His principle applies, supposedly serving the perfection of justice, even if the least advantaged representative man turns out to be comfortably affluent.

(ii) The Difference Principle does not take certain precautions that justice, as many understand it, would seem to demand respecting the amounts which people deserve to be paid as incentives to effort. Rawls relies in this connection on the marginal productivity theory of wages; and on the supposition that the Fair Opportunity Principle will ensure competition within every category of skill (87, 304–6). Then the marginal value product of any specially skilled worker may plausibly appear to be a fair enough wage, even though he takes the whole of it. There will normally be an intramarginal surplus of goods over wages for workers in his category, part at least of which can be transferred to the least advantaged at the bidding of the Difference Principle.

Even given fair opportunity, however, and the connection with improving the lot of the least advantaged, does the skilled worker deserve the whole of his marginal value product? If there were just one worker in the category, the Difference Principle would paradoxically allow him to approach taking the whole of the value product added by workers in his category, leaving a vanishing small amount to be transferred to the least advantaged. (In fact, he might take even more. In the absence of competition, the marginal productivity theory would not apply to him; he would be indispensable to one or another process of production and would have the chance of a monopoly income.) The real difficulty, however, is that even with a number of workers in every category and competition among them for jobs, the distribution of natural talents may be so skewed that the marginal value products of the most talented categories soar above those of the least talented, even with the application of the Fair Opportunity Principle for training and for jobs [though perhaps repeated application of the principle over generations might reduce or offset the advantages of the most talented].[29]

It may not be practical, of course, to pay the workers in the most talented categories, category by category, any less than the marginal value products. Otherwise they may not be given enough incentive to put forward the related effort; they may even emigrate. But do they deserve so much? The early Christians would not have thought so; nor would Marx, though he was willing to contemplate conceding so much to bourgeois motivations as a temporary expedient.[30] Provision under the Equal Liberty Principle and the Fair Opportunity Principle for transfers of income to ensure the effective exercise by the least advantaged of their rights under these principles will certainly mitigate the envy and resentment that the least talented might feel in view of the splendid wages paid to the most talented. On those splendid wages Rawls suggests levying a proportional expenditure tax (278), which, moved by the justice of the transfers mentioned, the talented may accept.

The differences remaining may be accepted quietly enough by the less talented – but then so might violations of the Equal Liberty Principle or the Fair Opportunity Principle or the Difference Principle itself. Quietly accepted or not, are the differences in income justified? One need not be a doctrinaire egalitarian to believe that they are not; that justice does not require giving exceptionally talented people so much;

on the contrary, that those people deserve to be reproached for being so greedy; and that they should be specially invited to cultivate a spirit of noblesse oblige, extending in this connection beyond the somewhat less than progressive acceptance of a proportional tax. Rawls himself gives great weight to the objections against awarding people special economic advantages on the basis of their possessing, as a gift of nature, specially useful talents. He intends the Difference Principle precisely to limit the rewards going to natural talent. So it does; but it does not limit them closely enough; and it requires, in the name of justice, rewards that a finer sense of justice evidently opposes. (It also, in the absence of good information about necessary incentives, lends itself to abuse: a person getting any multiple whatever of the income going to the least advantaged representative man may claim, or have it claimed for him, that without just that multiple he would not have enough incentive to do his work.[31])

(iii) There is another side to the issue of incentives. Whether or not the marginal value product paid as wages to workers in a given category seems excessive, compared to the wages paid other people, it may represent much less than whole-hearted effort on the part of the workers in question. Will it not be unjust – wrong at least, morally contemptible – for them to withhold from their community the benefits of further effort? Again, the talented may not be justified in merely conforming to the Difference Principle, which in this connection requires that they be paid only for amounts of effort which benefit the least advantaged, and paid only as much as is necessary to elicit those amounts of effort. This time it must be said, too, that the least advantaged may create a problem. The least advantaged, or at least some of them, may not be justified in accepting the benefits assigned them by the Difference Principle. Will they deserve any benefits if they have not put forth any effort? The feeling that no able-bodied people should be supported in idleness by other people willing to work has lent itself, under cultivation by reactionary politicians, to grotesque exaggeration. Does not the feeling nevertheless have a strong connection with most people's sense of justice – in socialist economies as well as in capitalist ones?[32] The Difference Principle, however, is so far preoccupied with justice on the side of consumption that it has not taken even the elementary precaution on the production side of requiring people in the least advantaged stratum to do as much work as they can, up to an amount normal for the society. Consistent with the Difference Principle as Rawls gives it, the least advantaged stratum that it is concerned to favour may be composed entirely of talented, able-bodied people who choose to be for the most part idle.[33]

The Principle of Fairness, which Rawls supposes would be chosen by the agents in the original position after they choose the Equal Liberty Principle, the Fair Opportunity Principle, and the Difference Principle, looks as though it might do something toward requiring full effort on everybody's part. The Principle of Fairness says, 'A person is required to do his part as defined by the rules of an institution when two conditions are met: first, the institution is just ... and second, one has voluntarily accepted the benefits of the arrangements' (111–12). Applied to the institutions of the basic social structure taken as a whole, does not this principle require everybody to do her share in supporting those institutions so long as they are just and she is accepting benefits from them? One may well think it does; it nevertheless falls short of implying that everybody's share amounts to full effort. In many connections, the share will consist more in forbearance than in activity; and though resentment about less-than-full effort may threaten the stability of institutions otherwise just, this empirical argument for full effort remains to be made out. Insofar as institutions fulfilling the other principles can be stable without full effort on everybody's part, they could evidently be unjust in this respect, without violating the Principle of Fairness.

The role that the Principle of Fairness has in Rawls's own eyes has to do with generating specific obligations binding upon particular persons rather than with ensuring that the basic social structure is just overall. Moreover, Rawls evidently believes that the principle is redundant, so far as it concerns efforts in support of the basic structure. He says, discussing the Principle of Fairness, 'We are not to gain from the cooperative labors of others without doing our fair share. The ... Principles of Justice define what is a fair share in the case of institutions belonging to the basic structure. So if these arrangements are just, each person receives a fair share when all (himself included) do their part' (112). In fact, like the rest of what Rawls has to say on this subject and other relevant matters, these statements leave the question of full effort wide open. There is an equivocation on 'a fair share' in the middle statement. In the statement preceding, the phrase meant 'a fair share of effort'; in the statement succeeding, it means 'a fair share of benefits,' which is all that (at most) Rawls's Principles of Justice do ensure.

It may be said that Rawls assumes full effort on everybody's part.

Does it suffice, however, for him to make this assumption? The agents in the original position can hardly make it safely. Why then do they not build the prescription of full effort into the Difference Principle along with other precautions? They cannot sensibly leave the prescription to precepts that the Difference Principle does not entail (303–10). They have as strong grounds to take precautions against less-than-full effort as they do against applying the Principle of Utility in situations where personal utility functions vary so widely as to invite perverse distributions – indeed, maybe stronger grounds: is there only anecdotal empirical evidence of less-than-full effort in every social class?[34]

(iv) Moreover, the assumption of full effort is not the last of the important empirical assumptions required to preserve the attractions of the Difference Principle. The very assumption of full effort generates a specific need for a further assumption. It must be assumed that, within the range of application for the Difference Principle, society does not reach a point at which some at least of its members might justifiably relax from full effort in favour of more leisure. Yet long before any efficiency frontier is reached, may not the relatively productive people on whose efforts further increases of material goods depend have tired of the game? Suppose at a certain stage, short of an efficiency frontier, there is a choice between a reorganization with the same flows of material goods but more leisure for the relatively productive strata and a reorganization with no more leisure for anybody but increased flows of material goods for the least advantaged. At this point, the relatively productive will perhaps have become civilized enough to prefer leisure to becoming richer.

We need not waste tears, before it comes to pass, over the possibility of a minority of people with civilized tastes being forced to work full time long after their desire for material goods has been satisfied, in order to increase further the flow of such goods to a less civilized least advantaged stratum, already materially comfortable but still unsatiated. It is nonetheless a limitation of Rawls's conception of justice that the Difference Principle takes no precautions against the effects of a divergence of tastes of this kind. (The circumstances in which such a divergence calls the Difference Principle into question are not excluded from 'the circumstances of justice,' which in this connection imply only that (some) cooperative labour on everybody's part is both necessary and useful; that implication has been left standing.)

Not only does the Difference Principle take no such precautions. With

a disregard for questions about tastes and about the blessings of techno-
logical development that will understandably excite objections from
Marxists and others, the Difference Principle calls for unlimited growth
in the quantity of material goods, so long as the growth favours people in
the least advantaged stratum and answers to their tastes, no matter what
the point of departure. As noted above, the Difference Principle applies
even if every member of the least advantaged stratum is already comfortably affluent. Does justice then still require full effort on the part of
the most talented to improve the lot of the least advantaged? Once again,
the attractions of the Difference Principle lapse, like the attractions of the
Capacity Principle, when the connection with needs is broken.

Let us suppose Rawls does assume, besides full effort, continuing
demand on everybody's part for increases in material goods. Are these
empirical assumptions not quite as far reaching as the assumptions that
the forms of utilitarianism offered by his chosen opponents require to
be attractive? Moreover, those forms, by resorting more directly to the
Principle of Utility than the Difference Principle permits, automatically
take care at least in part of each of the objections that I have raised
regarding efforts and incentives. By appealing to the humane concern
that the talented are supposed (by the champions of those forms of
utilitarianism) to have for the happiness even of people who are strangers to them, the Principle of Utility deters them from being so greedy as
to take the whole of their marginal value products, when it would be
greedy to take the whole; and it incites them to put forth at least as
much effort as is normal for the society at large. By appealing to the
humane concern that the least advantaged are supposed to have with
the happiness of the talented, it deters the least advantaged from pressing their claims for increased material goods so far as to deny the
talented any relief from effort. The appeals in neither case are likely to
be fully effective, given the recalcitrance of human nature; but should
they be left unused, as the Difference Principle leaves them?

A Better-Guarded Formula, Reached with Rawls's Help

A formula better guarded against the previous objections than Rawls's
Difference Principle can obviously be arrived at by making stipulations
that anticipate the objections. A better-guarded formula would run
something like this, assuming a society with a reasonably comprehensive money economy. Money income shall be distributed equally to
everyone willing to work as hard as is on the average normal in the

society, except (1) insofar as higher incomes for some people are indispensable incentives eliciting from them efforts that lead to improving or further improving the lot of people in the stratum least advantaged before these differential incomes are paid, compared with what their lot would be if these departures from equality did not occur; and except also (2) that no move toward greater equality is to be made which will lead to a least advantaged stratum with a lower income than the present one receives. If an opportunity arises to make an exception of the first kind, which does not itself lead to a least advantaged stratum, differently composed, with a lower income than the present one receives, the opportunity shall be seized, unless a move toward greater equality would produce an even more prosperous least advantaged stratum and unless everyone in the society already has enough income to cover what is generally agreed in the society to be his needs. (In the latter case seizing the opportunity is permitted but not required.) However, the resulting distribution will be just only if, in addition, the people receiving higher incomes are moderate in the incentives that they require; and only if they, too, work normally hard so long as anyone lacks enough income to cover his needs.

The formula, which I offer more as a means of summing up the effect of my criticisms of the Difference Principle than as a permanent acquisition of moral insight, could no doubt be improved. It does not need to be modified to allow the needs of the wilfully idle to be taken care of out of humanity when strict justice looks the other way; we can assume that in any decent society this will happen. However, with the introduction by judicious definitions of some technical terms, it might be both more compactly and more perspicuously expressed, even with certain additions – for example, a clause that would license increasing so far as they could be the incomes of other strata, once the basic structure supporting the least advantaged stratum with the maximum income (equally distributed) has been achieved (if it ever is) – thus attaining perfect efficiency. Among other additions, one might look for precautions against making moves that conform to the formula as it stands, but forfeit the possibility of moving to even better positions on subsequent moves.[35] Quite as important would be some precautions about respecting expectations not grossly at variance with the formula and established in good faith before its adoption as a social policy or during any pause in a sequence of reorganizations that it may dictate.

The attractions, such as they may be, of the principle expressed by the better-guarded formula have not, of course, all originated in the preceding discussion. On the contrary, the central idea and the major part of the attractions (which attach to the central idea) are due to the Difference Principle and to Rawls's insight into its importance. Moreover, if the present principle represents any advance beyond the Difference Principle, the major credit for the advance belongs to Rawls, too; without Rawls's efforts, the importance of working in this conceptual neighbourhood would not have been appreciated, and, as a contingent fact about intellectual history, there would have been nothing substantial to work upon.

Envoi: Reservations about the Terms of Discussion

My argument is finished; I wish to append a few remarks expressing my misgivings about the terms of discussion. I revised those terms, as offered by Rawls, to indicate that the object of discussion on this subject should be not to discover whether Rawls has offered an ethical theory superior to utilitarianism, but to discover whether the form of utilitarianism that he offers is superior to the forms that he objects to. The revision did not go far enough. Following Rawls, I have throughout talked about 'justice,' when in fact I do not think that 'justice,' strictly speaking, was always at issue. For example, I do not think that it is necessarily unjust (though it is a very bad thing) to deny people freedom of speech, or to disregard their needs (a very bad thing, too). Moreover, if Rawls had had more patience with linguistic analysis, he himself would have been led to appreciate, I think, how important to the received conception of justice in these connections and others is the question of established expectations.

He might also have been led, by appreciating the fluidity of linguistic phenomena, to suspect that there is something wrong with the whole notion of finding, once and for all, principles with which 'our considered judgments' about justice are in 'reflective equilibrium.' Every reasonable ethical theory may have to be a form of utilitarianism, combining the Principle of Utility with various constraints, but is it reasonable to ask for a permanent ethical theory in the terms accepted by accepting a choice between forms of utilitarianism?

I suspect it is not. In practice, teleological and deontological considerations are always found together, it is true, but I think the order in which they are found varies, so that every use of a teleological consideration demands support from deontological ones, and vice versa. The notion that there is a distinctive foundation for ethics in either sort of consideration is an illusion; moreover, both considerations are continually changing, along with the concepts that they involve. Instead of fundamental principles to be adopted in perpetuity, all that we can expect to learn from the phenomena of moral discourse are principles that sum up, more or less adequately, inconsistent past thinking and imperfectly coordinated current tendencies. In relation to future discussions, real or hypothetical, in which we must expect to encounter unprecedented problems continually, those principles can hardly serve as much more than rules of thumb – points of departure for the particularized ad hoc discussions in which we have to cope with novelty. The better-guarded formula that I offered a moment ago amounts to little more, as the indispensable use of such vague terms as 'moderate' and 'need' will already have revealed. The formula is not even retrospectively adequate, since it fails to preserve the genuine attractions of those forms of utilitarianism that relied on the Capacity Principle and that I have joined Rawls in rejecting.

General Comment (2005) on the Preceding Discussion of Rawls

Rawls did not propose to engage in any analysis of the use of the term 'justice' and cognate terms in the ordinary language of received moral discourse. Indeed, he explicitly disavows several times over any interest in doing so.[36] If he adopted this policy about the use of 'justice' because he thought analysis of this sort could not give any substantial results, he was mistaken. If he had asked 'What are typical examples in received moral discourse of the use of "justice" and "injustices"?' he would have been led to another argument for having the Difference Principle or some other approximation to equality of incomes and led as well to important conditions (taking the form of safeguards) to be associated with the Difference Principle.

Consider typical examples of what we call 'injustices': having one's property taken away in an arbitrary move to benefit another; being denied rights or privileges that are available to other people (like being able to vote; being able to work in a way suited to one's skills); losing one's freedom, temporarily or permanently. How do such injustices come about? They come about not always, perhaps, but time and again because people with greater income or wealth (or greater power, which Rawls treats as an increasing function of income or wealth) make oppressive use of it. A classic example, which has force for people who do not take the Bible as the fount of wisdom as well as for people who do, is Ahab's, or rather, in instigation, Jezebel's, seizure of Naboth's vineyard after murdering him (I Kings 2).

How is such oppression to be forestalled? In large part, by forestalling people from having overweening income or wealth, enough income to finance oppression. The Difference Principle does this to some extent, both by limiting the advantages of the richer members of a society [37] and by improving the advantages of the poorer members. Assuring the least advantaged of incomes adequate to meeting their needs gives them a greater capacity to resist oppression by the rich. This assurance can be got from Rawls's teachings in three ways: (1) by the assumption that the circumstances in which the original position is set up are the circumstances of a society in which after economic development people have enough resources to be ready to refuse to give up any liberties to get more material goods; (2) by the implication that in practice the 'transfer branch' of a government established under the Principles of Justice will give people a 'social minimum' of provisions for their needs; (3) by the explicit adoption, in work later than *A Theory of Justice*, of 'a lexically prior principle' that basic needs are to be met for everybody before the other principles begin to operate.

People with jobs that do no more than enable them to live from hand to mouth (and, of course, much more so, people who do not have even this advantage) cannot hold out against attempts at oppression to the extent that people can who have adequate incomes and some reserves of savings built up out of them. Perhaps the Difference Principle does not sufficiently limit the inequalities to which it gives rise; hence, it requires to be refined by amending it to impose upward limits to which the inequalities may be carried. This could be done by specifying the limit (after income taxes) as a multiple of the median income of the least advantaged stratum. It has to be borne in mind, however, that even small inequalities in income may facilitate oppression, for example, by enabling those favoured by the inequalities to run 'protection' rackets, or hire neighbours as henchmen, or threaten litigation. Besides the constraints on inequality, the Difference Principle needs some institutional supplementation to make sure that these incomes and reserves do not depend entirely on the goodwill of the rich. They must be secure, among other things, against harassing litigation by the rich. It will not suffice to have the courts nominally as available to the least advantaged as to the most advantaged if the latter can impose or just threaten to impose huge legal costs upon the former in lawsuits brought for just that purpose.

Institutional arrangements and the practices that they foster can help, if not so much with harassment as things stand, still, as things stand, in other connections. It is so far not so easy, even in the increasingly plutocratic United States, for the very rich to bend to their will, every time they are inclined to, a complex, well-established legal system, especially in the persecution of single persons. Many such systems are by and large uncorrupt, with provisions like contingency fee assistance and small claims courts for the poor to seek redress. Some helpful arrangements are not so obvious. Consider, in this connection, the protection against being pushed about on the job by their employers that Canadian workers have but American workers do not. Covered from cradle to grave by a national health care system, Canadian workers can leave jobs in which they feel mistreated without losing health insurance; American workers cannot.[38] It is hard for any particular rich persons, or even for the rich as a class, to set aside in individual cases the protections embodied in an arrangement like this.

Such supplementary arrangements, possibly useful to upholding the Difference Principle, may bear more directly on Rawls's first principle, about political liberty, which may be held to imply that the least advantaged are to have enough resources and enough security in having them to resist being bullied (cf. David Estlund again). Might one then wonder what work is left for the Difference Principle to do? Does it become a merely hypothetical resource? Perhaps it assists in persuading people that if the least advantaged are to be helped to the extent required by the Difference Principle, it is reasonable to go further and under the Equal Liberty Principle make sure of the protection against various sorts of oppression to be ruled out there. This would give the Difference Principle no more than a psychological role. Especially in a long-run, transgenerational view, however, it would still have a part to play in supplying incentives for economic innovation. Moreover, given adequate supplementary institutions, the protection of liberty for the least advantaged may require less than the Difference Principle will award them. Then, within the scope allowed by the upward limit on inequality of incomes and by the supplementary institutions, the Difference Principle may have significant room to operate.

I found in my review, as others have found after me, a number of problems about the motivations of the people who are to live under the Difference Principle. One has to do with the readiness of people, should they not be taking the *non-tuistic* view that is rational in the original position, when they find themselves with rare abilities or with current privileges, to accept the limits imposed by the chosen principles on the returns to these things. While they engage in original position thinking, they operate and assume that all other agents, too, operate with no more than *non-tuistic* motivation. Will they go beyond that motivation when, outside the original position, they have to apply the deliverances of that thinking? Suppose, however, they are convinced that it would indeed be an advance toward justice to have Rawls's principles observed in their society; and their attachment to justice goes far enough to support having the principles observed, even if this means renouncing any current privileges that cannot be justified by the principles. If they have rare abilities, will it be just for them to take all that the Difference Principle would allot them in return for raising the income of the least advantaged?

G.A. Cohen holds[39] that a true sense of justice would work against people with rare abilities accepting special rewards for serving the least advantaged and their whole society as well as they can. Indeed, Cohen charges, it would be inconsistent with their commitment to the Principles of Justice, in particular, the Difference Principle; if they waived the special rewards, there would be more to share out, and the least advantaged would get more. They should do their part anyway, just as the least advantaged should do what they can. Rawls does not quite get to the point of assuming (see, in the text above, 206–8) full effort on everybody's part; but what he introduces as 'the Principle of Fairness,' spelling out an aspect of justice not literally captured by the Difference Principle, would encourage such full effort, if it did not dictate it. All members of a just society are to 'do their part.' Rawls intends the Difference Principle, as Sharon Lloyd insists,[40] to be a principle of reciprocal benefit; but insisting on this does not remove the inconsistency. Why should some get more in reciprocal benefit than others if all are really committed to maximizing the income of the least advantaged?

Cohen, taking over the term as used by Samuel Scheffler in oral debate,[41] allows for a 'prerogative' under which an agent might claim an exemption from the Difference Principle for special rewards answering to a 'reasonable regard for self-interest,' though Cohen does not give much content to this allowance. Estlund, citing the allowance, adds other 'prerogatives' with ingenious examples having to do with affection for family and friends; moral reparations; moral considerations other than equality. Sharon Lloyd offers further ingenious examples: a father facing some difficulties about financing his daughter's college education; a torch singer who will sing longer if the extra income can be used to pay someone else to do the work that she is doing as a volunteer for her church. Like Estlund's examples, Lloyd's make use of the fact that Rawls's agents in the original position are not egoists, but *non-tuists*: not concerned to advance the interests of others in the original position, but maybe ready to use in worthy causes much of any higher income they might receive in a just society. 'It is difficult to say,' Estlund declares, 'how different the ... inequality [resulting from giving full value to the prerogatives] would be from the inequality produced by shameless self-interested behavior.'[42] I presume he would say the same if we add Lloyd's list. His and Lloyd's examples certainly are not far-fetched, but are they, even taken together, common cases? If not, they leave a sizeable amount of room for Cohen's objection about inconsistency still to operate.

Room for this objection is left even if we shift under a lead given by Lloyd from a perspective on the Difference Principle that does not take explicit account of transgenerational considerations (a 'short-run' view, in just this sense) to a perspective that does do this. In this perspective, special rewards enable those with relatively rare skills (including, perhaps, the skills of leadership) to make serious commitments to encouraging their children to acquire equivalent skills in their turn. Lloyd reminds us that Rawls thinks that inequalities of this sort are inevitable; Rawls's purpose with the original position argument for the Difference Principle is at once to reconcile the people with such privileges to sharing the return to them with the other members of society and to make as much use of the inequalities for the other members of society as possible. Thus, Rawls intends to defend a class structure if generation by generation it has the overall effect – and is necessary to having the effect – of making the worst off better off than they would be otherwise. This transgenerational view should disturb Cohen even more than what he has made of the 'a short-run' view. What, were the privileges of the nobility in their time justified? Is the bourgeoisie to retain its status forever? How can specially productive people committed to the Difference Principle accept for themselves or for others with the same 'talents' continuing more than equal reciprocal benefit, even if they have these valuable transgenerational effects?

I think a strong answer to Cohen's objection can be given if we take Rawls's Principle of Fair Opportunity as subject, in what it specifically requires, to transgenerational change. Here, though inspired by Lloyd's work, I go beyond her lead and maybe beyond anything that Rawls was prepared to say. I not only take up the Principles of Justice with the idea of applying them in a transgenerational perspective; I argue for adopting them with the presupposition that they are going to change in what they call for as one generation succeeds another. Suppose we begin by accepting under the Difference Principle the transgenerational advantages of having people prepared for life in entrepreneurial households. We might respond to Cohen by conceding that these advantages are not to be held indefinitely. On the contrary, we might look upon commitment to the Difference Principle as something that itself operates in the long run, with the commitment becoming ever more stringent as we advance stage by stage in making the Principle of Fair Equality of Opportunity more effective. Begin with universal free education through (say) junior college; if that does substantially eliminate the advantages of some households, raise the standards of the education – extend it in years, perhaps years spread out over a lifetime, intensify it with more challenging courses and larger contingents of better-trained teachers; if that does not suffice to do what can be done to reduce the differences in skills, in a next stage make up with various devices for the fact that some children come from homes without any books. The specially favourable effects of being born into entrepreneurial households and a superior class may be offset stage by stage until at the asymptote they vanish, along with class privileges. In effect, we wring out of the rough and ready category of 'natural talents' the advantages that some people have from upbringing. But as this process goes on, the advantages of the more talented and skilful will come to seem more and more subject to further reduction by further efforts under the Principle of Fair Equality of Opportunity. They will seem, even to those who have the advantages, more and more at most only a transient basis for claiming larger rewards.

What is going to motivate such a use of the Principle of Fair Equality of Opportunity? I think the people supporting it, with their commitment to the Difference Principle changing all along, as will their sense of entitlements, will have to be motivated by more than the motivations allowed the agents in the original position. I presume, however, that Rawls would agree, and I can cite the sense of justice and sense of fraternity that arise in members of a society in which his Principles of Justice have been established.[43] Do the agents in the original position foresee these motivations? They are not their motivations; but they could foresee the conditions that by fostering these motivations would help entrench the Principles of Justice.

As these motivations develop over time, strengthening the commitment to the Difference Principle, will not Cohen's objection to the motivations licensed by the Difference Principle tend to lose its footing? Eventually, with a more and more effective Principle of Fair Equality of Opportunity, the motivations may all fall under one or another of the 'prerogatives' apart from self-interest identified in different lists by Estlund and Lloyd; and the limited prerogative of self-interest may be less and less often invoked. That is more of a limitation to the prerogative than Cohen asks for. However, in the end, at the asymptote, Rawls's view of the Difference Principle will join Cohen's view. Their views will coincide, in the sense that the Difference Principle will not have to allow for any special rewards inconsistent with a commitment to it.

I think there is something Utopian about these observations. Nevertheless, Rawls's position, taken as a position about future stage-by-stage developments, hardly invites Cohen's charge of inconsistency. The commitment to the Difference Principle tolerates only pro tempore the inequalities that Cohen objects to. Nor would the position, still forward looking, still prepared to change, be inconsistent if these developments never got more than part-way to the ideal combination of fully defined principles and motivations.

9

Sidgwick's Critique of Nozick

Henry Sidgwick's *The Principles of Political Economy* (1883) and *The Elements of Politics*[1] (1891) have long been out of print, consigned by The University of Texas library (and no doubt other libraries) to remote storage, if not to discard. Paul Lyon has brought them back to availability by putting them on the Internet. But who reads these books nowadays (in contrast with Sidgwick's *Methods of Ethics* [1874, and still in the public eye, at least among philosophers])?[2] Why, apart from antiquarian interest, should anyone read them in this progressive age? One telling reason is that those works contain a searching and unsettling critique of Robert Nozick's work, in particular of *Anarchy, State, and Utopia* (1974).[3] Of course, because Sidgwick wrote long before, and certainly did not have Nozick in mind, never having heard of him, it is an anachronism to rank him as a critic of Nozick. But this, one might reasonably say, is only a trivial technical point. The implicit critique in the works mentioned is not only, point by point, pertinent, it is right up to date; indeed, Sidgwick is much more up to date than Nozick and always has been. He was more up to date in relation to current society when he wrote; and to take into account developments in institutions and social attitudes since his time, what he says needs only straightforward amending (by adding certain topics to an agenda already inclined to be friendly to them). Nozick's views, on the contrary, have no easily intelligible relation to society at the end of the twentieth century, or to society in Sidgwick's time, or indeed to any society that has ever existed in history. If Nozick had only read Sidgwick's arguments before taking pen in hand himself, he might have been deterred from writing the things that he did write in *Anarchy, State, and Utopia*; and many naïve philosophers would have escaped the misleading spell of his ideas, beautifully lucid, but always untimely.

This global difference between the two authors, which I shall describe as a difference in realism, is what I most want to emphasize, though I do not at all want to discount the importance of the point-by-point counter arguments against details of Nozick's views that can be derived from Sidgwick's global position.

Sidgwick is much more realistic than Nozick, in the first place, because he does not abstract from the populous industrial society of his time (too populous to be supported except by industrialization). Hence, he is always ready to cite, against the more or less extreme theses of the libertarians that he knew (e.g., Herbert Spencer), the provisions that organized society has found useful to make (or continue to make) against some of the practical implications of those theses. Are the provisions entirely well conceived, or entirely efficient? Sidgwick does not say, or need to say: his point again and again is that without some provisions of the sort life in society would be much less agreeable to everyone. Without, for example, some protection against slander, everyone would be worse off; so everyone would be without bridges and streets in towns, most efficiently built as governmental projects. The argument, of course, is in general tenor consequentialist and utilitarian, as one would expect from Sidgwick; but he does not need to mobilize any more of a utilitarian apparatus for evaluating consequences than figures in finding that everyone will be happier for having these things.

In the second place, and even more fundamentally, Sidgwick is more realistic just in having some going society to refer to in mounting his arguments. As it happened, it was his own society, nineteenth-century England. But this can be taken to represent any of a number of societies, real or possible, that stand in a historical relation to the arguments. Nozick has no such society to appeal to. He goes back to Locke; and characteristically takes as the basis for his own thinking the unhistorical side of Locke: unhistorical, in the sense that the state of nature as Locke thinks of it was never historical. If you go back to the beginnings of human society, you are not going to find Locke's solitary gatherers of acorns, or his independent subsistence farmers; you are going to find hunter-gatherer societies living in families or small bands and sharing the day's catch.

Something can be made in Nozick's favour of the approximation to a society of independent subsistence farmers (independent short of having a few supporting artisans – blacksmiths, millers) that was set up in parts of the North American colonies in Locke's day. As an approximation, that sort of society survived long enough to give for a while a plausible basis to the protections of the first ten amendments to the U.S. Constitution. (The first of those amendments forbids the federal government to interfere with freedom of speech; that might have been enough protection for people economically self-sufficient.) But even the approximation demands multiple historical qualifications: the land on which the colonists set up was not land to which they had first claim; the colonies were organized to a large extent under grants of property from London (which did not really have a good first claim either); the colonists often came in organized groups, including tenants and indentured servants; they began very early to import slaves.

Nozick's views, like Locke's, fit best a society of independent subsistence farmers and independent artisans; but it is doubtful whether any current society originated in such a society. This is a problem that social contract thinking in the style of Locke creates for itself; and Nozick, taking the side of Locke – one side of Locke – arrays himself against philosophers like Aristotle, or St Thomas, or Sidgwick, who continually had in mind some current society – indeed, the society current in each case with himself.

Even if a current society did originate in a Lockean state of nature, how would the institutions that it found convenient have any special claim to precedence over other institutions that might be better suited to a populous industrial society? Nozick, by postulating as sacrosanct certain free-standing rights respecting the acquisition and exchange of tangible property, would like to hold that the claim to precedence lies in the justice of present claims to property, insofar as they are founded on acquisitions and exchanges that conformed to the postulated rights. Indeed, this is the centrepiece of his theory of justice. But as he admits, in a startling, but little-noticed, confession, there is no way of sorting out how far present claims to property are founded on rightful historical sequences. Hence, he suggests,[4] as a rough attempt to rectify the past injustices that have contaminated all present claims, a social policy of redistribution guided by Rawls's Differerence Principle, which he began by rejecting theoretically as an 'end-result' principle, unacceptable in itself and requiring (he had claimed) an intolerable amount of continual tinkering. (Cf. Sidgwick's discussion of inequality and his approach, perfectly consistent with his basic position, to endorsing the Difference Principle.[5])

Sidgwick never got so far from current society as to commit himself, like Nozick, to a thoroughly idle appeal to history – not really to history; at best to a sort of history-in-principle, history as it might have been, dream history. Nor does Sidgwick get so far from current society as to contemplate anything like Nozick's Utopia, of people (most likely, again, independent subsistence farmers and independent artisans with their own small holdings of capital) freely emigrating between associations that foster different lifestyles. Nozick acknowledges barriers to such mobility in the real world, but does he understand how formidable the barriers are, or how disinclined people may be to emigrate even when the barriers are relatively easy to surmount? Why should people leave Sweden or The Netherlands? There may be nowadays a trickle of people leaving who in accordance with Nozick's beliefs are moving to the United States to try their chances as entrepreneurs; but even they would not be leaving because they found the public provisions in those countries, for medical care, education, unemployment insurance, and pensions in old age, directly oppressive; or the comparatively honourable record of those countries in international aid an intolerable drain on their pocketbooks.

The unrealistic abstraction of Nozick's thinking from current society and real social problems lends itself to the abuse of his doctrines (for which, I daresay, he is not to be held entirely responsible). The agents at issue, though they are properly no more than independent subsistence farmers and independent artisans, are taken to be somehow typical and current, some of them ready to stand on their own feet, never mind that in the real world they would be employees at some level of hierarchical authority or other of large organizations, though some of them – who have not quite fit into the employment matrices – are not. The latter are called upon to make themselves self-sufficient, though that is not what for the most part their luckier fellow-citizens are themselves. There results a sort of populist rationale for policies that reduce the social benefits coming from government or dispense with them altogether – policies, in short, that favour the rich and disfavour the poor. This is not because Nozick's doctrines imply such policies; they are too remote from current society (or any historical society) to imply anything about current policies.[6] But they paint what some readers have found an appealing picture in which only a minimal state is justified and leave the readers to apply the doctrines in almost any way they like. So the doctrines end up reinforcing the conscious anti-governmental bias widespread in public attitudes in the English-speaking countries. Along with that conscious bias they reinforce the largely unrecognized bias tending to perpetuate and strengthen the plutocratic aspects of public policies.

In Sidgwick, there is none of this loony confusion between never-never land and current society with its real problems. In the perspective of current society, Sidgwick grapples with point after point on the libertarian agenda, shows what a balanced view of the issues will make of them, and leaves his readers with overall equipment suited to dealing with current policies.

He begins by setting up, in the face of the extreme libertarian position that governmental action (interference) is allowable only to directly protect people's liberty, what he calls 'the Individualistic Minimum,' that is to say, the minimum of government action or interference that accords with a principle derived from utilitarianism, of gaining as much as possible of the benefits of mutual non-interference. He expresses this minimum as consisting of government support for personal rights under three heads, namely, '(1) the Right of personal security, including security to health and reputation; (2) the Right of private property, together with the Right of freely transferring property by gift, sale, or bequest; (3) the Right to fulfilment of contracts freely entered into.'[7] All of these rights, he points out, go beyond serving directly to prevent people from interfering with each others' freedom, taking that in the basic sense of being free to do what they wish to do, unobstructed by force or fear of force. Hence, the Individualistic Minimum goes beyond – far beyond – what an extreme libertarian would demand.

What is the status of these rights? Sidgwick argues for them on the basis of the utility ascribed to them by current society; but he does not rely on any questionable procedure for aggregating personal utilities. It suffices for his purposes, as I have said, that everyone will find life more agreeable if these rights are protected than if they are not. But maybe there needs to be no reference to utility at all. We might simply begin with these rights, treating them as free-standing postulates, as Nozick treats the rights of acquisition and exchange. Will they not do just as well as Nozick's rights? Indeed (2) (private property) is equivalent to Nozick's Right of Private Property on the topic of exchange, and though it does not imply his right of acquisition, (2) might be developed to include it; and (1) (personal security) and (3) (contracts) seem to be natural supplements to his scheme, even arguably implications of it when it is fully laid out. But none of them, in Sidgwick's treatment, not even in respect to acquisition, imply going back to any original state of nature. It is, for example, only acquisition, given present resources and opportunities, that is to be covered. With funds saved from her wages, a worker makes a down payment on a house, or buys pots and pans and some crockery.

The importance given by Sidgwick to security of reputation deserves a moment's pause. In any real society, people are connected with one another in a complex network of personal relations, which they look to for various benefits. Those benefits will be jeopardized by slander. A woman cannot expect to marry as well as she could, unslandered; her parents will not be able to place her in a marriage favourable to them as well as to her; her children, if she does marry, will suffer directly or indirectly from the injured reputation of their mother. Nothing of this sort occurs with Nozick's farmers and artisans, who seem to be related to one another only by the exchanges that they make of tangible commodities. Is this a society, even a society in principle? It is only a rather implausible attempt at the skeleton of a society.

Sidgwick proceeds to argue that the Individualistic Minimum is not enough to gain all the benefits of government action consistent with the principle that endorses it as a minimum. These benefits include not merely punishing fraud, but taking precautions against it and other evils by having government prescribe weights and measures and inspect food and other goods; and by having government restrict 'the manufacture and carriage of explosive substances.' Sidgwick admits that cases like these fall on 'the disputed margin' of the Individualistic Minimum; and invite charges of paternalism, as do, even more so, goverment schemes for licensing medical practitioners and for refusing to enforce contracts with unlicensed ones. But he holds that in many of these cases the individualistic principle suffices to endorse government action; and he does not repudiate paternalism out of hand, even in dealing with sane adults, since even sane adults may be liable to victimization in one way or another.

In the next stage of his argument, Sidgwick goes beyond even the margin of individualism: 'There is no reason to suppose that a purely individualistic organization of industry would be the most effective and economical.'[8] Socialism, he holds, meaning in its most intrusive instances, not just regulation but production carried on by the government, is in order for education, managing forests, building bridges and streets in towns, providing roads, parks, and waterways elsewhere, making banking and insurance available to the poor. He thinks that there are drawbacks to government production, in particular in respect to motivation. It is not easy to make up for the acute interest that individual entrepreneurs, proprietors of their own businesses, bring to production. However, Sidgwick does not regard this as an insuperable disadvantage. In time, motivations may change, for example, toward public spiritedness, in ways favourable to extending socialism, even to the extent of having government production become predominant. He contemplates with equanimity the eventuality of having land come under national ownership (though this would happen with due compensation). In every one of these connections, it is a practical comparison between individualistic methods and socialist ones that will decide whether to go forward to more socialism. It is not the restrictions of an abstract doctrine of rights that govern the comparison, furthermore, but a comparison of benefits, in the simplest cases a comparison of the quantities produced with given amounts of resources.

I have been drawing mainly on *The Elements of Politics*, rather than on *Political Economy*. Sidgwick runs much the same argument when he focuses on the workings of the economy. Laissez-faire – 'the system of natural liberty' – invites the attachment of individualists. However, for a variety of reasons, including excessive value ascribed to goods consumed by the rich, the special requirements of dealing with public goods, and the need to make special provisions for training the poor in useful skills, an economy run entirely under the banner of laissez-faire will not achieve optimal production, even if everyone involved is a well-informed judge of her own interest. Nor is the system optimal for distribution, since, among other things, it does not distribute enough to the poor to enable them to improve their productive skills, and it allows landowners to appropriate unearned increments to the value of their land. (This is a point that Nozick, characteristically, does not mention; it is not a benefit that reduces simply to acquisition or the exchange of acquired goods, but one that supervenes on the interactions of a concentrated population.)

Sidgwick mentions monopoly, but does not give it special prominence or recognize the ubiquity that, according to the twentieth-century theory of monopolistic competition, must be ascribed to it, though it is radically questionable how much of the laissez-faire ideal on either the production side or the distribution side will be left relevant when the ubiquity is appreciated. More striking and more important is Sidgwick's omission to say how business cycles affect production and distribution. If full production under the laissez-faire ideal is realized only intermittently and the economy is periodically depressed, with effects on income and happiness falling with much greater impact on workers – who lose their jobs and livelihoods, and may fall into destitution – than on capitalists, must not these effects be taken into account? The economy must be judged not only on its performance at peak moments, but over periods of some length, where the net benefits realized under the system of natural liberty may be much less impressive. Sidgwick, however, is at least prepared to consider carrying on production in other ways and is open to experiment with socialist projects. Thus, amendments on this point will come in the form of extending further some allowances that he has already made.

On other points, the amendments will have to correct some shortcomings. Sidgwick did not appreciate how weak the bargaining position of a worker is vis-à-vis an employer, even when the employer is a small manufacturer. Hence, he objected to establishing minimum hours for work as an infringement of personal liberty. Nor did he appreciate the scope for petty oppression on the employer's part that is opened up by the worker's immobility, given, among other things, family attachments and the fixed location of some of his few assets (like a house partly paid for). These differences between workers and employers have not gone away as huge bureaucratic organizations have supplanted small employers in the economy private and public. Sidgwick, moreover, is very sceptical about the motives of typical workers; he finds some merit in the British workhouse as a deterrent to idleness. But even here, he is prepared to learn from other countries, and prepared, in principle at least, to go forward with measures of social insurance. It is also perhaps only fair to concede to him that what in U.S. politics is called the 'welfare' problem has not yet been wholly solved.

Is there anything here that is not now, as it has been for some time past, a commonplace in the discussions of economics? But Sidgwick has had a part in making the points at issue commonplaces, mostly a useful part, a part for good. Sometimes he plays a part for ill, with others who established the commonplaces – for ill, chiefly in beginning with the idealized merits of a competitive market and introducing realistic qualifications one by one as so many deviations, if not quite as abnormalities. That is the way economists still think, and the way that the public has by and large been persuaded to think, too. They would all do better to treat fully competitive markets as precarious and transient phenomena, deviations from a reality steadily unsuited to keeping them going.

Even if Sidgwick's *Political Economy* were no more than a systematic presentation of what have become commonplaces, it is a striking implication of the comparison with Nozick that points recognized at least by an exceptionally judicious thinker generations earlier just go missing in

Nozick's work. But Sidgwick's presentation is still useful as an introduction to the moral criticism of economic activity, especially if it is amended in the ways that I have mentioned, as well as in other ways. Furthermore, it shows how classical liberalism in economics – 'the system of natural liberty' – invited transformation under the pressure of utilitarian considerations into what has been called 'liberalism' in the United States since at least the time of the New Deal, and lately has been vilified under that name (as it was, formerly, under the name of socialism) in spite of its achievements in giving capitalism a human face. Sidgwick was a classical liberal, but he was also, like some other leading classical liberals though not all, a utilitarian, too. Still in current commitments a classical liberal, he looked forward to transformation in the direction of the welfare state, 'socialist' in his view, more or less 'socialist' in other people's usage; and he helps to get the transformation moving just by this looking forward.

The argument of *Elements of Politics* resists even more easily the charge of rehearsing commonplaces. The points advanced by the argument – the points made in *Political Economy* reflected, recast, and supplemented – are the views that experience with a market economy has installed in common sense. Anyone who disregards them, as Nozick disregards them, does so only at great risk of irrelevance. They are thus suitable places to begin reflecting on politics. In the course of presenting them, Sidgwick offers a rationale for what advanced governments do, including governments more advanced than that of England in his time; and in the course of doing so, he offers a rationale for the services that their citizens generally strongly favour, though in many cases this is hardly consistent with the anti-governmental (anti-'liberal') rhetoric that has been induced in them by libertarian doctrines and other ill-considered influences. Sidgwick also supplies grounds for improving those services when occasion to do so can be found. He is more inclined to contemplate additions to the services than subtractions from them – experiments with privatization – but that is an effect of his view of the future and his assumptions about progress. Subtractions, along with revisions of services that continue, are undeniable logical possibilities. Sidgwick, with some amendments, thus also offers a place to begin comprehensive reconsideration of current policies.

What does Nozick have to say about application to current policies and current politics? Essentially, nothing on his own. He supports a principle of rectification to be applied to present holdings, but, as I have pointed out, he can do no better in approximating it than go outside his own doctrine, indeed, go outside to borrow the Difference Principle from his main target. But if the Difference Principle is to work acceptably, it must go hand in hand with the Principle of Fair Equality of Opportunity, which Rawls brings in to help make sure that the people who arrive at various positions, top and bottom and in between, in the income-level scheme, are the people best qualified to hold them. Rectification will thus open up a far-reaching opportunity to reorganize (more or less comprehensively, more or less rapidly) the economy, and consider what is to be done not just about Rawls's principles, but also about all the points that Sidgwick argues must be provided for. Sidgwick, like Rawls, is ready with advice about the reorganization. Nozick has nothing useful to add.

10

Social Contract Theory's Fanciest Flight
(with Gauthier)

There is less to say by way of preface to this discussion of Gauthier's work, because I can offer it straightforwardly as a current critical representation of Gauthier's Morals by Agreement, *which I think is the technically most proficient of the grand programs in analytical political philosophy, and the most suited to inspiring rigorous criticism.*

I

Readers on the Right – any readers who stand with Milton Friedman and Frederic Bastiat or to the right of them – will rejoice in the political colouring given David Gauthier's *Morals by Agreement*[1] by its broad commitment to private property rights, its born-again enthusiasm for the market, and its repeated denunciation of 'free riders' and 'parasites.' Readers on the Left, one may fear, will view the book with dismay and derision as just one more instalment in a tradition inherited from Locke of mystifying anachronism. The hunter-gatherers contract again, but what has that to teach us about the distribution of authority and privilege in a society of mass production?

In respect to the abuses that Gauthier's theory will lend itself to, both these readings may be well founded. Locke's picture of property acquired by labour in the state of nature has been abused to accord riches gained from shuffling oil leases the same respect as land that a homesteader has made tillable. Robert Nozick's notions about entitlements have no doubt been invoked to favour current distributions of property rights by many people who, from confusion or cynicism, have ignored Nozick's confession that one cannot expect to trace the pedigrees of present possessions.[2] Similarly, Gauthier's theory may figure, by confusion or cynicism, in attacks upon the progressive income tax or upon public aid for fatherless households.

In respect to the justified use of the theory, however, both rejoicing on the Right and dismay on the Left are mistaken – indeed, mistaken three times over. Closely examined, the theory is not, even on the face of it, so reactionary as the colouring suggests. Gauthier expresses due concern about having people wholly at the mercy of the market (4.3.2), and he explicitly attaches to the theory a number of qualifications that tend to neutralize it. These include standard cautions against treating the market in the real world as the ideal market of theory and go beyond to embrace a conditional licence for taxing away inheritances (9.6.2) and an unconditional licence for redistributing unearned income (economic rent) (9.3.1, 9.3.2). Moreover, the reactionary colouring is not indelible. When the chief point has been attended to on which the theory, given the direction of its ambitions, still needs to be carried through – namely, accommodating the public-goods aspects of having a market – the political tendency of the theory will shift leftward in principle. All these considerations undermine the justification of using the theory for reactionary propaganda.

But the theory cannot be used for such purposes anyway – or for any other adventure in real politics. Readers on the Right may rejoice not only in the political colouring of the theory but also in the degree of technical perfection to which Gauthier has brought social contract theory. In their rejoicing, they may fail to perceive the irony that the perfection has been gained at the expense of depriving the theory of any possibility of effective application. Its demands for information are fantastic, too fantastic ever to be met or even to allow the theory to be used as a guide to improvements within the reach of present social policy.

Readers on the Left will be ready enough to see this irony. It is likely to redouble their scorn to the point of distracting them from appreciating the technical virtuosity that Gauthier displays and the threefold philosophical triumph that he achieves. Social contract theory flies higher and more expertly in *Morals by Agreement* than ever before. But it does not fly alone. Gauthier has carried, to the same height of sophistication, the project, often mooted by philosophers past and present, of deducing morality from rationality. The theory of the social contract is the most promising vehicle for the deduction project, bringing together the themes, all crucial to ethical theory, of consent, mutual benefit, and cooperation. No one previously has come anywhere as near as Gauthier to carrying the project through with perfect precision and rigour, incidentally – a third triumph – making better combined use than utilitarianism itself of the notions of utility and optimization.

Will anyone ever do better? This may well be the best chance of succeeding with the highest philosophical ambitions that social contract theory, the deduction project, and the combined use of utility and optimization will ever have. If the result is a theory that has no application, those ambitions need to be reconsidered.

II

Can we say that *Morals by Agreement* is the treatise that Locke should have written, had he had the means that Gauthier has assembled, from economics, decision theory, the theory of bargaining, and the theory of games? Locke did not have the same high ambitions for the contract, and though he thought ethics was, in principle, a deductive science, suited to discovery by the rational powers of human beings, notoriously Locke did not himself set forth a deductive ethics.[3] In both connections, Locke spared himself more than a little trouble. He never got to the point of conceiving, as Gauthier does, that the social contract poses a bargaining problem about reconciling many different personal utility functions. Locke never dreamed of a solution concept as sophisticated as Gauthier's dual principles of minimax relative concession and maximin relative benefit, which distribute the utilities gained from the contract as near to equally as can be defined without assuming interpersonal comparisons of utilities or ruling out certain formally intractable patterns of distribution (5.3.2). Gauthier is in techniques a much more sophisticated representative of the Lockean tradition than Locke himself. Have the techniques vindicated Gauthier's higher-flying ambitions?

Morality or justice, as readers of the book will quickly become aware, consists for Gauthier of a system of constraints on utility-maximizing behaviour (5.1.2). They are, he undertakes to show, constraints that utility-maximizing agents – agents rational just in the sense of being utility-maximizing – would agree to after bargaining (5.3.3) and put themselves in a position to comply with once agreed to (6.2.1). The constraints are not necessary within the market (4.3.1); for, if force and fraud are sufficiently checked to allow a market to operate and it is fully competitive, each agent will maximize utility from private goods simply by seeking on her own to make the best of her opportunities in the market. The agents accept a market on this understanding. The constraints are necessary to capture the maximum utilities at stake in the externalities, negative and positive, that even a fully competitive market leaves unresolved by voluntary action (5.1.2). These externalities can be remedied only by the production of public goods (9.2).

A problem stands in the way of producing such goods, however, for they are goods of the sort that people may hope, as free riders, to enjoy without contributing to their production. This is, with rational agents, a vain hope; if all the agents are unconstrained, as well as rational, none of them will give others a chance to free ride on his contribution. No one will contribute, and the goods will not be produced. To obtain the goods, the agents strike a bargain, constraining them to contribute, about the combination of their contributions and their benefits. Gauthier holds that contributions and benefits are to be so combined that in each agent's case the net benefit bears a certain relation to the maximum claim that the agent might make on the benefits from cooperating with the scheme of production and to the agent's minimum claim. That relation may be expressed equally well by saying that the concession for each from her maximum claim is to be no greater than the maximum concession that anyone has to make (hence, minimax relative concession) and that the net benefit realized is to be no less than the minimum benefit that anyone has to accept under any arrangement (hence, maximin relative benefit) (5.4.3).

The maximum and minimum claims by each agent may seem elusive, defined, as Gauthier insists, by subjective utility functions that are different for each agent (5.2.3). The maximum claims, elusive or not, may seem too overweening to count. Suppose that the agent can discover the utility for him of the arrangement most favourable to him: must the other agents take seriously his claim to all the benefits of cooperation under that arrangement beyond the portions that would just marginally make the arrangement beneficial for themselves, by covering their minimum claims? But a partial answer to this question is that, on Gauthier's view, the other agents, far from conceding this maximum claim, would, if they could, concede no more to the person who makes it than his own minimum claim. Moreover, if we are dealing with utility-maximizing agents, it makes some sense to identify their maximum claims with claims that push maximizing as far as it can go, to capture all the net benefits available. Each therefore makes the largest possible claim and is met, to begin with, by the smallest possible offer. So they must bargain.

How much of morality will follow from the bargain? Gauthier argues that the softer, more congenial – the kinder – aspects of morality, in a broader sense than he uses the term, will develop, along with an affective attachment to morality broad and narrow, in the course of the agents' taking part together in a common scheme of cooperation that they know to be just (10.2.5, 11.1.3). Indeed, such a scheme, answering to a bargain of the sort that he has worked out, will, he contends, open the way to ascending to a nobler level of sentiment-free affectivity, in which agents' affections for other people spring up wholly unforced (11.2.3).

One might wonder whether having every agent intensely preoccupied with getting the most for herself out of the bargain is psychologically compatible with the fullest development of affection for others. However, the preoccupation, so far as Gauthier's theory calls for it, is called for only in reconstructing a rationale for relationships and sentiments that may develop naturally quite otherwise (11.1.3). Moreover, Gauthier's argument here has a strength best brought out by putting it the other way around, as what might be called in a Benthamite-like phrase 'the injustice-disaffecting hypothesis.' Persistent gross injustices will undermine affection. Even the most affectionately related – lovers, happy spouses – might do well to consider from time to time whether the division of benefits between them does justice to their different interests.

It is in the grander orbits of ethical theory, however, that Gauthier's argument most shines. It shines doubly because, in the most impressive tour de force in the book, he demonstrates that the contract which the agents would come to, actually bargaining with one another given their maximum and minimum claims, can be struck again as a virtual bargain (8.4) reached by an original position argument that has, as Gauthier claims, distinct advantages in principle over Rawls's. An Archimedean agent, from whom a veil of ignorance conceals her identity, but who knows the capacities and the utility functions of all the agents, one of whom she will turn out to be, chooses on their behalf (simultaneously on her own) a social structure or scheme of cooperation. She proceeds by taking up the position of each agent in turn and considering what bargain, fixing on the scheme of cooperation, the agent would voluntarily agree to as a utility-maximizing agent (8.4.1). No special favour is given to any existing arrangement, and each agent is considered to be operating from an initial bargaining position corrected, as it is supposed to be in actual bargaining, by Gauthier's version of the Lockean proviso, which removes certain effects of previous victimization (8.4.2).

The result is that the Archimedean agent chooses, along with choosing to have a market, a scheme of cooperation answering to the twin principles of minimax relative concession and maximin relative benefit. Just as, in actual bargaining, rationality leads to an impartial result and thus to justice, so here the impartiality of the Archimedean choice leads to justice through rationality (8.1).

Once the veil is lifted, some agents may find that justice requires of them sacrifices of present position and privilege which they are not prepared to make. However, in principle, Gauthier has solved, so far as rational argument can solve, the compliance problem that remains in Rawls's argument for agents who, after the veil is lifted, find that they are not in the least-advantaged stratum. Every one of Gauthier's agents, winners or losers in character and skills, has grounds sensitive to his individuality for accepting the scheme that justice prescribes, because every one of them was represented, individually, in the choosing of the scheme. The other compliance problem, which Rawls simply assumed away,[4] of acting in accordance with the scheme indefinitely, once it has been accepted, Gauthier solves by arguing that the contracting parties will, as rational agents, induce in themselves a reliable disposition to comply whenever they have to deal with other agents whom they find transparent enough – translucent – to be relied on to comply in turn (6.2.2, 6.2.3). That is the way that they escape from the optimum-sacrificing trap of defection. (It is unlike Hobbes's way, in avoiding any resort to coercion, but it is Hobbesian in supposing that agents can recognize in each other dispositions to cooperate.[5])

The major advance over Rawls, however, lies in the project of deducing morality (justice) from rationality and in particular in the fact that Gauthier, unlike Rawls, operates without question-begging assumptions. I am not suggesting that Rawls was unaware, when he brought in 'the formal constraints of the concept of right' to circumscribe the range of principles considered in the original position, that he was begging questions about whether the choice of principles would proceed from rationality alone, without any moral restrictions.[6] Rawls chose to pursue a different, less radical deduction project. The point is that Gauthier does not assume any of Rawls's constraints, either as regards bargaining or in the original position argument. Gauthier's agents simply are to maximize their utilities in respect to cooperation (or have their utilities maximized for them, by the Archimedean choice), and from that aim Gauthier deduces the attraction of an impartial scheme of constraints and benefits that is just.

It is true that, recognizing the possibility of rational agents acting oppressively on occasion, while other agents rationally submit to their trespasses (7.5.2), he assumes the bargain will be voluntary on all sides and in all respects. Were it not, the outcome could not be just without question. However, that it is to be voluntary is the very least that every utility-maximizing agent would ask for himself. It is true, too, that Gauthier insists that the initial bargaining positions must be corrected by the Lockean proviso. That proviso implies for Gauthier certain rights, for example, rights as property holders precluding victimization by others, and these rights, which must be respected both in the market and in the scheme of cooperation, have some semblance of being a source of moral constraints independent of the scheme and the bargain that leads to the scheme. So far as it affects the bargain, however, the proviso simply prevents the bargaining from being biased by inflated minimum claims covering resources acquired through victimization. This, again, is something that the victimized agents might insist on as a condition of the bargain's being voluntary.

Without these assumptions, Gauthier would not have much chance of reaching morally convincing results; so, without them, the deduction would not, one might well think, end up in anything convincingly like even a part of morality as familiarly understood. However, that does not mean that the assumptions themselves are question begging. What it means is that Gauthier's model is not unique. From the aims of rational agents under other assumptions – assumptions that left predatory behaviour unchecked and allowed intimidation to overshadow voluntary entry into the bargain – a convincing morality very likely could not be deduced. But it is unreasonable to expect that the deduction project can be carried through for every model in which rational agents might be deployed. Besides the assumptions mentioned, the project requires and can reasonably demand the traditional Humean assumptions about there being neither abundance nor dearth, neither saintliness nor ferocity.

Gauthier's contract, like the morality directly entailed by it, leaves out of account people who are not in a position to contribute to producing any part of the cooperative surplus, even if it is only by forbearing to interfere. So does Rawls's conception of justice, which also presupposes 'a society for mutual advantage,'[7] but Gauthier is much more insistent on the point. 'Animals, the unborn, the congenitally handicapped and defective, fall beyond the pale of a morality tied to mutuality,' which is rationally defensible as such (9.1). So may people overseas, if an established society for mutual advantage concludes that it has nothing to gain from cooperating with them and is not moved by sympathy or a disposition to cooperate with all human beings (9.4.3). Many (I among them) will feel that this possibility of indifference – or of worse – toward other people, not to speak of other animals, is an enormous limitation on the morality that here emerges from the deduction project. It is not clear, furthermore, that the limitation will be overcome by the development of free affectivity within the charmed circle of contracting cooperators. Yet, again, I think that we are dealing with an inevitable limitation on the deduction project, rather than an objection that depreciates Gauthier's success in carrying it out as thoroughly as it can be done. Why should we think that all that any of us wants to find in morality or justice will be put there by reason alone – by merely rational agents, even rational agents ready on utility-maximizing grounds to put themselves under the constraints required for cooperation?

III

Has Gauthier advanced beyond Rawls in every respect? He has not advanced in every respect beyond Locke. Locke does not perhaps deserve much credit for forgoing sophisticated conceptual means that were not on hand in his time. Yet Locke's more modest means, employed in the pursuit of his more modest ambitions, do retain what Gauthier forfeits: the possibility of exemplifying the social contract in the real world – in history. Locke's social contract is something the terms of which agents who have lived long enough in a state of nature (perhaps only momentarily) to recognize its inconveniences could identify and give effect to. Moreover, whether or not the state of nature and the social contract have ever had priority in this sense, the priority of actual origins, Locke's state of nature can figure in history and, along with it, the conception of a specific social contract intended to improve on nature in a currently applicable test for the legitimacy of a social structure. (As ingredients of such a test, they would have priority as a jural hypothesis.) Does the government respect the laws of nature and the rights to life, liberty, and estate that the members of the underlying society have under the jural supposition of the state of nature[8] and keep while consenting to that society, and to the government that it has organized? Suppose that it is agreed what are to count as rightful estates – perhaps all holdings current five years ago plus certain additions to them. Gauthier forfeits current testability of this kind as well as the possibility of there being any historical instances of societies originating in a social contract as he conceives it.

A

The forfeiture occurs for two reasons. One – the less serious reason because it can be formally rectified – is that, as it stands, Gauthier's theory does not complete Gauthier's program for it. It excludes private goods from the social contract and assigns pursuit of them to the market. The theory regards maximizing behaviour in the market as requiring none of the constraints on maximizing utility that cooperating to attain public goods requires. This is an untenable position. Is not the market itself – having a market – a public good? Alternatively, is it not a public good to have the constraints on force and fraud that are both empirically and logically necessary to having a market (4.1)? If having them is a public good, however, the utilities obtained from them as effects of their publicness must come under the social contract for distribution according to the principles of justice that figure in the contract.

Are all the utilities that are obtained from or in the market to come under the contract? That may not be very plausible, but it is more plausible than denying that any of them do. Is there some principle for dividing the utilities obtained from the constraints on force and fraud from utilities obtained solely from the variable enterprise and variable success of agents entering into exchange? If there is such a principle, Gauthier has not yet supplied one.

Could Gauthier simply set aside any questions about the public goods of having a market or having the indispensable constraints on force and fraud? Then he would by stipulation be confining the social contract to other public goods. This would formally forestall the charge of its being inconsistent to ignore the former in the contract. But it would also be very anomalous, as well as more than a little arbitrary. Given the traditional prominence rightly accorded them, the constraints on force and fraud invite being looked upon as the greatest public goods of all. (How could a devotee of the market not look upon them as such?)

Locke and, after him, Hume avoid trouble with these questions. They do not seek comprehensive optimization over all public goods. Nor do they associate with such an optimization a comprehensive social choice under all required constraints. The state is an institution brought in to give certain constraints already present the reinforcement needed for their further perfection. Laid down by God, the constraints are, according to Locke, already present in the state of nature, along with the market.[9] Hume, too, incorporates the constraints in laws already effective prior to government. In Hume's view, a government, once set up, will turn out to be the instrument of obtaining other public goods, but the benefits that suffice to make having a government desirable consist, again, in the reinforcement that it will give constraints already recognized and effective enough for a market to be already operating.[10] If the government is to be brought in by a social contract, the other public goods need not figure in it, and the public goods of having some constraints against force and fraud to begin with and with them a market are presupposed.

Can Gauthier follow their example and assume that the market, with effective (though imperfect) constraints against force and fraud, already exists at the ideal starting point and has only to be endorsed by the agents who (after reading chapter 4 of *Morals by Agreement*) then turn their attention to the other public goods? It is not easy to do this without anomaly. For the constraints must have been there for the market to get started or have evolved along with an evolving market. How did this happen? Hume's explanation, Gauthier has contended elsewhere,[11] was that the constraints were, in effect, contracted for; agents concurred in cooperating, perceiving the mutual advantage of constraining themselves not to try to maximize utility independently. But Gauthier, rightly, does not pretend that Hume had any exact measure of the mutual advantage at stake, much less any idea that it would be distributed to accord with Gauthier's dual principles. It sufficed for Hume, evidently, to think that everyone would benefit, by comparison with a situation in which there were neither the constraints nor a market.

Are we to have a contract for vague benefits from the constraints on force and fraud, letting the market operate without further social attention and then move on to another contract for precise benefits from the remaining public goods? This is still anomalous. Moreover, treating the social contract proper as a second contract does not dispose of the problem of allowing for the benefits of the market. If government, set up by the second contract, does no more than reinforce the constraints, will this not increase the utilities received through the market? Are the agents not to bargain about this?

Everyone may benefit from the constraints on force and fraud, but not everyone benefits more from the market than from non-market arrangements, and not everyone who benefits more from the market benefits equally. There is a bargain to be struck about having the constraints and with them a market, if, indeed, there is to be a market. Some people may dislike having a market; it would be a public good for them not to have one. Others may expect to get a smaller income in private goods (or a smaller relative income) out of a market than from communal planning. Should not the maximum claims of both groups be defined on non-market arrangements? Can the principle of minimax relative concession and its twin properly ignore maximum claims so defined? Those principles cannot be confined to other public goods, or to public goods rather than private ones, without prejudicing the issue between market and non-market arrangements.

Still another set of people may do better out of the market than under any other arrangement but, even so, less well than others better fitted than themselves to succeed in the market. Is there not something to be bargained about here, too, with maximum claims and concessions defined on a mixture of market arrangements with measures of redistribution? Gauthier may wish to say 'No,' but on this point his rhetoric may blind him. He would condemn as 'parasites' the prospective losers who insist on having the prospective winners bargain away some of their private goods. They are truly, one might think, in an unlovely position. But what ground is there for condemning them before a morality has been agreed upon? They are simply pressing their own interest. If it is argued that by pressing their interest too far they risk not having a market at all, or at least not having enough private goods to redistribute to improve their positions, this invites applying to private goods the distinction between independent maximization and maximization under cooperation that is at the heart of Gauthier's argument respecting public goods.

Moreover, unexpectedly, the charge of parasitism can be turned around. Robert H. Frank has shown, in a book that was published only after Gauthier had finished his, that superior status is a good which people are prepared to pay for, and prepared to relinquish only when given compensation.[12] If those who succeed in the market get superior status with their wealth yet fail to compensate those who, with less success, are to be content with inferior status, they themselves will be parasites.[13]

All these considerations converge to imply that Gauthier, if he is to complete his own program, must carry it further to consolidate the treatment of the market with the treatment of the contract. Just how he is to do this I shall not try to specify; it is a challenge to which he can bring a degree of technical resourcefulness hard to match. Any form of consolidation, however, will have to give more weight than his theory now does to utilities obtainable from measures modifying the results of the market or to some degree superseding the market to begin with in favour of planning. In that sense the political tendency of the theory will shift to the Left, without necessarily corresponding to any prescriptions that critics of the market have actually advocated.

B

A second, more intractable reason remains for holding that Gauthier's social contract, unlike Locke's, cannot be applied in history, either by people who actually make such a contract to escape the state of nature or by people who might wish to invoke it as a jural hypothesis along with the idea of the state of nature in a current test of government. Gauthier, seeking terms for the contract that will meet the most rigorous standards that he can imagine, ends up making fantastic demands on information, which no contracting parties and no current critics of government could ever meet.

To establish their maximum claims, from which their relative concessions are to be reckoned, Gauthier's agents must each identify the social structures under which they would attain fullest personal development, having access to the appropriate public goods and consequently enjoying the greatest utility from them (8.4.4). How could they ever do this or have it done for them? Gauthier tries to mend matters by stipulating that they need consider only structures feasible with current technology. But do any of us know the whole range of public goods or combinations of goods that could be produced with current technology? None of us know our own utility functions even for the public goods now being produced, much less the utility functions of 24 million or 240 million fellow-citizens. Nor shall we ever know. We shall never know whether we have arrived at the social structure prescribed by Gauthier's theory either – the one in which the maximum relative concession made by anybody is less than the maximum relative concession that anybody makes under any alternative (feasible) arrangement.

Can we at least tell, sometimes, whether we are further from the optimum so defined in one social state s_1 than we could be in another s_2?

Then the theory might guide us in changing from one social state to another, which would make it helpful, even if the change in every case was only a small one: an incremental change. Two ways of using Gauthier's theory for such limited comparisons suggest themselves, but in neither case is it the principle of minimax relative concession or its twin that makes the comparisons telling – when they are. It is some simpler and more familiar principle, which either does not figure in Gauthier's theory at all or figures there without being a distinctive ingredient.

First, one might find that in s_1 someone had to accept a lower net return from public goods than anyone would get in s_2. Might this difference suggest that s_2 would be closer to providing maximin relative benefits than s_1? Perhaps, but there is no way of vindicating the suggestion without determining the maximum claims of the people involved. This cannot be done. Worse, if it could be done, it might overturn the suggestion. N, who would get the lowest net return in s_2, might (because of the magnitude of his maximum claim) be making a greater relative concession in accepting that net return than M is making in accepting the still lower net return that is the minimum in s_1.

Waiving any interpersonal comparisons of utility, we might restrict ourselves to cases in which no one gets a net return lower in s_2 on his own scale than he does in s_1, though M (and perhaps others) get larger returns. But then, of course, we are invoking not Gauthier's theory but the Pareto principle, and, if we are acting on the Pareto principle, we shall want to know, in addition, that the further improvements available from s_2 will not be less attractive than those available from s_1. If we refuse to restrict ourselves to acting on the Pareto principle and are willing to consider improving M's lot by reducing the returns to N or others (though not to the level of M in s_1), we must be assured that shifting to s_2 implies no injustice, as it might, for example, by rewarding wilfully unproductive people at the expense of productive ones. Indeed, we should want to know that justice or some other great good would be advanced by the shift, for example, meeting the needs of people in difficulty at the cost only of denying some people luxuries. But we do not need Gauthier's dual principles of benefit and concession for these purposes; and if we did, we would, again, not be in a position to use them.

A second way of using Gauthier's theory to guide at least incremental change, it might be suggested, is to point to features of s_1 that violate Gauthier's version of the Lockean proviso (Gauthier himself points to

South Africa; 7.1, 7.2) and thus justify a change to s_2, if in s_2 those features are removed without generating new violations. Indeed, that people now in privileged positions owe those positions to victimization of others in the past must, as things stand in the world (not only in South Africa), often be a very probable hypothesis. But here, at most, we have in hand one of the conditions on Gauthier's social contract, a condition which (though much more carefully worked out than is usual) is in no way distinctive of the theory. What is distinctive of the theory – the dual principles of minimax relative concession and maximin relative benefit – has no application.

IV

What lessons are to be drawn from this want of application? I think the chief lesson is that ethical theory should abandon the notions of utility and optimization. This is not an inductive lesson only, to be drawn after considering the range of efforts to use those notions, with Gauthier's the most sophisticated and rigorous. If philosophers ascribed more importance to application – to the possibility of application, less to sophistication and rigour – they might have learned the same lesson by reflecting that, early and late, the notions of utility and optimization have doomed utilitarianism to epistemological catastrophe. Compared with discovering maximum claims defined over all feasible social arrangements and then minimax relative concessions, it may look more practical to identify the utilities received by a given population in the alternative social states s_1 and s_2. In fact, this has never been done; one may be confident that it never will be done on any scheme of measurement, certainly not for *280* million people, or even *28* million. The optimum that ideal utilitarianism or ideal rule utilitarianism advocates lies at an even higher altitude, beyond this sublunary world, in a separate world of fantasy. Where utilitarianism may seem to work, it is giving way, like Gauthier's theory, to surrogates that do not presuppose it, like the belief that works of sanitary engineering meet certain basic needs. If choices in real politics ever became refined enough for exact information about the impact on people's utilities to make any difference, the information would be unavailable. Meanwhile, due concern with application of value considerations leads sharply and briskly away from utility and optimization to the surrogate principles. It is there that ethical theory can hope for real practical advances, first in understanding just what the surrogates amount to and then in seizing opportunities to improve them. This is the chief – ironic – lesson of utilitarianism. Gauthier teaches it better, precisely because of his superior virtuosity. If utility and optimization fail with him, in whose hands can they succeed? Does it follow that the two other themes on which Gauthier has achieved, however ironically, triumphs of sophistication – the idea of a social contract and the deduction project – must be abandoned, too? I do not think so. However, they are themes that we should learn to handle more modestly.

We must make do with a social contract like Locke's, designed simply to protect property rights under some effective definition. Or we must be content with a social contract on Rawls's lines, arrived at not in the original position but by agents who find his principles something that they can live with and settle for at least for the early stages of social reconstruction. (Rawls's agents do not reason about utility; they reason about primary goods, all of which, together with the incentives at issue with the Difference Principle, are matters within the reach of practical observation. Any advance that Gauthier has achieved over Rawls in pure theory is liable to be overshadowed by Rawls's enormous advantage in relevance.) There are other possibilities, for example, a social contract founded simply on upholding, to begin with, a Principle of Precedence for Matters of Need over matters of preference only.

We can pursue the deduction project simultaneously, but in every case it will be a deduction project governed by an unrefined conception of self-interest: one's property; one's liberties, opportunities, income, and power; one's needs. The principles that might reconcile interests so conceived under a social contract will be equally unrefined: uphold everybody's property rights; given equal liberties and fair equality of opportunity, distribute money income by the Difference Principle; heed anybody's preferences only insofar as it is consistent with meeting everybody's needs. Unrefined they may be, certainly unrefined in comparison with Gauthier's dual principles, but, unlike Gauthier's principles and like the principles (of which they are examples) that have served as surrogates for utilitarianism, they work as they stand.

They not only work as they stand and so get things done for us in social policy that we might well agree we want done. Such principles also offer in each case a ready and intelligible focus for their own improvement. If we have misgivings about protecting every bit of property currently held, however acquired, we might begin, without resorting to fantasies about tracing pedigrees of entitlement, to set some questionable categories of property aside, or we might reduce questionable accumulations by narrowing property rights short of inheritance. If we have the Difference Principle in hand, we may not only seek to join to it a more searching understanding of incentives; we may also adapt it to giving more egalitarian results once everyone in the population has become far too affluent to worry about meeting needs. (Those favourable circumstances, if they are ever reached, will be reached, let us suppose, by changing step by step from one social structure to another in order to come ever closer to realizing the Difference Principle.) If we are working with a Principle of Precedence for meeting needs, beginning with a brief list of basic needs and minimal provisions for them, we may, after realizing the principle so conceived, seek consent for expanding the list and amplifying the provisions.

In none of these cases do we have to beg, for purposes of the deduction project, any questions about moral concern, so long as we take the principles initially in hand as embracing just so many plausible ways of answering to self-interest and renounce any attempt (like Rawls's) to deduce them within a field of principles circumscribed by moral considerations. Each of the principles would offer agents who are merely self-interested some attractions, arguably enough to make belonging to a society contracting for the principle worthwhile. Moreover, a social contract based on any of the principles might be substantially as safe from attempts at self-interested violations by individual agents as a contract based (if it could be based) on more refined principles like Gauthier's. This safety might be doubly assured by making the contract depend on an understanding that the principle chosen will be subject, given consent, to revision and improvement as time goes on. And should not this understanding attach to the contract anyway? If the agents start, as they must, with unrefined principles, they will be wise to make specific allowance for improving the principles later.

Will improvement sooner or later inspire a transition from self-interest to moral concern? Whatever its want of practical application, Gauthier's perfect-information contract does show how a lot of what morality would prescribe may coincide with the results of a self-interested social contract. To infuse those results with moral concern, however, self-interest must be transcended or at least enlarged. One way of getting to moral concern, formally left open by Gauthier (1.2.3) though he does not rely on it, is to postulate (in the real world, to foster) an enlarged self-interest in which agents, in reckoning their self-interest, put a high value on having mutually sincere friendships. In the spirit of the deductive project, and of incremental practical improvement, one looks for a minimal postulate; this may suffice.

If it holds in association with a needs-based social contract, it will have the advantage of building on what is at least a close approach to moral concern. In accepting the terms of such a contract as they apply to other agents, every agent is not only accepting that the others' needs must be so far consulted if there is to be a contract. Every agent is also in effect accepting what mutual concern for needs requires morally: that they take precedence over every agent's mere preferences, including her own. To accept 'in effect' is not the same thing as accepting with moral concern. However, the acceptance is something that under the impulse of a recognized value on mutually sincere friendship may easily shift from being merely self-interested to being morally concerned. Some such impulse, some such shift, must occur if the deduction project is to connect with a full morality. It must occur, prompted by mutually sincere friendship or by 'free affectivity,' if an agent's attitude toward what I called above 'the injustice-disaffecting hypothesis,' when I mentioned finding it in *Morals by Agreement,* is to take on a genuine moral colouring. A social contract crude enough to be practical is in no worse position than Gauthier's to acquire the colouring.

With working moral principles – like the surrogate principles in familiar use – we can, as we must, follow the advice, formulated in several quarters but never more elegantly or profoundly expressed than by Herbert A. Simon,[14] to satisfice rather than optimize. With such principles, we satisfice in the choice of social policies – and of social structures, insofar as it is given to us to choose between social structures. We can also satisfice in respect to improving our principles. In accordance with Simon's formulation, repeated success with given principles – at first, relatively modest principles – properly leads to rises in our level of aspiration. Then we satisfice in choosing somewhat more exacting principles and satisfice again in applying them to the choice of social policies. The lesson about abandoning utility and optimization can be learned as a lesson about satisficing: the fanciest flights of ethical theory make no practical discoveries, and discover no practical advice. They teach us that satisficing is not a mere peripheral sport among comments on the theory of decision. It is an indispensable clue to understanding the human condition, the character of applicable moral principles, and the possibilities of moral improvement.

11

Comparisons of the Other Grand Programs, Especially Rawls's, with the Needs-Focused Combination Program

In the preceding chapters of this part, I have surveyed the grand programs of Rawls, Nozick, and Gauthier. Now I wish to compare them with each other and with the program of needs, rights, and well-considered rules – the needs-focused combination program, in comprehensiveness, in effect another grand program – arrived at earlier in this book by aggregating humbler free-standing analytical studies. I raise two questions: I ask of each program, first, can the program (that is to say, the principles that it offers for application to choices of policies) be understood by inexpert citizens? I ask, second, can it, so understood, be applied by inexpert citizens in real world politics, that is to say, to real political systems and the policies discussed and adopted in those systems? I take a very broad view of inexpert citizens, not only allowing for the fact that we are all inexpert citizens regarding most public policies, but also deliberately including people less educated and sometimes less mentally agile than average – people, for example, who dropped out of high school, but who can still follow the best arguments, sometimes reasonably good ones, offered amid the clutter of trivialities on the main television news shows.

This comparison will reduce very quickly to a comparison of Rawls's program with the needs-focused combination program. At the end of the chapter I shall prolong the comparison with Rawls's program to consider how far either program is capable of dealing with political turmoil.

It seems to me clear that Gauthier's program fails the tests of both these questions. What are even inexpert citizens more mentally agile than most to make of Gauthier's 'dual principles' of 'minimax relative concession' and 'maximin relative benefit?' Or of the optimum choice according to these principles of a social structure for the production and division of the cooperative surplus to which everybody who can contribute is expected to? Applying the maximin relative benefit principle, the optimum structure is one in which the maximin relative benefit (compared with what, varying from person to person, a given person would have in the absence of cooperation) received by anybody is no less than the maximin relative benefit received by anybody under any feasible alternative arrangement.[1] This is almost as hard to digest as the beautifully managed argument for it. (Coming back to Gauthier's argument after some twenty years, probably somewhat diminished in mental agility, but probably still above average in this respect, I find it requires strenuous thinking to appreciate it.)

(As we shall see in a moment, inexpert citizens may find Rawls's original position argument for the results embodied in his program somewhat difficult to understand, too. Yet by contrast with Gauthier, where both argument and results are difficult, Rawls's results are not difficult [and can be reached by arguments more straightforward than the original position argument].)

The imagination, logical ingenuity, and precision that invite admiration for Gauthier's program from philosophers stand in the way of inexpert citizens' understanding the argument that leads to Gauthier's results; and stand in the way, as well, more pertinent to answering my first question, of their understanding those results as principles for selecting policies. So Gauthier's program fails the first of my tests; but if a program fails the first test, it must also, by implication, fail the second test. This, of course, says nothing to derogate from Gauthier's philosophical achievement, which is to make the most refined case ever made for the philosophical hypothesis that an attractive ethics can be founded entirely on egoism (more exactly, in Gauthier's discussion, on *non-tuism*, something more liberal, which will take down egoism in its train). I think his case for relying on egoism (*non-tuism*) fails; it has nevertheless made an important permanent gain for understanding the relation between egoism and ethics.

Nozick's program passes the first test. Inexpert citizens understand already what property rights are, so far as they have to understand them to understand Nozick's program. They understand already how, other things being equal, labouring on something can justly establish property in it; they understand what it is to exchange (transfer) goods justly acquired. Nozick expresses his argument, and his results, with exemplary lucidity, as accessible to inexpert citizens as to experts. Where

Nozick's program fails, as he himself admits, is in answering the second test question. What has to be done in the way of establishing the pedigree of present holdings of private property is clear enough. They must be found to originate in past chains of just acquisitions. However, neither experts nor inexpert citizens have enough historical information, going back hundreds, perhaps thousands, of years, about past acquisitions and past transfers, to be able to establish the degree to which many, indeed most, maybe any present holdings are legitimate.

How do things stand in these connections with Rawls's grand program? The original position argument, taking everything about it into account (including, for example, its use of formal decision theory), does little better than Gauthier's on the test of being intelligible to inexpert citizens. However, Rawls has an advantage in respect to his results: the various aspects of liberty called for by the first principle are familiar to inexpert citizens and are substantially in their grasp; so is the Fair Equality of Opportunity Principle, both as things now are and as they might be after successive stages of modification aiming to make it more effective. The Difference Principle is not so familiar. What it calls for, both in theory and in application, is problematic, at least in respect to being sure what incentives it must offer more productive people. Yet, as I have said, and shall say again, some rough applications of the principle are intelligible enough.

Overall, therefore, in respect to the principles that emerge from it, Rawls's program seems to pass both tests. Moreover, if his original position argument does not pass the first test, there are alternative arguments – the argument about forestalling oppression, personal and political (given in the 'General Comment' in chapter 8 on Rawls); and an argument that Rawls himself offers (without granting it any explicit recognition as an alternative argument) in at least two passages of *A Theory of Justice*,[2] the argument, as I shall call it, from mutual accommodation. Rawls offers the argument in the course of explaining how the principles emerging from the original position offer the worse-off the satisfaction that higher returns in income go only to people who are increasing the incomes of the worse-off; while the people who are better off have, besides the willing cooperation of those worse-off, the satisfaction of special rewards for the exercise of more productive talents. We must add, in accordance with the discussion in the 'General Comment' in chapter 8, that those rewards enable them to keep up a style of life that transgenerationally benefits the worse-off. Here, I am amplifying what Rawls says, in the passage cited, by what I have made of Sharon

Lloyd's insistence[3] on the transgenerational character of the Difference Principle as Rawls intended it.

The beauties of the mutual accommodation argument may demand an illustration. Imagine a city in which the master artisans (who design the jewellery, the gold plate, the shoes, the pottery) have been at odds for years with the journeymen and apprentices (who make the artefacts designed) about shares in the income of the workshops. Someone proposes that they adopt what, in effect if not in name, is the Difference Principle. The masters will ask for no more in income to apply their talents for design than they reasonably deserve for efforts that raise the income of the journeymen and apprentices. The argument is that both sides will benefit, and benefit more than under any other stable agreement. Just how much more is problematic; perhaps a third party could be appointed whose income and position would depend on suggesting formulas acceptable to both sides.

I have extracted the mutual accommodation argument from a discussion of the original position. But the argument itself makes no reference to the original position. It stands on its own, with its own attractions. To be sure, philosophers may well think that ratifying it by the original position argument, as can be done, lends it greater strength. Inexpert citizens, however, may be content to leave the ratification to the philosophers; I shall join them in waiving the ratification when assessing the intelligibility and applicability of Rawls's argument, recast to rely on the mutual accommodation argument.

How effective are Rawls's principles in application? Effective enough, I think, to make important objections to present policies and drive social choices toward better ones. The Principle of Fair Equality of Opportunity, for example, applied transgenerationally, calls for periodic statistical evidence about changes in the representation in the specially skilled stratum of people originating at a different income level or having some specific difference in ethnic descent. There are some complications to take care of. Young people brought up in affluent households may not be so eager to train hard for professional careers (in engineering or medicine) as are young people in households not so affluent but more dedicated to the upward mobility of children. One might want to ask, were apparently less eager people given a clear chance to choose? Or perhaps recruitment to exacting professional careers should, for purposes of testing fair equality of opportunity, be lumped together with recruitment to other elite occupations like investment banking.

Period by period, the Difference Principle can be given effective application, even if it will never be as exact as it might be in theory. Certainly, it can make a broad cut into the present phenomena of income distribution and condemn the multimillion salaries going to film celebrities, star athletes, and – with perhaps even less justification, since the competition is less rigourous, or at least less unambiguously connected with performance – to American CEOs. No such salaries could be plausibly endorsed under the Difference Principle on the ground that they are no more than is required to bring about a certain increase in the money income of the least advantaged. (Nor, I expect, could the more modest but still ample salaries that Professors Rawls, Cohen, and Braybrooke have enjoyed. None of these salaries could plausibly be endorsed under one of the prerogatives identified by Cohen or Estlund or Lloyd.)

Redistribution from these salaries under the Difference Principle (and, as needed, to establish the conditions for exercising the liberties prescribed by Rawls's first principle[4]) would tend to assure the least advantaged of meeting their needs; and, beyond, to open up for them opportunities to carry out life-plans that accord with their conceptions of the good. The social minimum that Rawls would have guaranteed by 'the transfer branch' of government would figure here.

However, in respect to needs at least, Rawls calls, not only under these heads, for meeting them. The circumstances under which the original position is to be set up are circumstances in which needs are met to the extent of making people loath to give up liberties in return for increases in material income. The shift from the general conception of justice, in which such trade-offs are allowed, to the special conception of justice as a set of lexically ordered principles, chosen in the original position, presupposes that the basic needs (and maybe some less basic) have been met, and will continue to be met, for the people who are to live under the principles.

In work, the book *Political Liberalism*, later than *A Theory of Justice* Rawls even embraces 'a lexically prior principle of meeting basic needs.'[5] He does so in a rather perfunctory way, disregarding any conceptual difficulties presented by the concept of basic needs.[6] For example, he does not take up the tendency of economists to reject the concept; or consider the common, widespread abuses of the concept that give some grounds for this tendency.[7] He does not consider whether the presupposition about having needs met that figures in the setting up of the original position; whether this presupposition might make a lexically prior principle for needs redundant. Moreover, though in adopting this principle about needs he is responding to Rodney Peffer,[8] who would have the principle chosen in the original position, Rawls makes little more of its claim to attention in the original position than to use the phrase 'lexically prior.' Peffer argues that the presupposition is not explicit enough to be relied on; and he wants to have meeting needs unconditionally guaranteed. Rawls may be ready to accept both points, but in the discussion that follows in *Political Liberalism* of the principles chosen in the original position, the principles do not include any principle of lexical priority for needs. The principles that he continually treats are the same two (three) principles as in *A Theory of Justice*;[9] and in treating them, he continually works, not with the notion of basic needs, but with the notion of primary goods, where 'income' brings in a reference to basic needs only indirectly at best. Rawls does refer several times to the presupposition that basic needs are being met; and at one place he gives this presupposition the handsome honour of implying (through the place given to 'adequate all-purpose means') an essential place for it in 'the political conception of justice,' of which his own principles, he says, are just one alternative set among many. He never, however, examines basic needs or recognizes anything problematical about them.

Nevertheless, it is easy to see how argumentation in the original position could lead to the principle about needs. Agents concerned there to make sure that their condition, whatever it turns out to be once the veil of ignorance has been lifted, is reasonably acceptable, will look with favour on the idea of making sure that their needs are met; and (like Peffer) they might not want to rely on having them met by a presupposition that does not figure on the agenda of the original position or under other principles that do. What harm would it do, anyway, to spell out the priority of meeting them?

However, in my eyes, an argument running through the original position does not take the most desirable route to giving priority to basic needs. Any argument in the original position appeals only to the rational grounds that *non-tuistic* agents have for choosing principles. I would rather appeal immediately to something that in Rawls's scheme can figure only as a consideration in the search for reflective equilibrium, after the results of argument in the original position have been established, namely, to the moral sentiment – compassion – that arises in morally sensitive people given the spectacle of people denied provisions for their basic needs. (It is a test and a defining feature of 'morally sensitive.') The spectacle will strike such people as especially unseemly if they see side by side with the people so deprived other people, in a position to help them and even under an obligation to do so, who are enjoying luxuries.

In the mutual accommodation argument, the reliance on *non-tuistic* attitudes persists. Thus, even in this connection, what I would do about needs and the Principles of Justice is turn Rawls's emphasis upside down: first, after carefully identifying needs and adequate provisions for them, have people insist on policies that meet these needs for everybody; then, look for and act upon principles for distributing any resources that remain. (In practice, these things might go on simultaneously, so long as it was understood that if the program for distributing surplus resources begins interfering with provisions for basic needs, the program will slow down for the time being.)

The principles for distribution would not necessarily be Rawls's principles. On the other hand, Rawls's principles would be strong candidates for adoption, for the reasons that Rawls gives in the original position argument and in the mutual accommodation argument, for the reasons advanced in the argument from oppression, and maybe for other reasons. In a number of places (beginning with discussion in *Meeting Needs*[10]; again in *Utilitarianism: Restorations; Repairs; Renovations*[11]) I have contemplated adding Rawls's principles as supplements to any program of meeting needs, including now the needs-focused combination program.

Moreover, there are a number of features of the census-notion, of which that program makes so much use, that could be justified, if justifying them were called for, by arguments in the original position. The very idea that, stage by stage, the number of people in lower census-categories should be reduced and the number of people in higher categories increased would appeal, so far as it goes, to agents in the original position. It offers only slightly different grounds from the grounds in Rawls's scheme for giving priority to the returns received by the least-advantaged stratum. Another feature is the condition (expressed in part by the Gains-Preservation Principle) that, other things being equal, people should not be ejected from a higher census-category while others are being elevated into it or beyond. (Certainly, this should not be done merely to get greater numbers of people in higher categories – a better census-result in the sense in which a mere increase in the total quantity of happiness would be a better overall score.) This, too, is something that agents in the original position may be expected to want to make sure of.

Respecting these features of the census-notion amounts to heeding so many points of justice. Moreover, questions about justice arise under the other main heads of the program of needs, rights, and well-considered rules. Respecting rights accords with justice. Ignoring them or violating them are instances of injustice. (I am assuming agreement on the content of the rights at issue.) It is unjust, relying on conformity by others to a well-considered rule not to do one's part in the actions or forbearances called for. It is unjust, for example, to enjoy a water supply drinkable only because everyone else, or almost everyone else, is refraining from dumping waste into, and to pay no attention oneself to the rule about refraining. In other words, acting as a free rider is unjust. Justice is not the paramount feature of the needs-focused combination program, but it has many footholds there; together they may support all the aspects of justice that Rawls's program does. Even the Difference Principle may fall under my program as a well-considered rule.

What significant difference in ease of application remains, then, between Rawls's grand program and the needs-focused combination program? It is to be recalled, the differences that we are looking for are differences in their ready intelligibility to the inexpert citizens of a democracy, and in their ready application.

Here something might be made of the plausible suggestion that inexpert citizens would more readily understand the program of needs, rights, and well-considered rules if they are brought to it by an appeal to moral sentiment – to their compassion. The appeal of the program will connect their understanding with points familiar to them. This suggestion thus disfavours Rawls's program on the issue at hand.

Another disfavouring argument would hold that by not requiring acceptance of any overall social structure (like the structure of mutual accommodation) the combination program of needs, rights, and well-considered rules more easily wins general agreement. It wins the agreement piecemeal, issue by issue, and need by need, right by right, rule by rule.

However, let us concentrate on comparative intelligibility. Take Rawls's program to consist of (first) a lexically prior principle about meeting needs and (second) the two (three) Principles of Justice that early and late he argues for combined (third) with the mutual accommodation argument. All of these things, I am ready to acknowledge, are as intelligible if not so familiar to inexpert citizens as anything in the needs-based combination program. How is the latter superior in being intelligible to Rawls's program, so expressed?

I do not think that it is superior in intelligibility. However, it has never been my aim in aggregating my free-standing studies in a grand program to produce a program superior to Rawls's on the point of intelligibility or any other point. I was not giving any close attention to Rawls's program when I put it together; all that I am claiming to do, when I bring Rawls's program into the picture, is to produce a program comparable to his, if not in the grandeur of elevated vision, at least in comprehensiveness and practical attractions. That is enough to vindicate my studies in analytical political philosophy in respect to being able to aggregate them in something like a grand program.

That being said, I may maintain, notwithstanding, that my program has certain features to recommend it that Rawls's does not. Rawls's program has many fine things in it, which may give it comparable or superior recommendatory force, if not in respect to ready intelligibility, then in bearing on fundamental moral issues. It does not, however, offer a careful clarificatory analysis of the concept of needs and a construction freeing it of abuses. Nor does it offer a clarificatory analysis of the concept of rights. It does not offer, what is philosophically essential to understanding rights, a clarificatory analysis of the concept of rules. All of these concepts Rawls uses, perhaps for his purposes effectively enough, with the implicit assumption that he shares correct intuitions about them with his readers. Rawls also omits any attempt, in analytical discussion, to identify an adequate practice for dealing with consequences. Yet the application of his principles over time will require – just as much as the application of the needs-focused combination program, a practice of dealing stage by stage with the consequences of attempts to apply them.

All these things are present in the needs-focused combination program.

As I said, toward the end of the keystone chapter (chapter 6), which has guided my work on the present book, the idea of putting my free-standing studies together in one combination program had not occurred to me before I found myself putting them together in this book. The principle that may be said to have driven them all is to give inexpert citizens (that is to say, all of us as regards most questions of politics) confidence that concepts and procedures familiar to them are adequate for deciding ultimate questions in politics. Where would democracy be if this were not so? I mean, moreover, to give this confidence, if not straightaway in the reading of this book, then in patient discussion that the book might generate, part by part, to just about the whole variety of inexpert citizens, including the less educated and the less mentally agile. (Just give me some turns with the sorts of groups collected by deliberative opinion polls.[12]) Experts of one sort or another have cast elaborate doubts on the concepts in question. Inexpert citizens themselves have had conceptual misgivings about needs and about rights. In my view, however, the experts do not in the end win the day. A firmly analytical approach to political philosophy puts the experts in their place, often a place with only marginal relevance to real politics.

The sort of political discussions that I have been assuming up to this point in this chapter are discussions carried on in relatively calm circumstances, in which all the political institutions are functioning normally. There are circumstances, however, in which, it may be thought, none of the grand programs that I have considered is grand enough, in which great evils create political turmoil and urgently call for political actions that displace and transcend incrementalist, meliorative politics, which is just the sort of politics that I have associated (in the keystone chapter, above) with the needs-focused combination program. Many of them are evils impinging on the state from outside. An enemy armed to the teeth threatens an attack. A network of terrorists threatens multiple sorts of destruction in the homeland. A bellicose regime abroad seems on the point of acquiring weapons of mass destruction. Some of the evils, however, arise within domestic politics. A flood or a tsunami washes over a large part of the country. The whole country suffers a lethal epidemic of influenza. A militant nationalist movement or religious movement threatens to take over the government and abolish (at least for certain people) its more humane features, including those that safeguard rights and liberty.

Suspension of incrementalist politics is a different thing from suspension of the needs-based combination program. The emergency arises (or is purported to arise) precisely from the jeopardy in which it puts provisions for one or another of the needs that figure in the grand program. People will not have water or food or shelter or clothing (kulaks not shot out of hand were stripped to their underwear and beyond during the repressions of the 1920s and 1930s). Maybe everything that they need to go on living is in jeopardy. So far, the needs-focused combination program will not have been suspended. It will have acquired a dramatic focus, in several ways: concentration on some needs (first aid, food, shelter); urgent attention to the needs concentrated on. (The program and the focus may not be heeded; the emergency does not therefore vanish.)

But what about incrementalist politics? Can action wait on the processes of incrementalist politics? People will often (sometimes mistakenly) accept it without argument that there will not be time to wait for the Revisionary Process to refine policies, round by round, and round by round eliminate unnecessary costs and mistakes. They will accept the insistence by some political leaders that to avert an enormous evil, bold action – a massive response – is called for.

The insistent assertion that incrementalist politics must be left behind may come forward in the filmy but dirty garments of an illusion, the illusion that the emergency will require dropping everything but the massive response, leaving no room for any other activity, or any other politics. But the idea of departing from incrementalist politics may arouse immediate resistance. Did suspicions, to some degree plausible, that Iraq had weapons of mass destruction in hand or was on the way to acquiring them, justify an invasion? In this case, there was the alternative of continuing the regime of international sanctions with stepped-up inspections. It was argued at the time, and argued again afterwards, that these measures were keeping in check the ambitions of Iraq in weapons development. Very likely, if the ambitions were to be laid to rest, additional measures would have had to be taken, including measures to remove Saddam Hussein, his sons, and his cronies from positions of power. Many of these measures, like further increasing the frequency and scope of inspections or modulating sanctions, could have been incremental. I do not know if all could have been incremental, but increasing the threat of military action (which lent powerful and indispensable support to the inspections) and broadening under the United Nations the coalition of countries ready to take action could have been accomplished, I think, in incremental steps.

The departure from incrementalist politics, if it does occur, may be real but temporary. Sooner or later, other activities, and decisions about them that can be fitted into incrementalist politics, will have to resume. The city's defenders will have to be supplied with drinking water and food; almost as urgently, heating and lighting will have to be taken care of. Maybe it will only be much later that there can be general public discussions of the policies that are to take care of such things. Meanwhile, there will nevertheless be discussions among officials already assigned responsibilities or assuming responsibilities; and the discussions will extend to include the people served, not only in registering complaints, but also in other matters, like the scheduling of supplies. So long as the emergency does not destroy the community – Baghdad sacked by the Golden Horde – its continuing in being will bring back the business with which incrementalist politics and the program of needs, rights, and well-considered rules must also deal. I do not say, complacently, that this business and incrementalist politics will surely come back. The turmoil may be too great to cope with. Emergency measures taken to cope, when coping is possible, may become permanent drawbacks to ordinary politics. One can only say that the drawbacks are far from being inevitable.

Not all of these measures that are proposed are sure to be accepted, even temporarily. People may immediately reject what they deem unnecessary suspensions of rights. In favourable cases, efforts will come forth to keep the processes going through which the needs-focused program will reach fruition; and even, once the requirements for bold actions are allowed for, to improve delivery of the goods at issue in the program. Britain in wartime did not cease to care for the nutrition of poor children; on the contrary, where possible it substituted means (rosehip syrup for orange juice) and in some cases improved the provisions (poor children got better nutrition during the war than before). Many government policies will be carried over from the situations preceding the emergency; and in the interstices of these policies incremental improvements can be sought.

If the response to the emergency does set aside or override resistance associated with items in the grand program, in a healthy political system and minimally favourable circumstances there will be people and groups to bring up the points of resistance again after the response has got firmly underway. A Department of Homeland Security will be set up, along with legislation restricting rights, for example, giving the police broad powers to arrest people, immigrants or citizens, on suspicion; but the right to be brought before a court to hear the grounds for arrest will be restored soon afterwards (as the United States Supreme Court, 'conservative' as it already is in tendency, did even for 'enemy combatants'). A narrow definition of 'torture' will be adopted that disregards, outside the scope of the definition, cruel, inhuman methods of interrogating prisoners; but after the event, unfavourable public reactions may compel return to a broader definition. This is incrementalist politics working after the event.

What about the domestic turmoil generated by militant nationalist or religious movements? Once they have seized power and installed an authoritarian state, a form of fascism, a form of communism, or a theocracy, drastic restrictions on discussion may curtail the room for incrementalist, meliorative politics, which implies ample room for discussion. (Consider, in particular, how a healthy Revisionary Process takes up criticisms of all kinds from all quarters.)

Even before such movements have seized power and curtailed any discussion that might lead to opposition to its policies, the pursuit of the needs-focused combination program (or Rawls's or any other) through incrementalist, meliorative politics may be blocked. The militants in the movements may prefer street fighting and inflammatory mass meetings. They may simply shout down efforts to gain new attention for unrealized points in any grand program, or in the needs-focused combination program in particular, whether or not they pretend themselves to be taking care of all such matters. Will pale, mild, ineffectual dons be any better at dealing with bullies like these than the good-hearted ladies of church auxiliaries?

Here, it seems to me, critics of the grand programs slip into another illusion, which in effect pictures people propounding a body of ideas (philosophical teachings) confronting people using physical force or threatening to use it. The power that the militant movements rely on, before or after seizing the state, may be the power to intimidate or to liquidate critics. This is not the power of ideas. The champions of any grand or comprehensive program will be at a disadvantage in confronting such power if they do not organize their own power to keep the peace. But they can often do this. Even when they cannot, this does not imply being at a disadvantage in the conflict of ideas. The power of ideas is an entirely different matter from the power to exert or resist brute force. Only in an illusion would anyone think successful resistance to brute force by the proponents of a grand program a reasonable or even an intelligible test of the power of their ideas.

Yet there is a sense in which it might be contended that the needs-based combination program lacks the strength that may be essential in confrontations with the militants like those mentioned. Are its ideas, however meritorious from a moral point of view, exciting enough to rally adherents for strenuous, protracted struggles? The militants rally under the banner of deeply moving myths: myths about the heritage and destiny of the German race, about the historical mission of the proletariat, about the onset of Raptures, Tribulation, Armageddon, the Second Coming, Judgment Day. These ideas vividly colour not only the outlook but the lives of believers. Can the needs-focused combination program offer anything with the colour and excitement to counter this? In comparison with these world-historical myths, the word 'grand' may seem especially out of order, to its cost.

'Grand' may be in place, however, with programs less than cosmic, wholly secular, and without any special beliefs about historical destiny. The needs-based combination program that I have assembled from ideas in the free-standing studies, can claim, after all, to be in grand company: the Common Good, Community, World Community, the Community of Mankind.[13] The idea of Community should not be left in racist or ethnic hands, but the Nazis showed with *Volksgemeinschaft* what power the idea of community can lend to political efforts. The European Community uses the term, quite free of racist implications or ethnic connections; in Italy and other countries its flag is flown proudly next to the national flag.

The needs-focused combination program can be embodied in a document, indeed, as set forth in chapter 6, a very brief document, not much longer than the American Pledge of Allegiance to the Flag; no longer, even if there is a clause added to give it (as I would wish) international scope. It is for social psychologists, not me, to say whether the program as set forth could acquire anything like the revered multifaceted status of the United States Constitution; but the example of the Constitution does show that a document can be continually resorted to for criteria to guide public policy (not always in enlightened directions; but that may be only a contingent failing). The Constitution is so invoked, both in the courts and by members of the public, to forestall excessive, order-threatening, or freedom-threatening militancy. More than that: it has been portrayed by historians as the principal source, along with the Declaration of Independence, of a commonly felt American identity (the Pledge of Allegiance, of course, is another). The needs-focused combination program aims at more cosmopolitan allegiances, but the examples of the European Community and the Christian Church show that allegiances of this kind are perfectly practical, though they are often diminished by nationalistic attachments to particular countries.

The Church puts a lot of weight upon pageantry; maybe the European Community will develop pageantry, too. (On the political importance of pageantry and ceremonies there are insights of Rousseau to invoke.) The needs-focused combination program does not have to forgo pageantry, or let the streets be taken over by irrational militants. If marching about to the stirring music of brass bands is wanted, the

Salvation Army, unwilling to concede that 'the devil has all the best tunes,' has shown the way. Sir Arthur Sullivan's 'Onward, Christian Soldiers' more than matches the Horst Wessel Song.[14] Of course, the Salvation Army had a message about the Christian religion to propagate, but there is a significant intersection between the message of Christianity and the needs-focused combination program. (Consider 'Love thy neighbour' applied straightforwardly, for example, in the practice of the Salvation Army.)

None of these ideas do more than suggest that the needs-focused combination program has a chance of competing in conviction with noisier militant movements, while it avoids the evils that may come in the train of militancy. But this is not a chance that should be forfeited faint-heartedly.

AN EPILOGUE TO THE BOOK AND TO THE FOUR-BOOK SERIES THAT IT BRINGS TO AN END: TWO OLDER GRAND PROGRAMS

Prefatory Note to Part Five

In this Epilogue, I bring not only the present book to an end, but also the series of four books in which the preceding three have been *Moral Objectives, Rules, and the Forms of Social Change* (1998); *Natural Law Modernized* (2001); *Utilitarianism: Restorations; Repairs; Renovations* (2004). All published, like this book, by University of Toronto Press, they form a mutually reinforcing ensemble in which all the topics that have most preoccupied me in philosophy figure substantially; hence, together, if it were not a bit antique and a bit pretentious, they might claim the title that I mentioned in the Introduction: *Summa Philosophica Latirivuli.* Insisting on my little joke, that is what I shall call the ensemble anyway. Given the somewhat surprising presence in the ensemble of both a book favourable to natural law theory and a book favourable to utilitarianism, it is fitting that I should explain at the end of the series how in my view these two lines of thought are related. In doing so, I also wind up the present book by presenting two more grand programs in political philosophy that have won sustained attention from analytical political philosophers. This is a true statement, even if the number of analytical political philosophers who have reflected on utilitarianism and championed it far surpasses the number of analytical political philosophers who have championed natural law theory (at any rate, championed it under that name). I number among both; I have little company in the latter connection. But this does not mean that I am misguided in being there.

12

The Relation of Utilitarianism to Natural Law Theory

I

At first glance, especially if we have in mind the history of utilitarianism as it has descended from Bentham, it must seem that the relation of utilitarianism to natural law theory is adversarial. Philosophers will think of Bentham's scorn for natural rights ('nonsense on stilts'[1]) and its backing in the disparaging references to natural law in his review of alternatives to utilitarianism.[2] Moreover, is not utilitarianism a secular doctrine, in which God plays no part, and natural law theory a religious one, in which God's part is indispensable?

Yet whatever we make of Bentham's scorn, the doctrines are not opposed on this point. For the most part forgotten now, the name of William Paley may still have, besides some resonance as a proponent of the argument from design, a resonance, though fainter, as a proponent of a Christian utilitarianism, which sprang up in his writings and in the writings of others at about the same time as Bentham's *Principles*.[3]

Moreover, more important, at its core natural law theory is a secular doctrine, as it was for St Thomas as well as for Hobbes, Locke, Rousseau, and Hume.[4] Hume is the key author. To class Hume as a natural law theorist as well as what he is more commonly ranked, a utilitarian or proto-utilitarian, will astonish many students of philosophy. Commonly, the passages in which he seems emotivist in tendency get undue weight, even in comparison to the passages in which he approaches being a utilitarian. They commonly quite overshadow the central passages in which 'correct' and 'incorrect' figure as analogues of 'true' and 'false,' indeed as surrogates for them. The passages in which he ascribes 'true' and 'false' themselves to moral judgments get forgotten entirely. If all these various passages get the weight that they deserve,[5] Hume takes on the defining characteristics of a moral realist, which he has to be in order to be a natural law theorist. However, he does more than meet this necessary condition. He says (even if he is speaking ironically) that what he is propounding on the subject of justice are natural laws.[6] They are established as such by what is visibly an entirely secular argument, in which he makes no mention of God and draws no inference from God's will.

All the other authors do have God present in the perspective in which they set forth their natural law theories; but for none of them is any professed inference from the will of God indispensable to arriving at the content of natural law. One does not need to think about God to identify the social rules that foster the thriving of human societies and of the people who belong to them. When St Thomas cites Cicero on the *utilitas* (mark that word!) of the natural laws,[7] he comes close to this position.

Bringing imperative force behind that content is another matter. Only Hume is entirely clear about God's not needing to be invoked in this connection,[8] either, though Hobbes, in substance if not in form, comes close. Indeed, insisting that laws must have a lawgiver, and invoking God as such, may bring more trouble than help.

God is traditionally called upon not only to give the laws but also to enforce them. At least one theistically inclined natural law theorist of the present day holds that AIDS is God's punishment for defying the natural law for sexual activity. This theorist acknowledges that the punishment is not certain; and that it may be delayed by a generation or two. He does not seem troubled by the gross disproportion between the savagery of the punishment and the trivial nature of the offence, for example, putting one's weenie in an unauthorized place, when there are no complications about consent or age of consent. (This description is tendentious, I think, only by the use of the disrespectful term, 'weenie,' instead of, say, 'the male organ of generation,' a term that may be substituted for neutral effect.) The theorist in question is not troubled enough by the many innocent women and children who have shared the punishment.[9] It has not occurred to him, furthermore, that if people can avoid AIDS, and the punishment, by practising safe sex, whatever sexual activities they engage in, God, in providing this means of escape, seems to be prohibiting, not various deviant forms of sexual activity, but only the unsafe practice of them.

Believers might not regard these considerations as undermining trust in God as lawgiver and law-enforcer. Who are we to question the wisdom of God? Believers might cite God's answer to Job: 'Where were you when I laid the foundation of the earth ... [where were you] when the morning stars sang together and all heavenly beings shouted for joy?' (Job 38: 4–7) Magnificently eloquent. But how helpful? Better for religion, I think, to keep God out of the punishment business, and the aggravation that it brings to the problem of evil. If you are going to attribute to God the will to punish, you cannot avoid inviting questions about punishments that seem unwise and unjust.

Hume holds that the natural law as a matter of moral obligation rests on human beings' perception that adherence to the natural laws fosters thriving; and on the feeling of normal human beings, sharing this perception, that thriving in this and other instances is something to approve. Hume holds that people's commitment to the obligation on the basis of shared perception and feeling, not the will of God, is what is indispensable; and it suffices to give a robust answer to the question about imperative force. The law is a law that people give themselves, an idea now, with the spread of democracy in recent centuries, entirely familiar. It was an idea not entirely unknown in earlier epochs. St Thomas explicitly allows for it: human laws (through which the natural laws come to bear, as they are expected to bear, in established communities) are adopted either by the people of the community (often settling in as customs) or by their delegate. If we follow Hume in this connection, we have a natural law theory that is secular both in respect to the content of the social rules required for thriving and in respect to the imperative force behind them.[10] This is a natural law theory that clearly might have congenial relations, rather than adversarial ones, with a secular utilitarianism.

God might be brought back, after the content of the natural law has been established by reference to thriving, and even after imperative force has been given a secular basis, and said to endorse the overall system; and to supply a sort of answer to the question how human beings have had the wit and the inclination to hit upon it. But God might be brought back in the same way, for those who wish for His presence, to endorse utilitarianism. In neither case should believers lightly assume that bringing Him back is an advantage in getting people to accept the theory. For many people it will be, at best, an idle gesture; at worst, a stumbling-block.

II

If the relation between utilitarianism and natural law theory is not adversarial, what is it? How far do they go together? Where do they pull apart (and so become liable in the end to being to some extent opposed)? I shall emphasize three points: the comparative looseness of natural law theory, which is (especially from the point of view of utilitarianism) a mixed virtue; the insistent sociality of natural law theory, going deeper on this point than utilitarianism; the deeper commitment of natural law theory to common purposes in an established community.[11]

To get to these points, however, I must say something about familiar objections to utilitarianism, which, seeming not to apply to natural law theory, would make out other important points of difference. They do not make out points of difference, either because they fail against utilitarianism quite as much as they fail against natural law theory or because, when utilitarianism is repaired to meet the objections, it moves closer to natural law theory.

One familiar objection is that utilitarianism permits, even requires, the sacrifice on some occasions of some people's lives simply to make the lives of some other people happier or simply to extend their lives beyond their naturally assigned spans. But this objection can be refuted, again without departure from the original intentions of utilitarianism, by granting utilitarianism an elementary statistical point. The comparison of the whole group of people before the sacrifice of the lives of some with the whole group diminished by just the people who have been sacrificed is statistically irrelevant. It is not the same group that has a higher aggregative happiness score afterwards that had a lower score beforehand; it is not that group with whom there was initial concern, not that group whose condition has improved.

To deal with the related objection that utilitarianism may require, short of permitting or requiring the sacrifice of lives, painful sacrifices from some people simply to make other people happier (or happier still) we do best to move from associating utilitarianism with the felicific calculus to associating it with the notion of comparative censuses. In spite of repeated efforts on my part to make the census-notion a household idea in the discussion of utilitarianism, I do not think I can assume that it has become so. I shall pause to recall how it works, which means recalling how it has been working in everyday practice all along, sometimes with happiness, more often with other considerations.

Consider the two following tables as results of comparative censuses carried out on a population or sample of 100 people:

Table I (also Table III)			Table II		
Policies	A	B		A	B
Steadily Provided For	20	30	Steadily Provided For	20	30
Sometimes Provided For	20	20	Sometimes Provided For	30	10
Never Provided For	60	50	Never Provided For	50	60

'Provided For' may mean 'Happiness Provided For' or 'Provided For in Respect to One of the Conditions of Being Happy.' Table I shows a clear improvement on changing from Policy A (maybe last year's policy) to Policy B (this year's). But the censuses might have a mixed result like Table II; and even Table I may be a mixed result in a concealed way: some of the people now 'Never Provided For' used to be, say, 'Sometimes Provided For' or even better off before the change in policy. Let Table I stand for this possibility as Table III.

Shifting to the census-notion from the calculus is a repair to received utilitarian doctrine, but it is a repair authorized by the traditional slogan, 'The Greatest Happiness of the Greatest Number.' The slogan has been felt to be an embarrassment by those utilitarians aware that it gives contradictory advice on occasions when the Greatest Happiness, taken as a sum over the whole group of people affected, lies in one direction, and the happiness of the Greatest Number in another.[12] The calculus, which is commonly presupposed by writers on utilitarianism as effective in principle, encourages people to resolve the ambiguity of the slogan in favour of the aggregative score and lets go of the Greatest Number, with the distributive consideration that it signifies. The census-notion makes good sense of both parts of the slogan. It accords with the Greatest Happiness in favouring movement from lower categories to higher ones; it accords with the Greatest Number in favouring having more people in the top categories. Furthermore, it resists sacrificing some people's happiness to other people's by refusing to support unqualified endorsement of such changes. Instead, it poses a problem for the Revisionary Process ubiquitously present in real-world politics about inventing another policy that does not require such sacrifices. Both Table II and Table III pose such problems; they invite operation of the Revisionary Process and they direct its course – to find a way of improving the lot of the people put at a disadvantage.

I think the distinction that I have just drawn between the (almost always only projected) use of the calculus and the (familiar, everyday) use of the census-notion is fundamentally correct, but it is put too simply. (As it is in the discussion, a little too exuberant, on the same topic in my book *Utilitarianism: Restorations; Repairs; Renovations*.[13]) As Richmond Campbell has pointed out to me, in principle, the calculus could be used, like the census-notion, in a process that would not settle for a higher aggregative score when this was not accompanied by having as many people happy at a given level of utility as there were to begin with, or more. The process might also reject results that made some people unhappy (lowered their personal utility scores) who had been happy previously. In both cases, people invoking the calculus might call for the Revisionary Process to operate. Considerations of principle do not exclude using the calculus in a way parallel to the use of the census-notion. But this is not a possibility that the proponents of the calculus have exploited, or even recognized, in the absence of any consideration of the census-notion. Their idea of how the calculus was to be used has stood in sharp contrast with the idea that I have developed about how the census-notion is to be.

Shifting to the census-notion can also be motivated by the fact that utilitarianism, in the absence, which continues to the present day, of a practically applicable calculus for utilities, has had what influence it has had on social policy through surrogates like provisions for food, housing, bodily security, and employment that are tracked by the census-notion. The shift from the calculus to the census moves closer to natural law theory, not just by moving away from gratuitous sacrifices, but by opening the way to taking into account the distribution of consequences for such surrogates, which in natural law theory have a visible place. A community cannot thrive without meeting the needs of the people who belong to it.

A third familiar objection to utilitarianism arises as much if it is associated with the census-notion as with the calculus. The objection decries the supposed tendency of utilitarianism to undermine moral rules like the rules about promise-keeping and truth-telling. If one can in any given instance get away with violating the rule and violating it will actually lead to an unqualified increase in happiness, why not go for it? Giving way to such considerations would amount to treating the rules about promise-keeping and truth-telling as no more than rules of thumb, which can be set aside whenever doing so looks more attractive. If giving way is allowed, or at least if it becomes very common, no one will be able to rely on the rules any longer. The promise that a utilitarian made to you will not prevent her from looking for better things to do when the time comes.

However, as is now widely understood, utilitarianism may be given a rule-utilitarian cast that supports adhering to the rules even in circumstances where acting against them in those circumstances would have happier consequences (not only for the agent) than adhering to them. Those special circumstances can be lumped in the case of any given rule with the whole range of circumstances over a long run of time in which an issue arises about following the rule; and to obtain the greatest happiness over the whole range of circumstances agents must be held to the rule without exceptions. Hume's example of an industrious farmer returning property to a seditious bigot is a famous case in point.

If it is suspected that rule-utilitarianism is a departure from utilitarianism in its original intentions, one might recall that Bentham's *Principles* concerns itself as much or more with laws as with personal actions[14] – laws or rules that are to hold over many different occasions. It is quite in keeping with the utilitarian tradition to contemplate (as Richard Brandt,[15] among others, has contemplated) having an ideal set of rules that makes the most of opportunities for happiness. But then we arrive at the centre of natural law theory, which holds that the purpose of the set of natural laws is to promote the thriving of communities – the thriving of the people who belong to the communities, and the thriving along with their thriving of the communities. Is not natural law theory perhaps just a variant of ideal-set rule-utilitarianism, or vice versa?

III

I think the answer is 'No,' and I begin with the mixed virtue that natural law theory has of being a looser theory. My remarks, unless notice is given to the contrary, will apply equally to an ideal-set utilitarianism associated with the calculus as to one associated with the census-notion (see below). They will also apply equally to theistic natural law theory, current and past, and to the version secularized and shorn of various excrescences having to do with sex as well as with women and slavery, which under the name of 'Natural Law Modernized' I prefer. Natural law theory in both versions shares with utilitarianism a remarkable fecundity. William Shaw describes utilitarianism as requiring 'a very small number of ethical assumptions, [which] yield a powerful but structurally simple normative theory, capable of unifying our under-standing of a diverse range of ethical phenomena.'[16] The power that is shared includes the power (by invoking human thriving) to resolve conflicts between particular received moral rules, the job that both Mill and Sidgwick thought had to be done by utilitarianism.[17] But natural law theory is much more present oriented, concerned to make the most of the rules that currently prevail. It supports rules that it recognizes are susceptible of improvement, and it may even support them against introducing the improvements for the time being and in present cir-cumstances. Thus, St Thomas cautions that changing the rules is likely to be socially upsetting; in many cases it will be better to go along with imperfect rules rather than invite the upset.[18]

Natural law theory, moreover, is much more actively concerned with preventing social upset and with having rules that operate against patent dangers to thriving than with finding an optimum set of rules. One sign of this is the absence in St Thomas's writings of any attempt to work out in detail an axiomatic system of the natural laws, in spite of various allusions to deduction that he makes and might have capital-ized on in this connection. He does not really have a systematic vision of an ideal set of rules.

Moreover, if we shift from calculus to census, an ideal-set rule-utilitarianism will still be preoccupied with happiness – maybe with utility still, measured under some scheme of measurement like von Neumann's and Morgenstern's, which, in spite of not supporting addi-tions of utility over different persons,[19] can be used for the limited sorts of interpersonal comparisons required by a comparative census. (Thus, we could establish census-categories for people experiencing increases or decreases in their personal utility-scores.) Natural law theory, on the other hand, would incline to invoke the census to deal with surrogates for utility or happiness – with provisions for food, clothing, housing, employment, education.

Has utilitarianism been left behind? Certainly, the distinctive goal of utilitarianism to reduce the evaluation of consequences (including as-pects of the actions themselves) to one simple uniform measure that would settle all questions of morals and legislation has been aban-doned. We have arrived a much looser – a much untidier – position, to which natural law theory is more congenial than utilitarianism. On the other hand, the goal to be achieved with the calculus was not the only distinctive goal of utilitarianism. Another distinctive goal was to insist that statistics about consequences for all the human beings (nay, all the sentient beings) affected should be brought in to govern actions, in particular, the actions of lawmaking. With the census-notion, we are still insisting upon this goal and, in doing so, making a congenial amplification of natural law theory on a point that it has traditionally for the most part left only implicit.

IV

Insofar as utilitarianism, including ideal-set rule-utilitarianism, associated either with the calculus or with the census-notion, supports and draws upon social sentiments and feelings of solidarity – which it is ready,[20] even compelled, to do, since otherwise it can hardly count on people being motivated to accept and act on it – utilitarianism runs hand in hand with natural law theory. However, it does not go so far. For utilitarianism will treat – perhaps at some cost in motivation – social sentiments and feelings of solidarity as contingent sources of pleasure; and it will downgrade them or set them aside if other sources are more productive. Without getting to the point of approving of Nozick's conception of people hooked up individually to pleasure-machines (cited by Shaw[21]), utilitarianism would approve of arrangements in which social intercourse, not to speak of social sentiments and feelings of solidarity, would be minimized if this would create for the persons concerned the Greatest Happiness.

Natural law theory, by contrast, would turn away from arrangements under which people were not to some extent – a large extent – interdependent in their happiness and allied in the pursuit of common purposes falling within the scope of the Common Good of their community: providing for defence; reducing air and water pollution; establishing a market. Does this imply a radical conflict with the utilitarian position? Utilitarians might say that, if the presence of interdependency gives the Greatest Happiness, they agree with natural law theory; if it does not, natural law theory is taking an arbitrary stand against happiness.

But this is not so. Put aside for a moment the possible cases in which the presence of interdependency leads to a clearly lower happiness score; and the possible cases, too, in which it leads to a clearly higher happiness score. There will remain cases in which neither the presence of interdependency nor its absence leads to a clearly higher score. In the present state of the art of assessing happiness, whether by a calculus or a census, one might expect there to be quite a lot of such cases. In them, utilitarianism would be at a loss to recommend one or the other. Natural law theory, however, would firmly recommend embracing interdependency.

Moreover, human beings are plastic enough so that social training can shape them, indeed, does normally shape them, to find more happiness with interdependency present than otherwise. Natural law theory recommends training them for happiness with interdependency. Given equally happy results and equal effectiveness in producing stable attitudes, utilitarianism is neutral on this point. But the upshot is that, after the training has taken place, natural law theory will not have to deal with cases in which utilitarians imagine the Greatest Happiness achieved without interdependency.

V

Natural law theory, I say, would choose to have people brought up with social training to find happiness in interdependency, with social sentiments and feelings of solidarity as appropriate thereto. Would this mean no more than friendship and the solidarity that comes with mutual identification among friends? Natural law theory would go further. It would also have the social training prepare people to join in the pursuit of common purposes that aim at realizing one feature or another of the Common Good. Thus, in wartime people so trained would turn out to defend the community against external enemies; in peacetime they would join in cleaning up parks and in planting trees – join, too, in more dangerous activities, fighting forest fires and coping with floods.

The difference that, with the support of natural law theory, having common purposes makes can be brought out by considering the famous case of medical cannibalization, the organically intact young man in the doctor's office – call him 'Barnaby' – who, taken as a source of organs at the expense of his life, could enable four patients in need of one or another transplanted organ to live.

If we consider this case as coming up by itself without any preliminaries involving the choice of a social policy, then the elementary statistical point referred to earlier will block the rationale for cannibalization. The group of five (the other patients and the young man on the point of being sacrificed) could not be said, whether on the basis of a calculus or of a comparative census, to be happier without him, since it would not be the same group.

But we may consider the case as an instance of a general social policy, according to which whenever a situation is encountered in which sacrificing one person's life would enable two or more other persons to go on living, the sacrifice should be made. We may suppose that various conditions are stipulated: for example, the remaining lifespan denied to the person sacrificed is less than the sum of the remaining lifespans afforded to the people preserved by the sacrifice.

Then we can save Barnaby by pointing out that it would not be reasonable to suppose that he would have consented to such a general social policy. This is a point made by contractual thinking, which takes us to the frontier between utilitarianism and contractarianism. But not, I think beyond the frontier. We can invoke a contractual ingredient present in utilitarianism from the beginning. In the powerful footnote *d* to chapter II of his *Principles*, Bentham advocates the Principle of Utility on the ground that 'in point of right, it [and only it] can be properly justified ... by a person addressing himself to the community,' whose agreement is sought.

Nevertheless, I think that this way of saving Barnaby does not reach deep enough to explain just why the proposal to sacrifice him is so unsettling. To reach deep enough we have to go outside utilitarianism and take up ideas about the Common Good and community from natural law theory.

Barnaby and the doctor's other four patients do not form a community. They are an accidental collection of people. Our moral intuitions about how to behave in relation to such a collection do not go further than to decry doing them any harm (or perhaps decry standing in the way of their gaining some benefit when the cost to us is easily borne). (Something much stronger comes into the picture when we think of them as members with us of a world community, but then we would have to weigh the claims of the people in question against the claims of other members.)

By contrast, if Barnaby is considered to be a member of a community, then he is obliged in normal situations to support policies fostering the life-chances of every member of the community as they fall under aspects of one or another feature of the Common Good of that community. Questions of (substantial) sacrifice, whether of life or short of life, may come up only in abnormal situations – emergencies like external attack, floods, earthquakes, drought, famine. The sacrifices are justified if they are justified as necessary to save the Common Good of the community. In particular, they are justified as imposed on fully consenting members of the community,[22] and the assumption that Barnaby is a freely consenting member of the community is essential to justifying the sacrifices required of him.

It appears that utilitarianism has the defect (shown up by the doctor's office example) of applying without qualification as easily to any accidental collection of people as to a (at least minimally consensual) community. Sometimes the application is morally convincing without qualification; but sometimes, as Barnaby's case shows us, the qualification, which utilitarianism itself cannot be relied on to supply, is indispensable. In this respect, which goes further than being ready to endorse the Greatest Happiness achieved in individual pleasure cells, it is inferior to natural law.

VI

Why would natural law theory insist so much on common purposes falling in with the Common Good of a stable, persisting community? Why would natural law theory choose to train the young for happiness only with interdependency present? Only with common purposes in a persisting community?

One cannot, perhaps, help thinking that something like the Greatest Happiness, considered as something predicated on stable features of human nature, has come back in, surreptitiously, to give natural law theory direction in these connections. Choosing to promote happiness with stability is a different consideration from promoting it without taking stability into account.[23] But then utilitarians could say that they are in favour of stability, too, along with the Greatest Happiness in the long run.

Alternatively, utilitarians might say, it may turn out that the Greatest Happiness will be discovered, finally, to lie not with interdependency, common purposes, and community, but with none of these things. What rational grounds could natural law theory have for refusing to go along with this result?

These questions arise because, since I brought ideal-set rule-utilitarianism onto the scene, we have been comparing a project of optimization with a loose, present-oriented natural law theory. It can be pointed out, in favour of natural law theory, that the utilitarian project, in its ideal-set version and in others, remains very much unfinished. Utilitarianism cannot currently deliver a definite answer one way or another on the attractions of interdependency, common purposes, and community. Natural law theory, valuing those things, can claim to be in a firm position as an ethics pro tempore. Time enough, its champions might say, to concede the field to utilitarians when the utilitarians have finished their project. Even then – which may be as far off as forever – they might ask, would they have to concede everything? Would not there have to be some provision defending anyone who found herself in an accidental collection of people from being cannibalized?

There is something further to say beyond the pro tempore defence. Would the human beings brought up to do without interdependency, common purposes, and community in their pursuit of happiness be enough like the human beings that we know for us to judge that an ethics suitable for them is suitable for us? The human beings that we know long for the company of others, rejoice in working together to accomplish common purposes, take pride in aligning those purposes with the Common Good of their neighbourhood, of their town, of their province, of their country, even of the United Nations. Ideal-set rule-utilitarianism cannot go too far away from these aspects of our present life without losing touch with human beings as they have been, are now, and may be expected to be in the future, which is not what an ethical theory should lightly do. It is something that natural law theory, modernized or not, conspicuously avoids doing.

VII

I have been so preoccupied with ideal-set rule-utilitarianism that I may seem to have left little for utilitarianism to do in non-ideal situations but invoke (with questionable pertinence) the ideal. In fact, I have left quite a lot to do, by leaving utilitarians room to press demands that nobody's happiness be sacrificed, on any point of pleasure, without a good reason.[24] Those demands hit hard at traditional theistic natural law theory, which has had to abandon, in the face of objections that resonate with utilitarian thinking (to be sure, not with utilitarian thinking alone), its endorsement of slavery and of the subordination of women.[25] The traditional theistic theory, in its current versions, still keeps up its restrictions on sexual pleasure; but many of these, too, invite utilitarian objections, like former restrictions, promoted by religion, on dancing, theatre-going, and even the playing of music in church (in 'whistle-kirks,' churches with organs, preached against in Scotland). A Surgeon General of the United States (Joycelyn Elders) lost her office a few years ago because she dared say that as a means of relieving sexual tension masturbation was not a bad thing. Yet, if we set aside people who relish mortification for the sake of religion, what has been gained for human happiness by the miseries caused countless millions – adolescent boys, celibate priests – by the prohibition of masturbation?[26] The furore drew strength from pseudo-scientific claims that masturbation is physically and mentally debilitating; I take it that all of these claims have been discredited, though not yet widely enough to save the Surgeon General.

Sexual freedom, outside the bounds of the missionary position when this is adopted by man and wife when they are both ready to let conception occur, is still under question in other connections. Some of the most zealous supporters of the Bush administration demand that efforts to deal with AIDS forgo the distribution of condoms. (Could they be thinking that distributing them interferes with God's plans for punishment?) One motive for attacking the freedom to choose abortion is to limit the sexual freedom that sometimes leads to exercising the choice in question.

Utilitarianism will press objections on these points. I believe that pressing these objections is important work. The natural law theory that I prefer is not liable to them. It is a theory of natural law modernized, with God having at most an optional honorary role both as to content and as to enforcement. It relegates many of the restrictions on sexual activity (so far as that activity is voluntary) to the same moral junkyard as the defences of slavery and of the subordination of women. Perhaps betraying some vestiges of its theistic origins, natural law modernized may not be so forward as utilitarianism in arguing for pleasures. However, it can accept arguments for them without trouble – even, on due consideration of all the aspects of human thriving, applaud them.

The applause will not, perhaps, come naturally (if I may so speak) to some people with a background of adherence to traditional natural law theory. Experience shows[27] that such people will think that I much too blithely override differences in moral points of view. Maybe so. In particular, my idea of simply adding, where commitment to community in outlook and education is not at issue, religious endorsement to positions established by utilitarian reasoning will not, I expect, suit everyone who wants to give religion and belief in God serious weight in ethics.

It may suit some. Utilitarianism in my perspective joins belief in God as an extreme form of intellectualism (the position that God chooses what can be established as good at least tentatively before invoking His choice), but intellectualism has a long and honourable theological history. My idea of simple addition, moreover, besides giving new life to

Christian utilitarianism like Paley's, may fall in undisturbingly with the outlook of moderate theists of the present day, from Unitarians through Anglicans and other denominations of mainstream Protestantism. The theological virtues may take a place in which their compatibility with utilitarian prescriptions is assured. However, if some people give so much weight to some religious ideas as to contravene those prescriptions, maybe deriving from sacred texts prohibitions for which cogent utilitarian grounds cannot be found – for example, a prohibition against marrying people of the same sex, or even a prohibition against homosexual activity – my idea of simple addition will not work for them. Intransigent conflict may ensue. But maybe not: a prospect of extended dialectic may open up, in which practical compromises may occur on the way, along with modifications of positions on both sides. I shall not try to predict what modifications.

One might say – given my personal history, I might say – that utilitarianism did some work to improve natural law theory modernized before that theory entered the present discussion. One might hope – I hope – that utilitarianism, recast in an attractive form, will remain on the scene at least so long as it has a use in keeping natural law modernized up to the mark in sparing pleasures that can with good reason be treated as innocent.[28]

VIII

A further point comes up to be dealt with in a last word – the last word in this epilogue; the last word in the book; the last word in the ensemble of four books of which this is the last. How does the program of this book, which I have called the program of needs, rights, and well-considered rules and, alternatively, the needs-focused combination program, relate to utilitrianism and natural law theory?

It was no accident that, recast as I have recast them, utilitarianism and natural law theory converge (without becoming identical, which is precluded by their different histories and different relation to the status quo, among other things). It is no accident, either, that the needs-focused combination program, coming from the same source, a source preoccupied by ideas that figure in utilitarianism and natural law theory as well, should converge with both of these. Continue applying any of them, and you will end up in much the same place that you would arrive at by applying either of the others. Take up at any point the needs-focused combination program, and you will be taking up something that both utilitarianism and natural law theory will recognize as calling for morally worthwhile action, so far as it goes.

The grand program of this book is more like natural law theory than utilitarianism in respect to being ready to settle for a satisfactory result, where utilitarianism calls, in the way that I have touched on, for optimization. But it is unlike natural law theory in resting its main weight not on well-considered rules (including, optionally, rules for rights), but on needs. That creates a basic affinity with utilitarianism as I have recast it. Even more affinity with utilitarianism comes to light if we consider that what is for now a 'satisfactory' resolution of the problems posed for action by the program of needs, rights, and well-considered rules may, on reflection, awaken raised aspirations – for ampler provisions for needs, perhaps for an ampler list of needs. Thus, utilitarianism figures in a drive for improvement from one stage of resolution to another.

There is, nevertheless, an important difference in presentation (which may have to do with something more than presentation). Natural law theory asks for allegiance to a comprehensive system of moral rules. If it is not yet a system made entirely explicit, it is already impressively comprehensive; and one knows in principle how it will be filled out. Similarly, utilitarianism, even as I have recast it, requires adherence to a comprehensive principle: no longer the maximization of utility, but the principle of unremitting application of Bentham's Master-Idea, that social policies should be chosen to accord with statistical evidence about their impact on the welfare (well-being) of all the people affected.

By contrast, the program of needs, rights, and well-founded rules offers no comprehensive principle of this sort. (I set aside the suggestion that adherence to the program is itself adherence to a comprehensive principle.) It offers a miscellaneous array of familiar ideas already at work in the practice of many communities (including cities, nation-states, the European Union, and the United Nations). One can take it up by taking up any idea in the array and asking what it amounts to, and what it calls for in current policy choices, which will lead to considering how it fits in with other ideas in the program; but even this may remain a local question rather than a question about comprehensive systematization.

This has advantages. It accords better than the other grand programs with issues arising in practical politics. When obtaining a comprehensive agreement is impractical, it can lead to agreements (local in time and space) about what to do on various practical issues; it can lead by way of these agreements to relatively comprehensive ones. We begin where we are, amid the details of familiar practices – details to which, given their ambitions to be comprehensive, utilitarianism and natural law theory will have to adapt to or at least take into account. In Rawls's terms, as we work upon these details, we build up the context for pursuing reflective equilibrium on comprehensive programs, Rawls's Principles of Justice, natural law theory, or utilitarianism. But we may not feel the need to use the context to settle upon any grand program. One person who read the manuscript of this book commented that my arguments tended to 'debunk' grand programs. If this is so, offering one of my own may be more than a little paradoxical. But is my grand program so grand after all? It is not governed by a comprehensive principle that transcends the details of needs, rights, rules; its appeal to humanity lies mainly in those details, miscellaneous though they may be.

Notes

Introduction

1 'Stands to Reason: The Liberal Responsibility of Raymond Aron,' *Harper's*, December 2003, 89–95.
2 *Time* magazine, 26 April 2004.
3 (Oxford: Clarendon Press, 1995).
4 (London: Routledge, 1974).

1. The Concept of Needs, with a Heart-Warming Offer of Aid to Utilitarianism

1 (Princeton: Princeton University Press, 1987).
2 What I called in *Meeting Needs* a Selfgovliset – a self-governing subset of people with a common language – to make a philosophical point about the empirical linguistic basis for the construction.
3 All of these were present in the account given in *Meeting Needs*, but the Gains-Preservation Principle was not given a name there.
4 Dasgupta, 'National Performance Gaps,' *The Progress of Nations: 1996 UNICEF Report* (New York: UNICEF House, 1996), 33–4. This is one of a series of annual reports by the United Nations Children's Fund that rank with the annual reports of the United Nations Human Development Program in pressing forward for public policy purposes social indicators unequivocally related to basic human needs.
5 Indeed, in the chapter in *Meeting Needs* on 'The Expansion of Needs,' I endorse amending the Criterion to embrace 'the full development of human personality,' a notion that should make room for autonomy.
6 'Thou shalt not strive officiously to keep alive.'

7 Brock, 'Braybrooke on Needs,' *Ethics* 104, 4 (July 1994), 811–23.
8 Robert Nozick, *Anarchy, State, and Utopia* (New York: Basic Books, 1974), 231. The Difference Principle, of course, is advanced by John Rawls in *A Theory of Justice* (Cambridge, Mass.: Harvard University Press, 1971), and as an example of an 'end-result principle' it is one of the primary objects of attack earlier in Nozick's book.
9 See the essay cited in n. 4, above.
10 In *Meeting Needs*, I went on to generalize the argument away from the vulnerability that having needs imposes on people with less power and contended that assignments of resources under any system of justice are liable to be undermined by accumulations of wealth that give people some power to disregard it. But the argument is most poignant when we consider more specifically departures from a system of justice under which everyone is to begin with equally provided for in respect to needs.
11 An essay that appears in a book, *Moral Objectives, Rules, and the Forms of Social Change* (Toronto: University of Toronto Press, 1997), which collects selected essays of mine, argues for the attribution; the essay reappears, as an indispensable feature of the overall argument of another book of mine, *Utilitarianism: Restorations; Repairs; Renovations* (Toronto: University of Toronto Press, 2004). (I did not anticipate writing a book with that argument when *Moral Objectives* was published.)
12 Henry Sidgwick, *The Methods of Ethics* [1874], 7th ed. (London: Macmillan, 1907; reprinted 1963), 415–16.
13 F.Y. Edgeworth, *Mathematical Psychics* (London: Kegan Paul, 1881), 71–5; cf. 65.
14 Gillian Brock and Tara Smith have commented on drafts of this paper; and I am grateful to them for their helpful suggestions.

2. Where Does the Moral Force of Needs Reside, and When?

1 (Princeton: Princeton University Press, 1987).
2 Brandon is now inclined to invoke his grandfather (Sam Collins) rather than his father, as having the more explicit and trenchant position, but I shall keep them both in view.
3 For example, Sen and others, *The Standard of Living* (Cambridge: Cambridge University Press, 1987).
4 Ibid., 25–6, 105.
5 The qualification 'direct' allows for the application through surrogates that I am about to describe.

6 This is true not only of his contributions to *The Standard of Living*, but also of his later book *Development as Freedom* (New York: Knopf, 1999).

7 G.A. Cohen has said, 'Sen arrived at what he called 'capability' through reflection on the main candidates for assessment of well-being that were in the field [in 1979], to wit, utility, or welfare, and Rawlsian primary goods.' (See 'Equality of What? On Welfare, Goods, and Capabilities,' in Martha C. Nussbaum and Amartya Sen, eds, *The Quality of Life* [Oxford: Clarendon Press, 1993], 9–29, at 17). That is not so: it misdescribes Sen's reflection, even if his reflection was limited to 'the main candidates.' Provision for needs (something different from welfare reduced to preferences or other matters not needs) was a main candidate, as it had been from time immemorial, though disregarded by most sophisticated thinkers. Moreover, Sen has reflected on needs, and I expect he did so before 1979.

8 In an early writing, Marx says, looking forward to a transformed society, 'To take the place of wealth and poverty as political economy knows it, there comes forward the rich man, fitted out with rich human exigencies. The rich man is at the same time the man who, to live, has need of a totality of human manifestations, the man for whom his own realization is an interior necessity, a need' (*Economic and Philosophical Manuscripts of 1844* [London: Lawrence and Wishart, 1959], 111–2). The English here is my translation from the French of the *Pléiade* edition. This is the sense in which Marx is to be understood, late in life, putting forward, in the *Critique of the Gotha Program*, the principle, 'From all according to their ability, to all according to their needs.'

9 See, for example, *Development as Freedom*, 4, 64, 82, 84.

10 Thus, the concept of needs, in the use that I advocate for it, is not open to the fifth of the five criticisms of the concept that Sabina Alkire finds in Sen's writings, the only one to which she thinks final weight should be given; see *Valuing Freedoms* (Oxford: Oxford University Press, 2002), 166–70.

11 Karl Marx and Friedrich Engels, *The German Ideology* (Moscow, 1964).

12 A point made in 'Equality of What?,' 19–20, by Cohen, who detects an ambiguity in Sen's use of 'capability.'

13 These terms in comparisons of policies, serve as instances of what Sen calls 'distinguished capability comparisons,' in which 'concentrated attention [is] being paid to some particular capability variable, such as employment, or longevity, or literacy, or nutrition' (*Development as Freedom*, 82).

14 A comment by Bill Pollard has led me to recognize that I have brought

forward not just one, but two types of surrogate for the term 'needs': not just the term or phrase identifying the plight of the people in need – for example, that they 'have run out of drinkable water' – but secondly, this identifying term or phrase combined with a term or phrase that gives 'a respectable explanation' of how their plight came about. The surrogate without the explanation will sometimes suffice, especially in very urgent cases. We would move to extract Mencius's child fallen into the well without asking for an explanation about how she got there; and likewise move without further ado to rescue an old woman from a burning house. At other times, with some people, only the combination including the right sort of explanation will be moving.

15 See, for example, F.H. van Eemeren, ed., *Advances in Pragma-Dialectics* (Amsterdam: SicSat, 2002); or the special issue of the journal *Argumentation* (17 [2003], 513–35), of which I have been titular editor, and, in particular, the contributions from Amsterdam.

16 Gillian Brock, ed., *Necessary Goods: Our Responsibilities to Meet Others' Needs* (Lanham, Md.: Rowman & Littlefield, 1998).

17 See the moving passage in the Preface to *Development as Freedom*, which ends, after saying that the book is aimed at 'nonspecialist readers' for 'open deliberation and critical scrutiny' in 'public discussion,' with Sen's saying, 'I have, throughout my life, avoided giving advice to the "authorities." Indeed, I have never counseled any government, preferring to place my suggestions and critiques – for what they are worth – in the public domain' (xiii–xiv).

18 Is it as elusive in respect to time and place as the historical contract that Locke postulated as the foundation of English government?

19 In *A Strategy of Decision* (New York: The Free Press, 1963), C.E. Lindblom and I quoted Sydney Smith: 'Education has many honest enemies; and many honestly doubt and demur, who do not speak out for fear of being assassinated by Benthamites.'

20 A point emphasized in just these terms by Sen in *Development as Freedom*, 84.

21 This chapter was presented as a paper at a conference on the concept of needs held at the University of Durham in England in October 2003. It was on that occasion that Bill Pollard made the comment discussed in n. 14 above. An earlier version of the paper was read and discussed – much to its advantage – in a colloquium of the Department of Philosophy at Dalhousie University in June 2003. I have also benefited not only from Brandon Butler's bringing his father and grandfather into the discussion, but also from Brandon's comments on a version of the paper even earlier than the one discussed at Dalhousie. Mats Furberg's reactions helped me understand the paper better as well as to make some corrections.

3. The Analysis of Rights

1 *Three Tests for Democracy: Personal Rights, Human Welfare, Collective Prefer-ence* (New York: Random House, 1968).

2 I add the parenthetical reference to falling into a certain condition to take into account a point made by T.C. Pocklington in a valuable critique, con-tained in 'The Concept of Rights,' *Peace Research: The Canadian Journal of Peace Studies* 22/23, 4/1 (1990–1), 17–30. He gives the example of falling ill in a jurisdiction where *N* has the right to medical care. I have already suppressed, in response to one of his criticisms, the claim that '*N* has a right to do *a*' is more fundamental. At a number of other places in this revision I shall be responding to points raised in his critique.

3 These are Pocklington's examples of rights that he supposes have no correlative obligations.

4 Pocklington holds that pleading guilty amounts to choosing not to exer-cise the right. But we can hold, instead, that the right to a fair trial in-cludes protections and obligations that come to bear in the pre-trial phase. Pocklington would hold that there is no option of exercising the right not to be assaulted, since according to him this is an example of a right that cannot be exercised. But I think it can be: *N* might call on bystanders or the police to prevent her being assaulted and, if she is assaulted, call for the prosecution of the assailant afterwards or sue for damages.

5 G.H. von Wright, *Norm and Action* (London: Routledge, 1963), 104–5.

6 I originally said that the right here in question should be treated 'as if it had the force of law.' Pocklington rightly points out that it quite literally does not. I could perhaps make a stand that the 'as if' condition is consis-tent with that, but I have thought it more illuminating to change what I say.

7 See the discussion of this possibility in chapter 1 of D. Braybrooke, *Utili-tarianism: Restorations; Repairs; Renovations* (Toronto: University of Toronto Press, 2004).

8 Ibid.

9 See John Finnis, *Natural Law and Natural Rights* (Oxford: Clarendon Press, 1980); Richard Tuck, *Natural Rights Theories* (Cambridge: Cambridge University Press, 1979).

10 J.G. Fichte, *Grundlage des Naturrechts* (1796–7); translated as *Foundations of Natural Right* by Michael Baur, ed. F. Neuhouser (Cambridge: Cambridge University Press, 2000).

11 Philonenko gives a thorough exposition of his position on Fichte in *La liberté humaine dans la philosophie de Fichte* (Paris: J. Vrin, 1966). For his in-fluence in reviving Fichte for French philosophy see writings by Luc Ferry

and Alain Renaut, for example, Renaut, *Le système du droit: Philosophie et droit dans la pensée de Fichte* (Paris: Presses Universitaires de France, 1986).

12 This is the position that Wayne Sumner settles upon in *The Moral Foundations of Rights* (Oxford: Clarendon Press, 1987).

13 An account of rights written in the spirit of Hegel would portray the ultimately validated set of rights as the culmination of a historical development in which at last human beings arrive at social institutions, in which these rights are included, that are perfectly suited to human beings. As such, they can be endorsed as features of the institutions that it is supremely rational to choose, as the human beings present in this ripeness of time are (or will be) rational enough to appreciate. Is this another way of giving rights a foundation? It is another way in the sense that it brings in an unfolding pattern of social and intellectual development. But it is capable of absorbing the position of empirical natural law and Fichte's position as well. The suitability of social institutions is something to be endorsed on the basis of observation, and the residence of the concept of rights in the relation, important to Fichte, between subjectivity and intersubjectivity is something that can be appreciated at the end of the historical development in question.

14 I think that this is part, at least, of what Simone Weil might have had in mind, in a passage brought to my attention by Steven Burns, where she decries rights for being too 'commercial' in conception and spirit.

15 This is the line that Mary Ann Glendon inclines to take in her book *Rights Talk* (New York: The Free Press, 1991).

16 Thus, I am setting aside, somewhat to the peril of my argument, not only the costs that I have mentioned, but the full array of the financial costs of having a legal regime to protect rights, costs discussed by Cass R. Sunstein and Stephen Holmes in their book *The Cost of Rights: Why Liberty Depends on Taxes* (New York: Norton, 1999). I take some comfort from the fact that in a book published not much later, *The Second Bill of Rights: FDR's Unfinished Revolution and Why We Need It More Than Ever* (New York: Basic Books, 2004), Sunstein does not suggest that the costs of new rights similar to a right to a livelihood, even in effect approximately equivalent, stand in the way of instituting them. Indeed, he mentions a number of rights already accepted that are doing some of the work of a right to a livelihood.

17 *The Second Bill of Rights*, 18, 20.

18 I noted, in *Three Tests for Democracy*, from which much of the present chapter derives, 'My treatment of the concept of rights was strongly influenced in its inception by A.I. Melden's *Rights and Right Conduct*

(Oxford: Basil Blackwell, 1959). In its present form it resembles the treatment given by Hans Kelsen, in his *General Theory of Law and State*, translated by Anders Wedberg (Cambridge [Mass.]: Harvard University Press, 1945), 75–90, more than any other.' That is still true, first of 'the present form' then and of 'the present form' now.

4. Our Natural Bodies, Our Social Rights

1 Samuel C. Wheeler III, 'Natural Property Rights as Body Rights,' *Noûs* 14 (1980), 171–3. The present chapter, discussing this article, originally appeared under the title given here in the same issue of *Noûs*, 195–204. Page numbers for citations of Wheeler's text have been inserted.
2 On this point, see the discussion by Theodore M. Benditt in his recent book, *Law as Rule and Principle* (Stanford: Stanford University Press, 1978), chap. 8.
3 A lot more would have to be done, for which I do not have the space, to deal fully with the possibility that Wheeler's theory of bodily incorporation could be restated without reference to any sort of continuous variation and without resort to any notion of degree-vagueness. My examples connecting some rights with criteria that are subject to degree-vagueness would stand.

At least one of my colleagues thought that I need not have read Wheeler as intending to treat rights themselves as natural kinds; perhaps Wheeler meant to treat them only as properties of entities – persons – that do belong to natural kinds. I agree that there is something to clear up here; but my reading is sustained by the text, and for Wheeler the other semantic relation, between 'rights' and properties, would (I conjecture) be constrained by nature in a similar way.

Another of my colleagues thought, as I had thought myself, that Wheeler's distinction between the unchanging 'essence' of a right and its variable 'accidental' consequences simply spirits out of sight the facts about how the scope of rights is adjusted by social policy to fit changing circumstances. I judged it best, however, to develop other matters.

I have also omitted to press a good objection that I had not seen myself, but which my colleagues brought up: the right of agenthood on which Wheeler relies in his section IV may embrace parts of the body that the agent can use in the exercise of his powers or that are essential for him to exist at all; but how does it establish any right to parts (like the paralysed leg, section I) that are useless or inessential?

I wish to thank a number of my colleagues at Dalhousie for attending a discussion of Wheeler's paper and of this comment: Richmond Campbell, Robert Eden, Robert Martin, Jennifer Nedelsky, Susan Sherwin, and Terrance Tomkow. In its present version, the comment goes at least part of the way toward taking into account several of the points that they raised.

5. The Representation of Rules in Logic and Their Definition

1 *Ethics* 100, 4 (1990).
2 Wittgenstein, *Philosophical Investigations* (Oxford: Basil Blackwell, 1953). See, for instance, part I, paragraphs 54, 154, 198–9, 202.
3 Some people have carelessly thought that Wittgenstein in his studies of rules put an end to all work on rules in formal logic. Von Wright, whose main works on deontic logic came after Wittgenstein's death, was one of Wittgenstein's most intimate students.
4 (London: Routledge, 1963).
5 Parris, 'The Origins of the Permanent Civil Service, 1780–1830,' *Public Administration* (U.K.) 46 (Summer 1968), 143–66. My discussion appeared in 'Refinements of Culture in Large-Scale History,' *History and Theory*, Beiheft 9, 1969), 'Studies in Quantitative History and the Logic of the Social Sciences,' 39–63.
6 Von Wright holds that normative statements asserting that given norms or rules hold, not norms or rules proper, which to him do not have truth values, can figure as propositions in the propositional calculus. I am passing over this distinction, which I do not anyway give as much weight to as he.
7 The five paragraphs just set forth are taken by permission, with minor amendments, from Braybrooke, 'Refinements of Culture in Large-Scale History.'
8 Further illustrated: it has already been illustrated during the exposition just given of the structure of von Wright's logic.
9 The example just given is taken from David Braybrooke, 'The Logic of the Succession of Cultures,' in H.E. Kiefer and M.K. Munitz, eds, *Mind, Science, and History* (Albany: State University of New York Press, 1970), 270–83.
10 The following passage, to p. 98, comparing the Dalhousie logic of rules with von Wright's reproduces, except for some additional examples and formulas and minor variations in phrasing, a passage on the same subject in chapter 3 of *Logic on the Track of Social Change*, by D. Braybrooke, Bryson Brown, and Peter K. Schotch (Oxford: Clarendon Press, 1995), 63 (at the bottom) to 68 (at the top), along with notes.

11 Davidson, 'The Logical Form of Action Sentences,' in Nicholas Rescher, ed., *The Logic of Decision and Action* (Pittsburgh: University of Pittsburgh Press, 1966), 81–95.

12 Hamblin, 'Quandaries and the Logic of Rules,' *Journal of Philosophical Logic* 1 (1972), 74–85.

13 *Leviathan* (London: Crooke, 1651), chaps 17 and 18.

14 Lewis, *Convention* (Cambridge, Mass.: Harvard University Press, 1969).

15 For a current survey of paraconsistent logic see Bryson Brown, 'On Paraconsistency,' in Dale Jacquette, ed., *A Companion to Philosophical Logic* (Malden, Mass., and Oxford: Blackwell, 2002), 628–50.

16 See, for example, Philip Pettit, 'The Reality of Rule Following,' *Mind* 99, 393 (1990), 1–21.

17 David Braybrooke, in *Philosophy of Social Science* (Englewood Cliffs, N.J.: Prentice-Hall, 1987), 48–50.

18 Brad Inwood, ed. & trans., *The Poem of Empedocles* (Toronto: University of Toronto Press, 1992) (Greek with English translation en regard), 261.

19 No doubt, few historians would be quite so bold in their resistance as G.R. Elton, who, in *The Practice of History* (New York: Crowell, 1968 [1967]), extolled the 'instinctive rightness' with which a professional historian poses his questions and assesses his evidence, whether or not, we are to understand, he makes any systematic use of concepts from social sciences (17, 19, 73).

20 They were confirmed by the reactions expressed by George K. Behlmer, a historian from the University of Washington, at the conference for which the essay from which this chapter derives was written. Apologizing for the fact that he will have no opportunity for a rejoinder, I shall take up one by one the concerns that he expressed.

21 Porter, *The Abolition of the Slave Trade in England, 1784–1807* (Hamden, Conn.: Archon Books, 1970). See the discussion in *Track*, chap. 10.

22 See the discussion in *Track*, chap. 8, of Foucault's *La Naissance de la Clinique* (Paris: Presses Universitaires de France, 1963).

23 Thus, I accept, in particular, the case against rights being absolute claims, as made out, for example, by Judith Jarvis Thomson in *The Realm of Rights* (Cambridge, Mass.: Harvard University Press, 1990). Cf. St Thomas on rules and *epieikeia* (the virtue of being ready to make exceptions when they are called for).

24 All these features can be illustrated (indeed, are illustrated, in *Track*) by the right of private property asserted by the British plantation-owners in the West Indies.

6. (The Keystone Chapter) Aggregating in a Distinctive Grand Program the Free-Standing Studies and an Account of the Serial Evaluation of Consequences

1 John Rawls, *A Theory of Justice* (Cambridge, Mass.: Harvard University Press, 1971). A revised edition was put out in 1999 by the same publisher. I shall also make use of Rawls's *Political Liberalism* (New York: Columbia University Press, 1993); Robert Nozick, *Anarchy, State, and Utopia* (New York: Basic Books, 1974); and David Gauthier, *Morals by Agreement* (Oxford: Clarendon Press, 1986).
2 (Cambridge, Mass.: Harvard University Press, 2000).
3 Hardin, *Collective Action* (Baltimore: Johns Hopkins University Press, 1982).
4 Arrow, *Social Choice and Individual Values* (New York: Wiley, 1951; 2nd ed., 1963).
5 See, for example, Hardin, *Morality within the Limits of Reason* (Chicago: University of Chicago Press, 1988).
6 Hampton, *Hobbes and the Social Contract Tradition* (Cambridge: Cambridge University Press, 1986).
7 See the chapter on Rousseau in my *Natural Law Modernized* (Toronto: University of Toronto Press, 2001); and D. Braybrooke and A.P. Monahan, 'Common Good,' in L. Becker and C. Becker, eds, *The Encyclopedia of Ethics*, 2nd ed. (New York and London: Routledge, 2001).
8 ST, 1a2ae, Q.90, 4.
9 With Bryson Brown and Peter K. Schotch (Oxford: Clarendon Press, 1995).
10 Consider St Thomas on penalties being necessary to control fractious people (ST 1a2ae, Q.95, 1).
11 ST 1a2ae, Q. 90, 1.
12 See my *Natural Law Modernized*.
13 They would still be in a plausible sense 'natural' if they were only INUS conditions, that is, 'insufficient but non-redundant part[s]' of 'unnecessary but sufficient conditions' of thriving. See J.L. Mackie, *The Cement of the Universe* (Oxford: Clarendon Press, 1974), chap. 3, esp. 62, for a discussion of causation in which INUS conditions play a central part.
14 Simon, 'A Behavioral Model of Rational Choice' (1955), reprinted in Simon, *Models of Man* (New York: Wiley, 1957).
15 Lindblom, 'The Science of Muddling Through,' *Public Administration* 19 (1957), 79–88; Lindblom returned to the theme in Braybrooke and Lindblom, *A Strategy of Decision: Policy Evaluation as a Social Process* (New York: The Free Press, 1963). For further discussion of incrementalism, see Braybrooke, 'Scale, Combination, Opposition: A Rethinking of Incrementalism,'

Ethics 95 (July 1985), 920–33, reprinted in Braybrooke, *Moral Objectives, Rules, and the Forms of Social Change* (Toronto: University of Toronto Press, 1998), 311–30.

16 For further discussion see D. Braybrooke, *Utilitarianism: Restorations; Repairs; Renovations* (Toronto: University of Toronto Press, 2004), chap. 2.

17 A wide range of abuses are enumerated and given due weight, which is sometimes negligible weight, in the first chapter of D. Braybrooke, *Meeting Needs* (Princeton: Princeton University Press, 1987).

18 See, for example, Sen's discussion in his *Development as Freedom* (New York: Knopf, 1999), and my discussion of capabilities in chapter 2, above, and in *Utilitarianism: RRR*, 161–3.

19 See the section below on 'Justice.' The safeguards are thoroughly discussed in D. Braybrooke, *Utilitarianism: RRR*, chap. 4.

20 See chapter 1, above.

21 For further discussion, see again my *Utilitarianism: RRR*, chap. 3.

22 A. MacIntyre, 'Causality and History,' in Julia Manninen and Raimo Tuomela, eds, *Explanation and Understanding* (Dordrecht: Reidel, 1976), 137–58; and P. Winch, *The Idea of a Social Science and Its Relation to Philosophy* (London: Routledge, 1958).

23 See, for example, D. Braybrooke, *Philosophy of Social Science* (Englewood Cliffs, N.J.: Prentice-Hall, 1987).

24 For full discussion see Braybrooke, Brown, and Schotch, *Track,* chap. 10.

25 Again, for full discussion, see *Track,* this time chap. 8.

26 March and Johan P. Olsen, *Rediscovering Institutions: The Organizational Basis of Politics* (New York: The Free Press, 1989); Ostrom, *Governing the Commons* (Cambridge: Cambridge University Press, 1990).

27 S.E.S. Crawford and Elinor Ostrom, 'A Grammar of Institutions,' *American Political Science Review* 89, 3 (September 1995), 582ff.

28 Homans, *Social Behavior: Its Elementary Forms* (New York: Harcourt Brace, 1962).

29 See also the discussion of the burdens and costs of rights in chapter 3, above.

30 See chapter 17, 'Policy Formation with Issue Processing and Transformation of Issues,' in my *Moral Objectives, Rules, and the Forms of Social Change* and, in *Utilitarianism: RRR*, the intermittent discussion of Scanlon's animadversions on utilitarianism.

31 See *Meeting Needs*, chap. 1.

32 Fishkin, *Democracy and Deliberation* (New Haven: Yale University Press, 1991), *The Voice of the People* (New Haven: Yale University Press, 1995), and other works.

33 It is a familiar fact that there are people who want to have various sexual

practices proscribed by political action. It is less familiar that some people are ready to argue that some of the practices make people unfit to take part in politics. But Kant, in one of Kant's less judicious moments, has been cited to support the argument that masturbation is an instance of self-indulgence incompatible with a desirable civic character. See Thomas Pangle, *The Ennobling of Democracy: The Challenge of the Post-Modern Age* (Baltimore: Johns Hopkins University Press, 1992).

34 Carens, *Culture, Citizenship and Community* (New York: Oxford University Press, 2000); Gregg, *Thick Moralities, Thin Politics* (Durham, N.C.: Duke University Press, 2003); Moon, *Constructing Community: Moral Pluralism and Tragic Conflicts* (Princeton: Princeton University Press, 1993).

35 Stuart Hampshire told me he thought this during one of the supervisions he gave me at Oxford in 1952–3.

36 See chapter 8 in *Natural Law Modernized* on moral education.

Part Three. Analytical Political Philosophy Deals with Evil

1 Also see the essay (reflected in chapter 5, on rules, of the present book), which may be regarded as preliminary to this collaborative work, in which I apply von Wright's logic of rules to the political and social change that led to the non-political, permanent British civil service: 'Refinements of Culture in Large Scale History,' *History and Theory*, Beiheft 9 (1969), 'Studies in Quantitative History and the Logic of the Social Sciences,' 329–58.

2 In *Traffic Congestion Goes Through the Issue-Machine* (London: Routledge, 1974); in my essay, 'Toward an Alliance between the Issue-Processing Approach and Pragma-Dialectical Analysis,' *Argumentation* 17 (2003), 513–35.

7. Through the Free-Standing Studies and Their Aggregation in a Grand Program, Analytical Political Philosophy Can Deal with Evil

1 Until recently not an explicit preoccupation in analytical ethical theory or analytical political philosophy, evil has lately gained serious attention in both, with books by John Kekes, *Facing Evil* (Princeton: Princeton University Press, 1990); Jonathan Glover, *Humanity: A Moral History of the Twentieth Century* (London: Jonathan Cape, 1999); Claudia Card, *The Atrocity Paradigm: A Theory of Evil* (New York: Oxford University Press, 2002); and Adam Morton, *On Evil* (New York and London: Routledge, 2004). I shall be writing, in the main, independently of them, except that I shall make a little explicit use of Card's *The Atrocity Paradigm*, Kekes's *Facing Evil* and

Morton's *On Evil*. If it were my aim in this chapter to digest the leading current work on the concept of evil I would make much more of these texts, perhaps especially of Kekes's book, which puts forward a number of characteristically bold and trenchant theses. But my aim is rather to show that a creditable account of evil can be generated by the studies, including ordinary language analysis of political terms, put together in this book.

2 Neiman, *Evil in Modern Thought* (Princeton: Princeton University Press, 2002).

3 (Princeton: Princeton University Press, 1987), 34–8.

4 Lincoln Steffens, *Autobiography* (New York: Harcourt, [1931] 1958).

5 In my own thinking, I have been preoccupied with overcoming disregard and neglect in meeting needs, so much so that, when in the course of preparing this chapter I began to think about active obstruction to meeting needs, I wondered whether my paradigm List of Matters of Need, set forth in *Meeting Needs* and invoked in earlier chapters of the present book, answered to the range of measures of active obstruction. Had I had the wit to include sleep, for example, among the Matters of Need? Ordinarily, there is no issue about not providing people with sleep; they provide for themselves. However, as we have lately learned from American practices in Iraq, sleep deprivation has been a standard technique in interrogation. Other things being equal, it is certainly an evil. Did I include sleep on my List of Matters of Need? I held my breath. It turns out that I did, associating it explicitly with the need for periodic rest.

6 People may want to use a term that applies to the below-threshold cases as well as the above-threshold ones. 'Wrongs,' they suggest, or 'harms' serve better as general terms. I do not think that this is true: 'wrongs' implies someone doing wrong, whereas the basic evils on my (converted) List of Needs are evils whether or not they are the consequences of human actions; and 'harms' not only keeps company with 'wrongs' in this respect; its use as a verb overshadows its somewhat awkward use as a noun. 'Evils' does have the embarrassment of not fitting the below-threshold cases; and this embarrassment is aggravated, I think, by there not being any term that quite fits there. Is having to go without food for a couple of days simply a 'difficulty' or an 'irritant'? The terms 'wrong' and 'harm' are not specially called for by these cases. Is it 'a matter of distress'? This seems to make too much of it. There are almost always so many more serious things – genuine evils – to attend to. Perhaps we do best to speak of 'troubles,' as in the question (in Australian English), 'What's your trouble, mate?' 'Trouble' can range up to apply to genuine evils, but it is also at home below the threshold of significance. To reply to the question,

it is quite in order to mention that you missed dinner today; that's your trouble, and you are a bit upset about it.

7 Cf., in chapter 2, how the use of specific terms for needs requiring urgent provision makes the use of the term 'needs' redundant.

8 'Life-blightening' is a very uncommon term, but I revive it because it pairs better than 'life-blighting' with 'life-threatening.'

9 Here Sen's linked concepts of capabilities and functionings, discussed above in the chapters on the concept of needs, offer valuable resources for evaluating social policies. See, for example, his discussion in *Development as Freedom* (New York: Alfred A. Knopf, 1999).

10 Morton, *On Evil*, e.g., 56.

11 Card, *The Atrocity Paradigm*, 94.

12 Kekes, *Facing Evil*, 4.

13 To say, in general, having N and perhaps others in view, that something is evil leaves open the question whether anyone is to blame for its happening and, if so, who. It also leaves open the question whether or not it is an evil, 'all things considered.' But this question does not normally arise. From the information that an evil (a specific evil, like losing her power of speech) has befallen N, we proceed to ask how it happened; whether it is a permanent disability; whether it is an instance of an evil that has begun to occur surprisingly frequently. The question 'Is it an evil, all things considered?' diverts our attention to what is usually an unfruitful line of discussion. Someone who asks 'Is it an evil, all things considered?' will be expected to have in hand some special reason to think that it is not, some larger perspective in which it is not.

14 A greater evil comes from multiplying cases already evil. Do difficulties below the threshold of evil become evils if they are multiplied? A utilitarian in the grip of the calculus-notion would be inclined to say 'Yes'; but utilitarianism as I prefer to conceive it, relying on the census-notion, is not bound to agree. Ten thousand children missing their dinner just this once do not equate to one child who is actually starving after weeks of deprivation.

15 Samantha Powers, *A Problem from Hell* (New York: Basic Books, 2002), chap. 10.

16 It was approximated during the firestorm bombings of Tokyo in 1945, when thousands of desperate people tried to take refuge in the rivers and found the river waters boiling.

17 Morton, *On Evil*.

18 As Shadia Drury reminds us in her unsparing and unsettling review of the ethics of Jesus and of Christianity in *Terror and Civilization* (New York: Palgrave Macmillan, 2004).

19 This and all the following page citations in the text refer to *Evil in Modern Thought.*

20 My colleague Benjamin Gregg takes Adorno to be holding not that these things cannot be written, but that they will be garbage.

21 This assertion and the previous one make a point that goes beyond the second understanding of outrunning concepts. I shall not follow it up.

22 Neiman takes the conceptual difficulties more seriously than Jean-François Lyotard. Lyotard has attached great importance to Auschwitz; and though something might be made of his inclination as a post-modernist to find in it a challenge to conceptual innovation that we cannot find any uniquely settled way to meet, the main line of his thought on Auschwitz seems to be that it has once and for all refuted the grand narrative of human progress in all of its versions. See *La condition post-moderne* (Paris: Editions de Minuit, 1979) and *Le post-moderne pour les enfants* (Paris: Editions Galilée, 1988) (both, incidentally, lucid works, especially the latter).

23 When I read this chapter to a colloquium at Dalhousie in September 2004, Sue Sherwin expressed some misgivings in the neighbourhood of this point.

24 Recounted in the colloquium at Dalhousie by Christina Behme, who wondered how I would deal with evils that people afflicted with them did not regard as evils.

25 Or so I am inclined to think, agreeing with Steven Burns, who brought up genocide at the Dalhousie colloquium.

26 Mentioned at the Dalhousie colloquium by Rainer Friedrich.

27 Steven Burns, in a personal communication before the colloquium was held.

28 See remarks on fragility in *Natural Law Modernized,* in chapter 8, on moral education, 217–20.

29 See Ed Vulliamy, 'Return to Omarska,' *Guardian Weekly,* 10–16 September 2004. Some of the surviving Bosniaks, defiantly returning to the places the Serbs intended to drive them from by terror, find themselves living again in the same towns alongside their persecutors.

30 That is a complementary lesson from Milgram's and other experiments. See Stanley Milgram, *Obedience to Authority* (New York: Harper, 1974).

31 Particularly instructive and horrifying was the 'animalizing' diatribes of Vyshinsky, the prosecutor in some of the most notorious trials. *The Black Book of Communism* (Cambridge, Mass.: Harvard University Press, 1999), 749–50, cites the style of his attacks on defendants in the Moscow trials: 'Shoot these rabid dogs! Death to this gang who hid their ferocious teeth, their eagle claws, from the people! Down with that vulture Trotsky, from whose mouth a bloody venom drips, putrefying the great ideals of

Marxism ... Let's put an end once and for all to these miserable hybrids of foxes and pigs, these stinking corpses!' and so on. Introducing this citation, the text mentions that Vyshinksky was 'an intellectual with traditional classical training.'

32 In an article famous among sociologists, Everett C. Hughes emphasizes the effectiveness of the Nazi movement in expanding its power with divisive mobilization of this kind; 'Good People and Dirty Work,' *Social Problems*, 10 (1962), 3–11.

33 Discussed instructively by Stanley Cohen in his book *States of Denial* (Cambridge: Polity Press, 2001), 81–2.

34 Ibid., 77, 60–1. Cohen also mentions 'moral indifference,' but this does not seem to me on the same footing as the others, since it does not presuppose even a prima facie charge to answer.

35 Milgram, *Obedience to Authority*.

36 Both Yoo and Gonzales had a hand in writing the all-too-permissive memorandum on torture, which not only attempts to entrench the narrow definition, but also argues that there is no legal barrier preventing the President, as Commander-in-Chief, from ordering torture. The memorandum was signed by Jay S. Bybee, then Assistant Attorney General of the United States. See, among many sources recoverable on the Internet, Jane Mayer's review of the issues in 'Outsourcing Torture,' *New Yorker*, 14 February 2005. The language that Congress used in approving the International Torture Convention lent itself to a narrow definition of torture, as Yoo pointed out in the *Los Angeles Times*, 11 June 2004 (quoted in 'On the Fringes of the Public Sphere,' on Discourse.net). Neither Yoo nor Gonzales showed any uneasiness about the abuses to which the narrow language and narrow definition might lead.

37 The memorandum explicitly sets aside, as not amounting to torture, various 'cruel, inhuman, or degrading' acts. Mayer supplies some examples: suspension from a ceiling or a door frame, with feet just touching the floor; being forced to stand for hours on tiptoe in water up to one's chin.

Part Four: Three Famous Grand Programs in Analytical Political Philosophy, with Comparisons

1 (Cambridge, Mass.: Harvard University Press, 1971).
2 (Toronto: University of Toronto Press, 2001), chap. 1.
3 (New York: Macmillan and the Free Press, 1968), Vol. 11, 80–5.

8. Utilitarianism with a Difference: Rawls's Position in Ethics

1 This chapter originated as a critical notice, an early review, of John Rawls's *A Theory of Justice* in *Canadian Journal of Philosophy* 3, 2 (December 1973), 303–31. References to the text of *A Theory of Justice* (Cambridge, Mass.: Harvard University Press, 1971) are given in parentheses throughout.

2 Including one led by me at Dalhousie University during the academic year 1972–3, of whose collective effort this notice is a report – from my point of view, no doubt not fully freed from my personal prejudices. Everyone who attended the seminar, both students and colleagues, made a significant contribution; but I think everyone will consider it fair that I should mention by name, as having made especially significant contributions reflected in this notice, Florian Bail, John Devlin, and Kenneth Smith, among the students; and Richmond M. Campbell, among my colleagues. I have had the benefit of reading impressive papers by Bail and Smith; and, before its publication in *Dalhousie Law Journal* 1 (September 1973), 210–23, Professor Campbell's own excellent review of Rawls's book. I have also profited from reading, in Professor E.F. McClennen's unpublished doctoral dissertation, his treatment of Rawls's Equal Liberty Principle in an earlier form in which liberty is generalized.

3 Tawney, *Equality*, 4th ed. (London: Allen & Unwin), 192.

4 Wootton, *End Social Inequality* (London: Kegan Paul, 1941). She called here for a ceiling on incomes along with a levelling up of incomes from the bottom.

5 David Hume, *An Enquiry Concerning the Principles of Morals* (1777), Part 1, Section V, at the end. Jeremy Bentham, *An Introduction to the Principles of Morals and Legislation* (1823), chap. I, fn. 1.

6 Rawls follows J.S. Mill, *Utilitarianism* (1861), chap. V, in citing Bentham.

7 F.Y. Edgeworth, 'The Hedonical Calculus,' *Mind* 4 (1879), 394–408, at 404. The article was reprinted as 56–82 of the same author's *Mathematical Psychics* (London: Kegan Paul, 1881), where the passage in question appears on p. 74.

8 'Hedonical Calculus,' 402–3; *Mathematical Psychics*, 56–82, 72–3.

9 Mill, *Utilitarianism*, especially chaps II and III.

10 Bentham, *Principles*, chap. II.

11 Cf. S.E. Finer, *The Life and Times of Sir Edwin Chadwick* (London: Methuen, 1952) on Chadwick's utilitarian milieu and on his vigorous pursuit of sanitary reform.

12 He gives three principles in two groupings; so, grouping the Fair Oppor-

tunity Principle with the Difference Principle, he speaks of two principles, one the Equal Liberty Principle. I shall deal with this trivial but annoying complication by speaking of three principles.

13 Hart, 'Are There Natural Rights?' *Philosophical Review* 64, 2 (April 1955), 175–91.

14 David Hume, *A Treatise of Human Nature* (1740), Book 3, Part 2, sec. 2, toward the end.

15 Wicksteed, *The Common Sense of Political Economy*, ed. L. Robbins (London: Routledge, 1933), vol. I, 173ff.; cited by J.M. Buchanan and G. Tullock in *The Calculus of Consent* (Ann Arbor: University of Michigan Press, 1962), 18.

16 Lyons, 'Rawls versus Utilitarianism,' *Journal of Philosophy* 69, 18 (5 October 1972), 535–45, at 541–4.

17 Edgeworth, 'Hedonical Calculus,' 398; *Mathematical Psychics* 64; cf. vii.

18 Sidgwick, *The Methods of Ethics* [1874], 7th ed. (London: Macmillan, 1907), 417, fn.

19 During the quarter-century that followed the publication of 'The Hedonical Calculus' in 1879 no one took issue with Edgeworth on this point, either in the pages of *Mind*, or in the *Proceedings of the Aristotelian Society*. No one, at least in those places, raised the point against Sidgwick either, whose *Methods* first appeared in 1874. In a careful and searching discussion of *Methods* on the occasion of a later edition, H. Rashdall, not an obtuse man, came nowhere near mentioning the point (*Mind* [1885], 200–26).

20 'Some Fundamental Ethical Controversies,' *Mind* 14 (1889), 473–87 at 483.

21 'Silly' is not a word strong enough to describe the passage in which Edgeworth effervesces in praise of 'the privilege of man above brute, of civilized above savage, of birth, of talent, and of the male sex' ('Hedonical Calculus,' 405–6; reprinted without second thoughts and without change in *Mathematical Psychics*, 77–8).

22 In fact, in a footnote, though he approaches stating the principle in a later passage (432). The principle – which he calls in the footnote 'an obvious and incontrovertible deduction from the Utilitarian principle' – is directly contradicted by another, later passage (447), in which Sidgwick, mixing means and ends, says that 'in any distribution of pleasures and privileges, or of pains and burdens' where 'considerations of desert do not properly come in,' 'the Utilitarian' will fall back with 'Common Sense' on 'Equality' as 'the principle of just apportionment.' I cite the contradiction not to belittle Sidgwick's logical powers, but as evidence of his remarkable inattention to the point at issue.

23 The first formula was uttered in *A Fragment of Government* (1776), Preface, par. 2; the second, in chap. 1, fn. 1 (added 1822), of *Principles*. As has

often been noted (see, e.g., Edgeworth's very apt comment, *Mathematical Psychics*, 117–8), the use of the phrase 'the greatest number' renders the first formula ambiguous; the phrase nevertheless unambiguously expresses a concern for distribution.

24 *Utilitarianism*, chap. II.

25 Rawls does not say 'median money income'; he says 'median income.' However, he must mean money income; the median of real income (goods and services in various combinations) will vary as the index for measuring it varies: one index, because one ordering of combinations, according to preference, if it is founded on one person's tastes; possibly a very different index, because a different ordering, if it is founded on the tastes of any other person. The indeterminacies exposed in the following arguments would not be removed by turning to real income for an index; they would be aggravated.

26 A defect vigorously criticized by G.A. Cohen in 'Where the Action Is: On the Site of Distributive Justice,' *Philosophy and Public Affairs* 26, 2 (Winter 1997), 3–30; cf. Cohen, 'Incentives, Inequality, and Community,' in S. Darwall, ed., *Equal Freedom* (Ann Arbor: University of Michigan Press, 1995), 331–97 (originally published in G. Peterson, ed., *The Tanner Lectures on Human Values*, Vol. 13 (Salt Lake City: University of Utah Press, 1992), 263–329.

27 David Estlund, in his discussion of Cohen's opposition to the Difference Principle, notes that the capacity to exercise the basic liberties implies a minimum income; see 'Liberalism, Equality, and Fraternity in Cohen's Critique of Rawls,' *Journal of Political Philosophy* 6, 1 (1998), 99–112. In a comment appended to this chapter I shall be discussing Estlund's article along with the articles by G.A. Cohen, cited in n. 26.

28 Rawls's generality condition (131) would not be violated; the agents in the original position need not be supposed to know which of them would be in (say) the 111th and 112th positions in any ordering; nor would a definite description of the form 'the person in the 111th position' suffice to identify the person beforehand.

29 In the 'General Comment (2005)' that follows this early review, I take a hopeful view of the repeated applications of the Fair Opportunity Principle.

30 Acts 4:34–7. (I presume that the language 'distribution unto every man according as he has need' would have applied to any current production as well as to the fixed stock of lands and houses mentioned.) Cf. Karl Marx, *Critique of the Gotha Program* (Moscow: Foreign Languages Publishing House, 1947), Part I, sec. 3.

31 At a time when eleven of the eighteen highest-paid men in U.S. industry were officers of one company – Bethlehem Steel – A.B. Homer, the presi-

dent of the company, who himself got $670,000 a year in salary, told a Senate committee that it was questionable whether he or the others would have the incentive to do all that they did for the company without the full amount of their current salaries; see *Study of Administered Prices in the Steel Industry*, 85th Congress, 2d Session. U.S. Senate Report No. 1387 (Washington, D.C.: U.S. Government Printing Office, 1958) and detailed testimony in associated publications.

32 It is written and St Paul commanded that 'if any would not work, neither should he eat.' II Thessalonians 3:10. Von Wright holds that something very much like the Principle of Fairness is not only central enough to be called 'the Principle of Justice,' but is the very 'cornerstone of morality': 'No man shall have his share in the greater good of a community of which he is a member, without paying his due'; *The Varieties of Goodness* (London: Routledge, 1963), 208. But this approach to justice seems to overstress justice on the side of production as much as Rawls overstresses it on the side of consumption.

33 Everyone is familiar with some cases, for example, those of some managers in British industry, who prefer long weekends to keeping up with world competition; of some skiing enthusiasts, who sojourn at Banff on the strength of unemployment insurance; of some university professors, who drop anchor when they gain tenure.

34 See n. 33.

35 How close the society can be brought to the efficiency frontier, or even to the point at which everyone's needs are satisfied, may depend on the path taken, that is, on the sequence of reorganizations initiated. An improving move on a dead-end path is not to be recommended without question. In a forthcoming article on the Difference Principle by Professor Douglas Rae, which I have seen in draft, this objection is raised against the Difference Principle, as applied to moves short of the efficiency frontier; the objection holds against my formula, too, as it stands.

36 See *Theory of Justice*, most explicitly p. 9, but cf. the disdain colouring pp. 44–5. Rawls does not rule out a role for linguistic analysis; and later in the book, comes close for better or worse to engaging in it himself (for example, his discussion of the features of moral sentiments, beginning on p. 420; the footnote on the same page; and his discussion of the distinction between shame and regret on p. 388). See also his 'A Note on Meaning,' *Theory of Justice*, 355–8.

37 See *Political Liberalism* (New York: Columbia University Press, 1993), 6–7.

38 Some of them may be able to continue the insurance temporarily under the COBRA provisions if they have the means to pay the premiums without out the help of the employer's share.

39 In 'Site' and other articles.

40 In a paper not yet published, 'Self-Interest, Citizen Virtue, and Justice in a Liberal Democracy: A Rawlsian Reply to G.A. Cohen,' which I have been discussing with her.

41 Cohen, 'Incentives,' 370–82.

42 Estlund, 'Liberalism,' 107.

43 Does the concession that toward the end of part IV of 'Site' Cohen mentions Rawls making about erring at places in *A Theory of Justice* by treating his principles as giving a comprehensive conception of justice stand in the way? Even given the concession, some use can be made of the senses of justice (as a sense of attachment to the Principles of Justice) and of fraternity (as something that develops among people recognizing their shared attachment). I am not using them to rebut the objection that it is inconsistent for people to be attached to the Difference Principle and require more return for a more productive contribution.

9. Sidgwick's Critique of Nozick

1 *The Principles of Political Economy*, 3rd ed. (London: Macmillan, 1924 [1883]); *The Elements of Politics*, 4th ed. (London, New York: Macmillan, 1919 [1891]; reprint (New York: Kraus, 1969).

2 *The Methods of Ethics*, 7th ed. (London: Macmillan, 1907 [1874]); reprint (Indianapolis: Hackett, 1981).

3 *Anarchy, State, and Utopia* (New York: Basic Books, 1974).

4 Ibid., 231.

5 *Politics*, 160–3.

6 Cf. his own caveats: *A., S., & U.,* 231.

7 *Politics*, 55.

8 Ibid. 151.

10. Social Contract Theory's Fanciest Flight (with Gauthier)

1 Gauthier, *Morals by Agreement* (Oxford: Clarendon Press, 1985). All references to the book are to chapters, sections, and subsections. Gauthier and Oxford University Press kindly allowed me to use photocopies of a final draft of the book in the seminar on advanced ethics that I led at Dalhousie University in the spring term, 1985. I wish to thank them for their helpfulness. I wish to thank also, for close reading and pointed discussion, the members of the seminar, in particular, Colin Macleod and my colleague Richmond M. Campbell.

2 Nozick, *Anarchy, State, and Utopia* (New York: Basic Books, 1974), 230–1.

3 For an assessment of this omission, see John Dunn's latest book on Locke, in the Past Masters series, *Locke* (Oxford: Oxford University Press, 1984), 66–8.

4 With his assumption of 'strict compliance'; see Rawls, *A Theory of Justice* (Cambridge, Mass.: Harvard University Press, 1971), 8.

5 'Every man ought to endeavour Peace, as far as he has hope of obtaining it' (Thomas Hobbes, *Leviathan* [London: Crooke, 1651], chap. 14, par. 4). The first Law of Nature, like others, begins by being a disposition that each agent finds in himself and ascribes to others; see chap. 15, toward the end.

6 Rawls, *Theory of Justice*, 130–6; cf. 584.

7 Ibid., 14–15; also see 127. It is true that Rawls deliberately limits his theory to the 'special case' of 'a closed system isolated from other societies' (8). He still faces a problem about extending a theory constructed for a closed society where, as assumed, mutual advantage exists, to persons and groups outside it.

8 Cf. John Dunn, *The Political Thought of John Locke* (Cambridge: Cambridge University Press, 1969), 103–10, who is correct, it seems to me, in insisting upon Locke's conception of the state of nature as 'a jural condition' but misleading in denying it historical and logical priority.

9 On constraints effective in the state of nature, see Locke's *Second Treatise* (1690), par. 6; on the market operating in the state of nature, see pars 46, 47.

10 Hume, *A Treatise of Human Nature* (1740), Book 3, Part 2, esp. secs 2, 4, 5, 7, and 8.

11 Gauthier, 'David Hume: Contractarian,' *Philosophical Review* 88 (1979), 3–38.

12 Frank, *Choosing the Right Pond* (New York: Oxford University Press, 1985).

13 For example, see ibid., 124.

14 Simon, *Models of Man, Social and Rational* (New York: John Wiley, 1961), 61, 70–1.

11. Comparisons of the Other Grand Programs, Especially Rawls's, with the Needs-Focused Combination Program

1 In the preceding text, I am relying pointedly on the paragraph overlapping pp. 264–5 in Gauthier's *Morals by Agreement* (Oxford: Clarendon Press, 1986) and disregarding Gauthier's qualification to this most simply stated view of the optimum choice of structure.

2 (Cambridge, Mass.: Harvard University Press, 1971), 13, 88.

3 See her unpublished paper, 'Self-Interest, Citizen Virtue, and Justice in a Liberal Democracy: A Rawlsian Reply to G.A. Cohen.' See also chapter 8.

4 See Estlund's point in 'Liberalism, Equality, and Fraternity in Cohen's Critique of Rawls,' *Journal of Political Philosophy* 6, 1 (1998), 99–112.

5 (New York: Columbia University Press, 1993), 6–7.

6 For instance, ibid., 373.

7 Perhaps his disdain for linguistic analysis is operating again, in combination with a view (one of several views, which I discuss and take the measure of in *Meeting Needs* [Princeton: Princeton University Press, 1987], put forth by economists to discredit the concept of needs) that in any advanced society, at least, it is so easy and inexpensive to meet needs that, grant them what priority you like, they cannot count for much in resolving controversies over public policies. The answer to that claim is twofold. If meeting needs is inexpensive, still they are not met for everybody even in advanced countries: in the United States and France old people die off during heat waves for want of air conditioning; in Britain, they die off during cold waves for want of heating. But needs, even basic needs, are not, as a set, inexpensive to meet: supplying pure drinking water in the cities of advanced countries and carrying off sewage are very expensive matters. Moreover, again, Rawls's disdain for linguistic analysis is misplaced. Such analysis of the concept of needs not only leads to rescuing the concept of needs from abuses and confusions; it also leads to the census-notion, and a basis for recasting utilitarianism in a way that removes the grounds for Rawls's objections. See my *Utilitarianism: Restorations; Repairs; Renovations* (Toronto: University of Toronto Press, 2004) for details.

8 Peffer, *Marxism, Morality, and Social Justice* (Princeton: Princeton University Press, 1990), 383–5.

9 *Political Liberalism*, 223.

10 Indeed, even earlier, though not in a discussion following the same pattern, in twin essays, 'Making Justice Practical' and 'Justice and Injustice in Business,' originally published in 1982 and 1983, respectively, both reprinted in my collection *Moral Objectives, Rules, and the Forms of Social Change* (Toronto: University of Toronto Press, 1998).

11 (Toronto: University of Toronto Press, 2004).

12 See the references in chapter 6, above, to the work of James Fishkin.

13 No doubt the eloquence that Arthur Monahan and I tried to achieve in our detailed account of the Common Good could be improved on, but it shows one route to eloquence. See L. Becker and C. Becker, eds, *The Encyclopedia*

of Ethics, 2nd ed. (New York and London: Routledge, 2001), 262–6, especially 263–4; condensed in a further effort by me in *Natural Law Modernized* (Toronto: University of Toronto Press, 2001), 78.

14 Another example of a march inspired by a good cause is 'Esperanto,' in which the Swedish bandmaster Sam Ryberg expressed his hopes that a common language would help achieve world peace. Touching and naive, perhaps, but perhaps no more to be dismissed as naive than 'Onward Christian Soldiers,' which in music and other ways admits of very sophisticated treatment, given it, for example, by Thomas Carter in the Salvation Army march 'Boston Commandery.' I cite the Salvation Army with a respect that originates in my father's: like other British soldiers in the First World War, he had admired the distinctive courage of the Salvation Army, which, unlike other helping organizations, came into the front-line trenches.

12. The Relationship of Utilitarianism to Natural Law Theory

1 B. Parekh, *Bentham's Political Thought* (London: Croom Helm, 1973), 269, in an excerpt from Bentham's discussion of the French Declaration of the Rights of Man.

2 Early in the *Introduction to the Principles of Morals and Legislation* (London: University of London Press, 1970 [1789]), chap. II, fn. d, secs 6, 9.

3 Paley, *Principles of Moral and Political Philosophy* (1785); James E. Crimmins, in *Utilitarians and Religion* (Bristol: Thoemmes, 1998), anthologizes a number of other Christian utilitarians. Cf. J.S. Mill: 'the hope of favour and the fear of displeasure from ... the Ruler of the Universe' as a motive that can attach itself 'to the utilitarian morality, as completely and as powerfully as to any other'; *Utilitarianism*, chap. III.

4 Rousseau ranks as a natural law theorist in spite of himself, mainly because of his illuminating contribution to the conception of the Common Good. See David Braybrooke and Arthur P. Monahan, 'The Common Good,' in L. Becker and C. Becker, eds, *The Encyclopedia of Ethics*, 2nd ed. (New York and London: Routledge, 2001), vol. 1, 262–6. See also in my *Natural Law Modernized* (Toronto: University of Toronto Press, 2001), chap. 3, 'Rousseau and St Thomas on the Common Good.'

5 They get carefully balanced weights in chapter 5 of my *Natural Law Modernized*.

6 *A Treatise of Human Nature* (1740), Book 3, Part 2, sec. 1, at the end.

7 *Summa Theologiae*, 1a2ae, Q.91, 3.

8 He does allude to the deity at the end of appendix I to the *Inquiry*; but this

is just a throwaway line, unconnected in respect to God with the arguments in the preceding text. See my comment in *Natural Law Modernized*, 137.

9 J. Budsiszewski, 'The Revenge of Conscience,' *First Things: A Journal of Religion and Public Life* (June/July 1998). The title of an earlier version was 'Conscience Will Have Its Revenge: Natural Law and Social Collapse' in W.D. Gairdner, ed., *After Liberalism: Essays in Search of Freedom, Virtue, and Order* (Toronto: Stoddart, 1998). The article in *First Things* elicited a number of letters published in a subsequent issue, but no reader or contributor to *First Things* seems to have risen up to challenge, on God's behalf, what a friend of God might think were unworthy imputations.

10 John Finnis, as learned, acute, and committed a scholar of St Thomas as we have in our time, and as pious, says of natural law, with St Thomas in mind, 'Natural law can be understood, assented to, applied, and reflectively analysed without adverting to the question of the existence of God'; *Natural Law and Natural Rights* (Oxford: Clarendon Press, 1980; reprinted with corrections, 1984), 48–9. Its content is thus discoverable by non-Christians (and non-Jews); and not even adherence to natural theology is necessary for the discovery. Finnis does hold that God must be brought in for 'further explanation.' So, of course, would St Thomas. I would deny the need for further explanation, but not deny that people who believe in God would insist on the need.

11 The points made about utilitarianism in the following passage reflect the more detailed, more comprehensive, and more rigorous account, intentionally innovative, that I give in my book *Utilitarianism: Restorations; Repairs; Renovations* (Toronto: University of Toronto Press, 2004).

12 See F.Y. Edgeworth, *Mathematical Psychics* (London: Kegan Paul, 1881), note VI.

13 See 123–5.

14 See Bentham, *Principles*, holding in the first paragraph of chapter I that the Principle of Utility is the foundation for law, and referring in the second and seventh paragraphs to 'a measure of government' as the typical object of application for the principle.

15 Brandt, *Ethical Theory* (Englewood Cliffs, N.J.: Prentice-Hall, 1959), 396–7.

16 *Contemporary Ethics: Taking Account of Utilitarianism* (Oxford: Blackwell, 1999), 96.

17 Mill, *Utilitarianism*, chap. II, at the end, and also in chap. V, after a review of contending views of justice; Sidgwick, *The Methods of Ethics* [1874], 7th ed. (London: Macmillan, 1907; reprinted 1963), Book IV, chap. V.

18 *Summa Theologiae*, 1a2ae, Q.97, 2.

19 R.D. Luce and H. Raiffa, *Games and Decisions* (New York: Wiley, 1957), 34.
20 Shaw, *Contemporary Ethics*, 76.
21 Ibid., 50.
22 John Locke, *Second Treatise of Government* (1690), par. 122.
23 Cf. Bentham, *Principles*, chap. IV, pars 2 and 4, on 'duration' and 'certainty'; also on 'fecundity.'
24 Ibid., chap. I, par. 2; chap. II, pars 4 and 16.
25 See Finnis, *Natural Law and Natural Rights*, 217; more fully treated in his book *Aquinas* (Oxford: Oxford University Press, 1998), 171–6; Robert P. George, *In Defense of Natural Law* (Oxford and New York: Clarendon Press, 1999), 206, 219.
26 Is 'countless millions' an exaggeration? Thomas Walter Laqueur, the author of *Solitary Sex: A Cultural History of Masturbation* (New York: Zone Books, 2003), reports that though masturbation was long a subject of religious condemnation, it was only for something like 200 years, beginning in the eighteenth century, that it incited a furore of attention. But that was time enough, given the rapid increase in the population of Europe and North America, for countless millions to be affected.
27 Experience giving this chapter as a paper to philosophers at the Jagiellonian University in Krakow showed me.
28 A number of nuances in what I say are responses to comments by Mats Furberg, who in this connection, again, did me the kindness of reading my work critically.

Index

Adorno, Theodor, 162
affirmative action, 40
agency, 38, 157–8
AIDS, 266, 278; God's punishment
  not for deviant sex, but for unsafe
  sex, 266; obstruction by Bush
  administration of distribution of
  condoms, 278
Albright, Madeleine, 157
altruism, not the same as concern for
  other people's needs, 41
analytical political philosophy, 3, 4,
  7, 8, 9, 115, 116, 140, 147, 149,
  176–7, 263
Anders, Guenther, 162
ants, 35
Aquinas, St Thomas, 8, 118, 120, 124,
  161, 221, 265–7, 272
Arendt, Hannah, 163–4, 170
argumentation theory, 8, 43
Aristotle, 177, 221
Aron, Raymond, 5
Arrow, Kenneth, 115, 138
Auschwitz, 149, 161–72; said to
  outrun our concepts , 161, 162,
  163, 164, 168–9; especially with
  respect to intentions, 164

authority as dimension of rule-
  formulas, 110
autonomy, personal, 22, 152

bargaining, 33, 232–5, 239
Bastiat, Frederic, 229
battered wives, 24
Bentham, 15, 29, 129, 177, 184, 197,
  198, 233, 265, 271, 275, 280; anticipates contractual thinking, 275;
  Master Idea, insistence on statistical evidence, 280; rejects asceticism and caprice, 184
Berlin, Isaiah, 35
'best' in 'best policy' compared with
  'true' in 'true statement, 126, 135;
  neither tentative nor categorical,
  126
Bill of Rights (first ten amendments
  to U.S. Constitution), 73, 74, 221
blocking, and blocking operations,
  99–100, 106–7, 120; in definition of
  rules, 99; equivalent to imperatives, 99; not punishments, 99
Bosnia and Bosniaks, 150, 169–70
Brandt, Richard, 271
brass bands, in pageantry, 259–60

Dante, 158–9

Dasgupta, Partha, 20, 27

Davidson, Donald, 95–6

deliberation in politics, 8, 9, 140

Descartes, 69, 169

democratic theory, 137–44; competence and confidence of inexpert citizens, three problems, 138–9, 140; cultural diversity, 141; demands respecting character of citizens, 141; pretensions of elites to superior knowledge, 142

deontic logic. *See under* rules: the logic of rules

dialectic of history, 104

Difference Principle (Rawls), 27, 117, 176, 180, 181, 195–9, 199–209, 209–11, 215–18, 221, 228, 243–4, 248–50, 253; besides argument for the Principle in the original position, an argument from oppression, 213–14, and mutual accommodation argument, 248–9; a better-guarded formula for the Difference Principle, 209–11; borrowed by Nozick, 221, 228; comparisons of money incomes of representative persons, 181; correcting a lapse in other utilitarianisms, 195–9; defects: compelling productive people to serve people no longer in need, 201,208–9; defects: considered as formula for distributive justice, 199–209; defects: difficulty about conceding to the relatively productive the whole of their marginal value product, 201, 204–6, 215–18; defects: disregarding present expectations of income through institutions, 202–3;

defects: not safeguarded against less than full effort, 201, 206–8; defects: possibly skewed distribution of income in least advantaged stratum and unjustified sacrifice there, 201–4; definition of least advantaged stratum, 200, change in composition of stratum over time, 200–1; loses force when needs not in view, 201, 209; trans-generational considerations qualifying limits on income of the best-off, 216, 248–9

discourse analysis. *See* argumentation theory

Dworkin, Ronald, 115

Edgeworth, F.Y., 29, 182–3, 194–7, 199; emigration, 29, 183; limit to reducing means of happiness going to the lower classes, 182

egoism, and limits of egoism, as basis for ethics and ethical theory, 176, 192–3, 244–5; vs moral concern with other people, 244–5. *Also see* Gauthier: deduction project, from rationality to morality

Elders, Jocelyn, Surgeon General of the United States, 277, 278

elites, in politics, checked by democracy, 138

emotion, expressed in utterances, 48, 265; as a feature of Hume's ethical theory, 265

Empedocles, 98

empirical social science, benefits from free-standing studies, 131–5

employees, as such more vulnerable to oppression than self-sufficient farmers, 73, 77